ORGANIZATIONAL TRANSFORMATION

ORGANIZATIONAL TRANSFORMATION

Approaches, Strategies, Theories

Amir Levy
Uri Merry

PRAEGER

New York
Westport, Connecticut
London

Library of Congress Cataloging-in-Publication Data

Levy, Amir.
  Organizational transformation.

  Bibliography: p.
  Includes index.
  1. Organizational change. I. Merry, Uri.
II. Title.
HD58.8.L48 1986   658.4'06   86-9389
ISBN 0-275-92147-6 (alk. paper)

Library of Congress Catalog Card Number: 86-9389
ISBN: 0-275-92147-6

First published in 1986

Praeger Publishers, One Madison Avenue, New York, NY 10010
An imprint of Greenwood Publishing Group, Inc.

Printed in the United States of America

The paper used in this book complies with the Permanent
Paper Standard issued by the National Information Standards
Organization (Z39.48-1984).

10 9 8 7 6 5 4 3

Contents

Part II
TRANSFORMATION STRATEGIES

Part III
RESEARCH AND THEORIES

Part IV
SUMMARY

Preface

This was an exciting book to write, and we hope it is exciting to read. It is a book about transforming organizations. It examines what transformation is, what approaches have developed to facilitate transformation, what kinds of interventions are used to do this, the different strategies possible, and the theories behind all this.

Organizational transformation is a completely new field of practice and theory. It is almost an infant, yet growing very fast. It is hard to believe that the first symposium on organization transformation took place in New Hampshire in 1984. Yet there has not been, as yet, any comprehensive publication covering the field. This book attempts to close that gap.

Organizational transformation deals with a radical, basic, total change in an organization, in contrast with improving the organization and developing it or some of its parts. Transformation often deals with a condition in which an organization cannot continue functioning as before. In order to continue to exist, it needs a drastic reshuffling in every dimension of its existence: its mission, goals, structure, culture. Some call this second-order change; others call it transformation. We will begin by using these concepts interchangeably and later will give them different meanings.

Organizational transformation is on the cutting edge of science. It is in the forefront of the field of organizations, and draws insights and ideas from pioneering, innovative thinking in such other sciences as physics, chemistry, biology, and psychology. It is an exciting, thrilling, mind-blasting subject to deal with. The mind is opened to possibilities, vistas hardly dreamed of before. Transformation deals with topics and concepts that touch on the very core and essence of human existence and being. It deals with core processes, spirituality, consciousness, creativity, and evolution. It applies approaches such as changing myths and rituals, envisioning and creating new paradigms, energizing, and raising consciousness.

This is the first attempt to survey the state of the art in this young and growing field. Although it is a child of the 1980s, it has made giant steps in its development. Different approaches to transformation have been developed; alternative strategies have been tried out; a plethora of change interventions have been used in practice; and a whole new world of theories has begun evolving. Yet all this vast array has not yet been collected, documented, organized, and analyzed in a methodical, understandable, and available form. This book attempts to do so. It is the first major effort to provide a comprehensive survey of organizational transformation in practice and in theory.

Many of the approaches to transformation described in these pages have never appeared in book form: They are data from presentations at conferences, first drafts of papers, and such. The case studies that illustrate the approaches are hardly known and often are not thoroughly researched. Since much of the material is so new and in the process of development, evaluative research has not had sufficient time to catch up with it. This truly is the first opportunity to develop a comprehensive, up-to-date overview of an exciting new field of science in the process of development.

We have attempted a task that is not easy. We have tried to write a book that is simultaneously comprehensive, well researched, integrated, and understandable. We have covered all the material developed to date in the field of transformation, with sufficient detail to enable the reader to grasp the essentials of each approach and theory. We have based ourselves on the original sources, whether in writing, lecture, interview, or correspondence. Seventy letters were sent to scientists in this field. Fifty-six replied, and 44 sent at least one written paper. The authors interviewed 21 consultants on their experience with facilitating second-order change and recorded their views on the subject.

The book tries to be both practical and theoretical at the same time. It describes each approach to transformation by conceptual clarification, by concretization in the form of a case study, and by describing and evaluating different interventions using the approach. Alternative strategies to transform an organization are compared, and the theoretical sources and underpinnings of transformation are elaborated, analyzed, and integrated. The book intertwines a wide array of practices, techniques, approaches, and strategies with a rich mine of concepts, theories, and models.

Many people could find much of interest in this kind of book. The organization development convention in Los Angeles, in 1984, which dealt with transformation, raised great interest among organizations in the United States and in the rest of the world. Many are looking for reliable resources in this field. Managers will, for the first time, find here a detailed, comprehensive, understandable description of this new and revolutionary way to change organizations. Organization consultants and practitioners who wish to thrust beyond their usual way of working will find here new openings, new directions, fresh strategies, and previously unknown interventions. Courses in management, organizations, and organizational behavior and development will have at their disposal a first scholarly attempt to review, summarize, organize, and analyze this new area of theory and practice. Organization development consultants may debate the issue of whether transformation is part of organization development, a legitimate child, or a completely separate field. Be that as it may, here is a work that describes transformation and surveys its manifold forms.

The book is divided into four parts. The first and largest describes in detail all the approaches that have been developed to transform organizations. Each chapter surveys a different approach, clarifying it conceptually, illustrating it with a case study, detailing the different forms it takes, describing the variety of interventions and techniques used to apply it, and finally evaluating all this. The second part describes and compares some of the basic strategies used in transforming organizations. The third part provides the reader with a wide array of theories and research on organization transformation. The final part conceptualizes and integrates all that has gone before. The strands of theory that underlie all this are tied together to create a number of models that try to integrate the wide array of practices and theories.

Chapter 1 opens by describing briefly what transformation is. Building on a variety of scientific approaches, an attempt is made to distill the essential characteristics of organizational transformation. Chapter 2 describes the approach to transformation by changing the organization's paradigm, its basic world view. Chapter 3 concentrates on transformation to achieve "high performance" and "excellence." Chapter 4 focuses on changing the symbolic aspects of the organization's culture, its myths and rituals. Chapter 5 analyzes an approach that focuses on reframing the context in which the organization views its reality. Chapter 6 deals with ways to revitalize organizations and create energy for transformation. Chapter 7 emphasizes raising and expanding individual members' consciousness to set the stage for a transformative process.

In the second part, Chapter 8 compares the strategies of transition and transformation. Chapter 9 examines and evaluates the strategies of renewing an existing organization versus creating a new organization. Chapter 10 describes the "top-down" and "bottom-up" strategies, and concentrates on examining the less known strategy: "bottom-up."

In the third part, Chapter 11 reviews studies on organizational change, with emphasis on why organizations change and what is the driving force of radical change. Chapter 12 examines theoretical perspectives, such as the evolution of living systems, from which transformation theory draws its roots. In the last part, Chapter 13 provides conceptual models for capturing the dynamics of transformation. Chapter 14 tries to integrate the different approaches, strategies, and theories into a comprehensive and contingent change process. In it we present some evaluations, thoughts, and suggestions for further study.

Thanks are due to Prof. S. Shapiro, Prof. L. Iannoccone, Prof. N. Glassman, and Prof. G. I. Brown for their helpful criticism, suggestions, and assistance in many ways. We owe a great debt to many practitioners of transformation who found time to answer our queries and send us material. We wish especially to thank Linda Ackerman, Will McWhinney, Harrison Owen, Linda Nelson, Frank Burns, Danny Miller, John Adams, David Nicoll, Charles Kiefer, Michael Brown, Robert Johnston, and James Ritscher. And, last but not least, our deep thanks to our wives, Nira and Ruth, who encouraged and supported us in this endeavor.

Amir Levy
Uri Merry

PART I

APPROACHES TO TRANSFORMATION

1

Organizational Transformation

This chapter is a stepping-stone to allow us to begin examining different approaches to transforming organizations. These different approaches will be the subject matter of the first section. But before dealing with approaches to transformation, we need an initial understanding of what transformation is about. In the final, theoretical section of this book we will deal with this at length and in depth. At this stage we need a description that will allow us to begin our journey. That is what we will be dealing with in this chapter.

PLANNED CHANGE

The concepts "planned change" and "managed change" refer to changes that are deliberately shaped by the organization members (managers, consultants, groups). What distinguishes between the two concepts is the type of people they refer to. "Planned change" usually refers to how experts, outside or inside the organization, can help the organization cope with difficulties, and to plan and implement desired changes. "Managed change" usually refers to how managers can plan and implement changes. We will use the term "planned change" in both cases, as planned and implemented by managers only or when experts play a major role. In many cases, as will be shown later, the two perspectives (management and consulting) are intertwined and managers become the agents of change and the experts at the same time.

Lippitt, Watson, and Westley (1958) have distinguished between spontaneous or evolutionary change, fortuitous or accidental change, and planned change. The first two types are unplanned. Unplanned change, according to their definition, originates outside of the system experiencing the change. Planned change, on the other hand, originates with a decision by the system to improve its functioning.

Bennis, Benne, Chin, and Corey (1976) added to the above definition the utilization of scientific knowledge. Margulies and Raia (1978) contributed to it the importance of the decision to engage in change, and Huse (1982) added the importance of power sharing (power that derives from knowl-edge, skills, and competencies) between the agent of change and the client system. Hence, the characteristics of planned change, distinguishing it from other forms of organizational change, are as follows:

1. Planned change involves a deliberate, purposeful, and explicit decision to engage in a program of change.
2. Planned change reflects a process of change.
3. Planned change involves external or internal expertise.
4. Planned change generally involves a strategy of collaboration and power sharing (power derived from knowledge, skills, and competencies) between the expert and the client system.

We suggest adding a further note to the above description. The process of second-order planned change is usually started when needs, problems, crises, or opportunities are recognized by means of threshold phenomena (Prigogine & Allen 1982). Hence, "planned" refers to both intended and realized; that is, planned change has both intentional (explicitly planned for) and realized (emerging from the situation) aspects. According to Tichy (1983), organizational change is very rarely based on strategies that are explicit, purposefully developed, and planned in advance. In cases of second-order change this preplanning often turns out to be both unrealistic and not descriptive of many change efforts.

SECOND-ORDER CHANGE

In order to describe and characterize second-order change, an effort will be made to summarize definitions provided by scientists in different fields, and to analyze and form them into a more integrated, conceptual framework. Among the few who have dealt with this issue in organization theory is Smith (1982); his definition is very broad and unspecified, yet provides the basic framework for distinguishing between two types of change. Smith borrowed the terms "morphogenesis" and "morphostasis" from biology. He writes:

> **Morphogenesis** . . . is of a form that penetrates so deeply into the *genetic code* that all future generations acquire and reflect those changes. In morphogenesis the change has occurred in the very essence, in the core, and nothing special needs to be done to keep the change changed. (p. 318; emphasis added)

According to this definition, second-order change is in the organization "core" and is irreversible. Smith defines first-order change as follows:

> **Morphostasis** encompasses two types of changes. First there are those that enable things to look different while remaining basically as they have always been. . . . The second kind of morphostatic change occurs as a natural expression of the developmental sequence . . . the natural maturation process. (p. 318; emphasis added)

According to this definition, first-order change is those minor improvements and adjustments that do not change the system's core, and occurs as the system naturally grows and develops. In order to characterize second-order change, more specific definitions, given by scientists from various fields, are provided, then summarized and integrated into a conceptual model. Table 1.1 displays the terms and definitions provided by these scientists.

Table 1.1 provides a reasonable consensus about the definitions of the two concepts and what distinguishes them. While the above scientists use different terms, take different perspectives, and focus their attention on different change dimensions, their definitions are complementary rather than contradictory. Table 1.2 summarizes the characteristics of first- and second-order changes.

Summarizing the essence of the above in one sentence leads to this description of second-order change, which we will also temporarily use to describe organizational transformation: "Second-order change (organization transformation) is a multidimensional, multi-level, qualitative, discontinuous, radical organizational change involving a paradigmatic shift." This description will suffice to allow us to examine different approaches to transformation, detailed in the following chapters of this section. We will return to reexamine the concepts, in greater depth, in the final, theoretical section of this book.

Table 1.1.
Definitions and Descriptions of First- and Second-Order Change

Author	First-Order Change	Second-Order Change
Lindbloom (1959, p. 79) Management theory	Branch change: ". . . successive limited comparisons that continually build out of the current situation, step-by-step and by small degrees"	Root change: "A rational comprehensive approach starting from fundamentals anew each time, building on the past only as experience is embodied in a theory and always prepared to start from the ground up"
Vickers (1965, p. 27) Management theory	Executive change: ". . . gives effect to policies by maintaining the course of affairs in line with governing relations, norms, and standards"	Policy-making change: "Forming the governing relations which assume, express, and create a whole new system of values"
de Bono (1971, pp. 4, 9–10) Creative thinking	Vertical change: ". . . seeks to establish continuity, one thing must follow directly from another"	Lateral change: "Works with the hope that a better pattern can be arrived at by restructuring; it seeks to introduce discontinuity"
Greiner (1972, p. 40) Planned change	Evolutionary change: "The modest adjustments necessary for maintaining growth under the same overall pattern of management"	Revolutionary change: "The serious upheavals and abandonment of past management practices involving finding a new set of organizational practices that will become the basis for managing the next period of evolutionary growth"
Putney (1972, p. 32) Organization theory	Linear quantiative changes: ". . . occur within a steady state; they tend to be gradual and readily predictable"	Nonlinear qualitative changes: ". . . disrupt a steady state; they tend to be abrupt and difficult to predict"
Grabow & Heskin (1973, p. 476) Planned change	Rational change: ". . . does not change its internal structure at all because it does not question the fundamental assumptions upon which it is based"	Radical change: ". . . is a paradigm shift and system change"

continued

6

Table 1.1. Continued

Author	First-Order Change	Second-Order Change
Gerlach & Hines (1973, p. 8) Change theory	Developmental change: ". . . is a change within an ongoing social system adding to it or improving it rather than replacing some of its key elements"	Revolutionary change: ". . . is a change that replaces existing goals with an entirely different set of goals steering the system in a very different direction"
Skibbins (1974, pp. 4–7) Organization theory	Homeostasis: ". . . internal and external forces are nearly in equilibrium. The managers operate with limited short-range goals and tend to run such systems pretty much as they are"	Radical change: ". . . high spread, large-scale processes that occur within a single organization like caterpillars turn into butterflies, the organization retains its identity yet is transformed into something new"
Watzlawick, Weakland & Fisch (1974, pp. 10–11) Problem solving	First-order change: ". . . involves a variation that occurs within a given system which itself remains unchanged"	Second-order change: ". . . involves a variation whose occurrence changes the system itself. . . . it is change of change . . . it is always in the nature of a discontinuity or logical jump"
Golembievsky, Billingsley, & Yaeger (1976, p. 135) Planned change	Alpha change: ". . . involves a variation in the level of some existential state"	Gamma change: ". . . involves a redefinition or reconceptualization . . . a major change in the perspective or frame of reference within which phenomena are perceived"
Hernes (1976) Systems theory	Transition: is a change in two dimensions: output and values	Transformation: is a change in three dimensions: output, process, and values
Argyris & Schon (1978, pp. 2–3) Learning theory	Single-loop learning: ". . . permits the organization to carry its present policies or achieve its present objectives"	Double-loop learning: ". . . involves the modification of an organization's underlying norms, policies, and objectives"
Kindler (1979, p. 478)	Incremental change: ". . . step by step movement or variations	Transformational change: ". . . is a variation in kind

continued

Table 1.1. Continued

Author	First-Order Change	Second-Order Change
Planned change	in degree along an established conceptual continuum or system framework . . . it is intended to do more of the same but better"	that involves reconceptualization and discontinuity from the initial system"
Miller & Friesen (1980a, p. 592) Organization theory	Momentum change: ". . . momentum is expected to be a dominant factor in organizational evolution . . . reversals in the direction of change in strategy and structure are expected to be rare"	Revolution change: "Organizational adaptation is also likely to be characterized by periods of dramatic revolution in which there are reversals in the direction of change across significantly larger numbers of variables of strategy and structure"
Sheldon (1980, p. 64) Management	Normal change: "The fit between the organization and its environment and among its components is so rarely perfect, so . . . organizations are constantly tinkering with one dimension or another"	Paradigm change: ". . . involves several or all dimensions at once . . . radical change in the world and world view"
Carneiro (1981, p. 179) Neoevolution theory	Growth: ". . . is usually manifested by growth of structures already present and is essentially quantitative. . . . Growth tends to be continuous"	Development: ". . . is characterized by the emergence of new structural forms and is essentially qualitative. . . . Development is generally discontinuous and proceeds by a series of jumps"
Ramaprasad (1982, pp. 387–88) Management theory	Minor change: ". . . merely improving the efficiency of current operations"	Revolutionary change: ". . . redefines the system. The redefinition may be entirely conceptual, structural, or processual, or a combination of the three"
Davis (1982, p. 65) Management	Change: ". . . a shift in the content of anything referred to herein as change"	Transformation: ". . . a shift of the context will be referred to as transformation"

Source: Compiled by the authors.

Table 1.2.
Characteristics of First- and Second-Order Change

First-Order Change	Second-Order Change
A change in one or a few dimensions, components, or aspects	Multidimensional, multicomponent, and multiaspectual
A change in one or a few levels (individual and group levels)	Multilevel change (individuals, groups, the whole organization)
Change in one or two behavioral aspects (attitudes, values)	Changes in all the behavioral aspects (attitudes, norms, values, perceptions, beliefs, world view, behaviors)
A quantitative change	A qualitative change
A change in content	A change in context
Continuity, improvements, and development in the same direction	Discontinuity, taking a new direction
Incremental changes	Revolutionary jumps
Logical and rational	Seemingly irrational, based on different logic
Does not change the world view, the paradigm	Results in new world view, new paradigm
Within the old state of being (thinking and acting)	Results in a new state of being (thinking and acting)

Source: Compiled by the authors.

2

Changing the Organizational Paradigm

The recent literature on organizational change features more and more articles on "organizational paradigms" and "paradigmatic shift" (Chase 1983; Sheldon 1980). These concepts were taken from Kuhn's theory of "scientific revolution" (Kuhn 1970), which explains how science develops and changes. But what is an "organizational paradigm"? What is "organizational paradigmatic change"? How can one facilitate and manage this type of change? What is the model that guides this change strategy? These are the basic questions addressed in this chapter.

This chapter deals with a change strategy that focuses on the organizational world view, belief system, and presuppositions underlying its operation. The basic theory that guides this strategy, as suggested here, is Kuhn's theory of scientific revolutions, as translated and applied to organizational change. The implicit assumption of this change strategy is that organizations have a "world view," high-level abstract beliefs that shape and guide members' values, perceptions, attitudes, and behavior; these beliefs also shape and guide the organization's purpose, policy, priorities, procedures, and structures. Therefore, once this world view is changed, other elements will change accordingly.

A CASE EXAMPLE: THE RENEWAL OF THE MENTAL HOSPITAL*

This is a short description of paradigmatic change managed by Dr. V., a psychiatrist who, with the help of two consultants, transformed a

---

*The case was taken from Sheldon 1979.

large psychiatric hospital at Ermel, Holland, from a custodial care institution into a modern mental health facility providing enlightened psychiatric treatment.

The psychiatric hospital served a large community of about 500,000, providing a full range of mental disorder services. It had 800 beds, 30 members on the medical staff, and a staff of 800. The hospital belonged to a group of six that worked together and acted as its board. In 1963, the board nominated Dr. V. to run the hospital. When he came, the hospital was 75 years old, with run-down buildings and crowded wards. The hospital had a bad reputation, and there were few admissions. Patients were treated more or less cruelly. There was much fighting among them and not much variety in active treatment. The wards were dirty, and the organization displayed closed, centralized, authoritarian, and bureaucratic characteristics. Among the staff, morale was low and turnover was high. The organization was facing bankruptcy.

The internal crisis and external opportunity — governmental financial aid depending on improvements — triggered the process of change. The original case description included a long interview with Dr. V. revealing that the transformation of the hospital involved the personal transformation of Dr. V. from a professional liberal psychiatrist into a participative and political leader. His first actions involved a political campaign: gaining the support of the outside authorities, gaining the support of the board, bringing new people with him, networking, and making the new ideas visible, all of which demanded political awareness and ability.

Having minimal external and internal support, the next step was to challenge the old paradigm by providing alternative ideas, to discuss them openly and widely, and to encourage the staff to search for and discover better alternatives for mental treatment. This step was followed by physical changes in the buildings. The goal of changing the organization paradigm could not be done without first changing the buildings so that people could imagine something else, could feel themselves in another environment.

Besides managing the political aspects of the change, Dr. V. established trust and collaboration through participative strategy, that is, creating a climate and structure that enabled everyone to take an active part in the process, to discuss freely and openly their concerns, anxieties, and emotions. Mixed groups were established to discuss the crisis, search for new alternatives, and explore the new ideas provided by Dr. V.

Dr. V.'s ideas and ideals certainly represented a new paradigm. He wanted to transform the old custodial-authoritarian paradigm into an open, ever developing, democratic paradigm. Interviewed by Sheldon, Dr. V. explained:

> I thought a mental hospital should be not a hospital alone, but a **school for life** where you can learn how to live.... The patient should participate in the treatment, where the treatment goals were based on learning principles. I thought it was important for them that they could learn to bargain with the doctors and psychologists about how their treatment should be done. I thought that it was important that they could speak about their problems and feelings, not only in a psychiatric way, but also in a human way, based on **repair of relationships.** (1979, p. 172; emphasis added)

The transformation process was actually a learning and discovering process for those who participated in it, because redefinition of old concepts and generation of new concepts does not automatically entail different procedures. The problem was to translate the new paradigm into operating concepts, procedures, and structures. This could be done by establishing task teams of various types of people who tried to find common practical ideas about how to put highly abstract concepts into action. Further, the new paradigm included changes not only for patients but for the staff as well. For example, the abstract concept "a school for life" was applied:

> We agreed that promotion is not the only goal in life. We introduced a learning philosophy that we call "permanence education." . . . What is most important is to grow personally, to develop yourself. Therefore, permanent education is a very important issue now. A lot of people are following courses, developing themselves either professionally or managerially. (Vernon 1979, p. 174)

The transformation process was not a smooth, easygoing one. It went through crisis periods and encountered strong resistance from the medical staff. They were the most powerful people in the hospital and were anxious about the nursing staff gaining power, and about having to change their world view, values, attitudes, habits, and behaviors. In order to obtain their collaboration and motivate them for change, the consultants interviewed members of the nursing staff, whose feelings, anxieties, and perceptions were openly expressed in small groups. They were assured that they would participate in the process, and that their needs and ideas would be an inseparable, important part of the process. Those who did not want to change were assisted in finding jobs in another hospital.

The process was slow and painful. It involved mourning the old paradigm and the old days, letting go of old presuppositions, values, and habits. It involved changes in buildings, facilities, treatment, structure, procedures, and management. It meant changes in beliefs, values, attitudes, perceptions, and behaviors at the individual, group, and organizational levels. The process took about three years to establish trust, motivation for change, and a "critical mass" that supported a paradigmatic change. And it took four more years to translate the new paradigm into an action plan and to implement it.

ORGANIZATIONAL PARADIGM: DEFINITION

The term "organizational paradigm" is used in two different ways. In the first, the term is used very broadly, to imply the organizational philosophy, beliefs, values, structure, policies, and operations. In the second, the term is used more explicitly, to imply the basic presuppositions that unnoticeably define and shape structures, policies, and operations.

The definition of organizational paradigm that takes a broad, all-embracing perspective is based on Kuhn's (1970) description of a scientific paradigm. According to this description, a paradigm is composed of four basic elements:

1. Symbolic generalization — the ways that problems within the paradigm are posed and solved
2. Metaphysical assumptions — the taken-as-given beliefs about what will be treated as real
3. Values that embody the basic priorities and choices of what problems to pursue and what goals to serve
4. Exemplars — those worked-out approaches and solutions which display the whole world view as a coherent gestalt.

Kuhn's definition is applicable to the organizational domain, and indeed was used to describe the organizational frame of reference and culture (Burns & Nelson 1983), and the organization world and world view (Sheldon 1980).

In this book we use the term "organizational paradigm" in a more explicit, concise way. This term is similar to several other concepts, including "shared meanings" (Pfeffer 1981), "master scripts" (Sproul 1981), "world-view" (Starbuck 1982), "meta-rules" (Smith 1983), "context" (Davis 1982), "conceptual framework" (Nicoll 1984a), and "interpretive schemes" (Bartunek 1984). These concepts vary slightly but have in common the underlying assumption that any given experience can be understood in multiple ways. The way an organization's members perceive what is important, right or wrong, problems and solutions, is dependent on their world view.

Davis (1982), for example, uses the concept "organizational context" to describe the unquestioned assumptions through which all experience is filtered and gets meaning. It provides the ground for being from which content derives. Ranson, Hinings, and Greenwood (1980) use the concept "interpretive schemes" to describe the cognitive schemata that map our experience of the world, identifying both its relevant aspects and how we are to understand them. Interpretive schemes operate as shared, fundamental (though often implicit) assumptions about why events happen as they do and how people are to act in different situations. The interpretive schemes, world view, and unquestioned assumptions are expressed in the organization's values, policies, structures, and approach to problems. They provide the logic, validation, and legitimization for organizing.

The explicit, concise definitions seem to be more practical and operational, and therefore preferable. From this perspective, the organizational paradigm is, first of all, the metarules, or the conceptual framework and precepts, or the unquestioned assumptions that shape the organization's beliefs, values, and operations, and provide meaning and direction for members' actions. To put it more precisely, the organizational metarules or basic assumptions are highly abstract mental constructs, some of which are taken for granted; others operate at the subconscious level and define the reality in which the organization operates. These abstract constructs are translated into a lower level of constructs that are more specific and concrete, the values and beliefs. Values and beliefs are interpretations regarding what is correct and incorrect, right and wrong, good and bad.

THE PROCESS OF PARADIGMATIC CHANGE

Understanding the theoretical stages of the paradigmatic change process is important for the diagnostic step and for the role that managers and consultants may take. Therefore, in this section an effort will be made to summarize some of the studies on the paradigmatic change process.

Kuhn (1970) noted that paradigmatic change typically passes through five stages:

1. Preparadigm research
2. Normal science (normal changes: discoveries, inventions, and developments within the current paradigm)
3. Growing anomalies and crisis
4. Accumulation of new ideas and methods, and paradigm revolution
5. Normal science within a new paradigm

In the organizational domain, Elgin (1977) conducted a field study on the transformation cycle in a large sample of organizations. He found a process very similar to that of Kuhn's:

1. Growth and efficiency
2. Decline
3. Crisis
4. Muddling through and procrastination
5. Chaos
6. Back to basics
7. Transformation and revitalization

Elgin suggests that when the organization's belief system no longer explains reality, or helps to shape policy and operations, the organization passes through crisis and chaos. In this situation dominant coalitions tend to stick to the old paradigm, to increase centralization, and to call for "back to basics." These actions deepen the crisis until a turning point is reached. The organization either stops functioning or "suddenly jumps" into a higher order and a new paradigm.

The phenomena of decline, stagnation, centralization, and pressure to hold on to the old paradigm, as a response to crisis, were noticed by Miller (1982) and Miller and Friesen (1980a).

A detailed model explaining the stages of paradigmatic change is suggested by Nicoll (1980). The model is based on longitudinal field observations and suggests the following stages:

1. Fertilization. The necessary precursor to paradigm shift is the birth of a new paradigm outside the organization. The process starts with new ideas framed as presuppositions, assumptions, and beliefs that explain, rationalize, and define reality in a totally new way. New ideas of this sort are necessarily part of a wider paradigm shift, and hence enter the organization from outside. Ideas are usually suggested by individuals and groups on the periphery of the system. These new ideas may come to a specific organization in different modes:

- Invasion occurs when a new model or idea sweeps an industry ("excellence," "management by objectives").
- New technology, demanding new modes of organizing, typically opens new ways of thinking about the world (computers).
- Pragmatic calculations are valuable sources of new ideas, particularly when current ideas do not work.
- Play. Under this category are such human activities as creativity, loose and relaxed thinking, and associations.

2. Crisis. Paradigm shift needs a catalyst to begin — usually a crisis. It begins when a disruptive event threatens the system. If the event cannot be handled, it sets up a demand for a new paradigm that will help explain the "glitch," diagnose the problems, and remedy them.

3. Incubation. Disruption does not immediately overturn an organization's established paradigm. A substantial time lag generally occurs between perception of a crisis and reorganization of the prevailing paradigm. Nicoll (1980) argues that this is because an organizational paradigm shift is part of — and needs the support of — changes in the higher-level paradigm, such as the wider culture, organization as a science and profession, and the industry.

4. Diffusion. For a new idea to become systematically potent, it must have widespread acceptance. At this stage, ideas come from the periphery into the center through communication systems and public relations. Scattered ideas become familiar, palpable, and coherent. They get labels that ease their spreading (such as Theory X and Y).

5. The struggle for legitimacy. The use of an idea, however, is not necessarily manifest when it is broadly publicized and recognized. To gain the power to determine purpose or policy, explain events, or attract funding, paradigmatic ideas must compete with the older ways of

"seeing" and the established work methodologies that reflect the organization's old views of causality, truth, and reality. This stage is characterized by conflicts and resistance.

6. The politics of acceptance. A paradigm shift involves political struggle, the establishment of parties, the management of open conflicts, and networking. This is where leaders play an important role.

7. Legitimization. For a new paradigm to shape the organization, it needs legitimization. It must become habitual and implicit in the thought processes and work routines of managers and workers. Ideas must be used again and again before they are perceived as consistently producing the desired results.

Nicoll's study is important because it is based on longitudinal field observations. Furthermore, it not only provides a logical sequence of the process of paradigmatic change, but also incorporates an important, widely neglected aspect of second-order change: the political aspect. The study, however, omits an important element stressed by Owen (1983c). During the stage of accepting the new paradigm, there is a very explicit and deliberate acknowledgment of the value and contribution of the old paradigm. The new paradigm is described as "building on" or encompassing the old paradigm, not usurping it.

A slightly different perspective on the process of paradigmatic change is taken by Sheldon (1980), who studied the overall patterns of organizational paradigmatic change. In an empirical study on mental institutions, he found that change may take one of the following patterns:

1. A side-by-side overlap in the existence of the old and the new paradigms. In complex organizations, subsystems may have totally different ideologies and perceptions about basic concepts and ways of doing things correctly.
2. A transformation in which the old paradigm is dying, or dead, before the new one is born.
3. A superimposition of the new on the old.

Sheldon found that dominant paradigms are those of the dominant coalition. Hence, it is possible that when dominant coalitions leave the organization or when the organization fails, the old paradigm will die before a new one has been born. Sheldon's finding that a paradigm may die before a new one is born is inconsistent with the claims and findings of the other studies provided here, but is consistent with the authors' observations. One can solve this inconsistency by arguing that "born" means "explicitly and consciously manifested." This is a matter of perspective. What seems to be "nonexistent" and in "need of coming to existence" or "invention," can be seen as "exists at the subconscious level" and "in need of discovery." However, all the above scholars agree with the idea that it is possible for organizations to enter a long period of crisis and/or "muddling through," or "back to basics" processes while no clear, consistent, organized new paradigm exists.

The literature on death and dying points to the possibility that there are some typical characteristics of the process of each of the previously discussed stages. These elements are denial and avoidance, strong resistance, restriction, multilevel confrontation, and mourning.

1.   Denial and avoidance. This behavior is typical of the very first stages of the process. When new ideas representing a new paradigm emerge within or without the organization, the old paradigm is challenged. Members tend to collude (or collaborate) in order to avoid awareness of both the need to change their paradigm and of the existence of other choices, other directions, other paradigms. They collude by creating a "facade," or by a false mapping of reality. Organizational behavior displaying denial and avoidance has been studied by a few scholars. Harvey and Albertson (1971) and Warren (1984) describe how organization members collude in creating different kinds of delusions, fantasies, and illusions in order to avoid radically needed changes; Merry and Brown (1986) describe avoidance mechanisms such as glorifying the past and living in the future, and how an organization's members collude to avoid incoming information that conflicts with the present paradigm by distorting its meaning, ignoring its existence, and blocking it from awareness. Bibeault (1982) shows the relationships between organizational decline and what he calls "functional blindness" of senior managers who tend to ignore warning signals for needed drastic changes. The results are deepening crises, "muddling through," chaos, and deterioration in the organization's functioning.

2.   Strong resistance. Scholars tend to agree that every change causes resistance and arouses related emotions such as fear and anger. Studies on resistance to change show that the more abstract and the more high-level beliefs are, the more they become resistant to change, and the more fear and anger they arouse (Hultman 1979). Tannenbaum (1980) suggests that what we believe is what we are. Therefore, tapping the belief system is tapping the organizational identity. The closer we get to

this identity, the more fear and resistance are evoked. "Better the certainty of misery, than the misery of uncertainty," concludes Tannenbaum.

3. Restriction. This type of organizational behavior is typical of the advanced stages of the process. Once a new idea or procedure that represents a new world view emerges and exists within the organization, the dominant coalition colludes to restrict its expansion and diffusion. The coalition uses different types of restriction mechanisms. It redefines boundaries and keeps these new ideas and procedures at the margin of the system. Organizations tolerate these marginal areas, and the people and ideas they harbor, only if they come in playful or harmless forms. When a new concept from the periphery becomes a "cause" for "weirdos" or presents itself unexpectedly from all sides, it will be held back from conscious attention, neglected in a kind of intellectual never-never land, or repressed. All too frequently, new perspectives are consciously and vigorously disconnected from action. They are restricted by limiting funding, limiting status, and using other "negative incentives" (Nicoll 1984a).

4. Multidimensional confrontation. This type of organizational behavior is typical of the more advanced stages of the process. When the new perspective begins to diffuse in the system, it challenges an unquestioned view of reality. Members are encouraged to define their attitudes, parties are created, and conflict is almost inevitable (Warren 1984). Paradigmatic conflicts are highly charged. They involve emotional and affective judgmental, ethical, and moral tones, and also abstract and even philosophical debate, all of which are inherent in one's world view (Tichy 1983).

5. Mourning. This behavior is typical of the last stages of the process. A paradigmatic change is typically followed by deep sorrow and mourning for the old world that is disappearing. Without going through this important process of "letting go," members would find it difficult to internalize a new world view and would remain dissatisfied with the change (Tannenbaum 1980; Sheldon 1979; Albert 1984). This includes valuing and acknowledging the worth of the old paradigm, and seeing it as the basis and "parent" of the new.

To summarize, the cycle of organizational paradigmatic change is not a smooth one. It includes periods of crisis and chaos. It involves political campaign, conflict, perturbations, and power restructuring. Typical of this process are the call for "back to basics" and the denial or avoidance of new ideas that represent a new paradigm. The process of paradigmatic change is characterized by behavioral patterns such as denial, avoidance, resistance, and anger in its first stages; by restriction and multidimensional debate in its advanced stages; and by mourning in its final stages. In her book *On Death and Dying,* Elisabeth Kübler-Ross describes behavioral patterns of dying patients that resemble, in many ways, those of members of transforming organizations. She has observed that individuals confronted with death go through stages that include shock, denial, anger, accommodation, depression, and finally a quiet acceptance of the reality that death will come.

Under these circumstances, first-order change techniques and interventions that involve a large measure of rationality cannot work (see, for instance, Albert 1984; Burns & Nelson 1983; Merry & Brown 1986; Watzlawick et al. 1974). Sheldon (1980) studied the process of paradigmatic change in health institutions and concluded that "paradigmatic change is only partly rational. . . . Obviously, techniques appropriate in dealing with *normal change* are not at all appropriate in dealing with *paradigmatic change*" (p. 63; emphasis added).

APPROACHES FOR FACILITATING AND MANAGING PARADIGMATIC CHANGE

This section describes three approaches aimed at facilitating and managing the change of the organization's paradigm: facilitating the process of paradigmatic change, strategic planning and change, and future envisioning.

Facilitating the Process of Paradigmatic Change

Three approaches are presented: a model developed by Burns and Nelson (1983), an approach developed by Nicoll (1980, 1984a), and a model developed by Albert (1984).

High-Performance Programming

Burns and Nelson (1983) developed a model to illustrate a way of thinking about the processes and strategies that can assist in transforming an organization into a higher-performing system. The model provides a "nested structure" for diagnosing current levels of functioning as well as for understanding the potential for performance at the higher levels. The model, called *high-performance programming,* provides four different organization paradigms and their characteristics, and specific change strategies are outlined for creating the conditions that elicit high performance from individuals, teams, and organizations.

The basic assumption underlying this model is that performance is a function of an organizational frame of reference and culture, or its paradigm. Therefore, only change in the organization's paradigm can elicit high performance. Moreover, every paradigm shift needs to be anticipated by a change in the strategies and method for facilitating the next level of paradigm shift. As in Kuhn's theory on scientific revolutions, Nelson and Burns propose that (with the exception of the "reactive" frame) organizational paradigms or frames are nested one inside the next. Each new paradigm is an extension of the old one, providing a larger frame of reference in which the two coexist.

The four frames are the reactive, the responsive, the proactive, and the high-performing. The model, by trying to describe complex phenomena such as organizational change both in theory and in practice, might be seen as "too simple to be true"; nevertheless, it was developed out of practice and has already been used for facilitating radical changes in the U.S. Navy. Nothing, so far, has been published as evidence on its utility. The model is shown in Figure 2.1.

The model consists of two interrelated parts. The lower part describes the four frames or paradigms in a developing order. The upper part describes the three strategy modes appropriate for facilitating the change to a higher order. Each paradigm is changed by utilizing strategies of the next-higher-order paradigm. For example, the transformation of the reactive organization to a responsive one is possible by using responsive strategies, which are actually traditional organizational development interventions.

The above model, because of its simplicity, might have some advantages for explaining the concept of organizational paradigm and paradigmatic change. Moreover, theoretical models, in the form of conceptual maps, can be, by themselves, a major instrument of change technology. Members' perceptions of reality and definition of the situation can be changed by providing them with a conceptual model that changes their perspective. If the model resonates with people's experiences of reality, it can open new doors to their perception of the organization (Blake & Mouton 1978). Theoretical models as intervention tools are very popular among managers and consultants. The

Figure 2.1. The High-Performance Programming Model

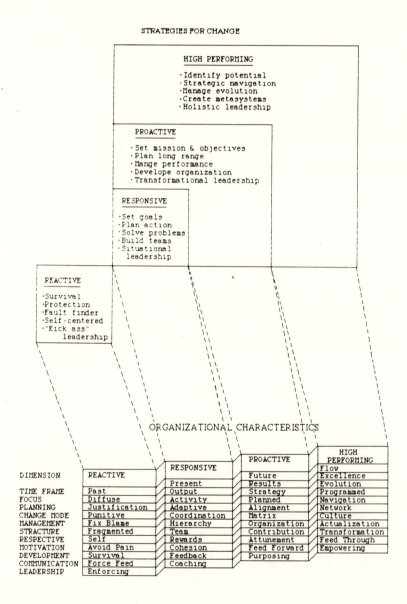

STRATEGIES FOR CHANGE

HIGH PERFORMING

·Identify potential
·Strategic navigation
·Manage evolution
·Create metasystems
·Holistic leadership

PROACTIVE

·Set mission & objectives
·Plan long range
·Mange performance
·Develope organization
·Transformational leadership

RESPONSIVE

·Set goals
·Plan action
·Solve problems
·Build teams
·Situational
 leadership

REACTIVE

·Survival
·Protection
·Fault finder
·Self-centered
·"Kick ass"
 leadership

ORGANIZATIONAL CHARACTERISTICS

DIMENSION	REACTIVE	RESPONSIVE	PROACTIVE	HIGH PERFORMING
TIME FRAME	Past	Present	Future	Flow
FOCUS	Diffuse	Output	Results	Excellence
PLANNING	Justification	Activity	Strategy	Evolution
CHANGE MODE	Punitive	Adaptive	Planned	Programmed
MANAGEMENT	Fix Blame	Coordination	Alignment	Navigation
STRACTURE	Fragmented	Hierarchy	Matrix	Network
RESPECTIVE	Self	Team	Organization	Culture
MOTIVATION	Avoid Pain	Rewards	Contribution	Actualization
DEVELOPMENT	Survival	Cohesion	Attunement	Transformation
COMMUNICATION	Force Feed	Feedback	Feed Forward	Feed Through
LEADERSHIP	Enforcing	Coaching	Purposing	Empowering

Source: Prepared by the authors from the illustrative models of Burns and Nelson (1983).

22

"managerial grid" (Blake & Mouton 1978) and "Theory X and Y" (McGregor 1960) exemplify the strength of theoretical models as instruments of change.

An important aspect of this model is its proposition that organizational paradigm change entails first a change in the change methods. According to the model, each paradigm change can be facilitated by using change methods that represent a higher paradigm level. From that perspective, organizational development methods of change may be used for facilitating paradigm change of a special kind only: the transition from the "reactive" to the "responsive" paradigm. The next level of change demands the use of the subsequent level of change methods. This idea is of major importance and coincides with the view that organizational transformation necessitates new change approaches such as those described in this book.

Paradigm Reframing

Nicoll (1980, 1984a) has pointed out that the nature of interventions aimed at facilitating paradigmatic change depends upon the stage in which the organization is located in the cycle of paradigmatic change. Nicoll suggests the following interventions:

1. Focus the organization's attention on the role of its paradigm. Paradigms exist below an organization's level of consciousness, and therefore are neither examined nor understood. Most of the time they are not even recognized. In this case rational foolproof interventions are inappropriate. Nicoll suggests focusing the system's attention explicitly on the paradigm change process by "reframing paradigmatic symbols" (such as "patient" to "client"), and focusing and guiding imagery.

2. Supportive, creative work on the periphery. Nicoll argues that paradigmatic change starts at the organization's periphery. In this context, a possible strategy is to encourage marginal, vanguard roles and the "brokers of new ideas." Another way is to encourage the "steeping" of ideas by facilitating cross-fertilization, review of new technology and structures, and free-form play.

3. Separating problem-solving and paradigmatic change processes. Problems are defined and solved within a specific paradigm. By exploring the presuppositions underlying the problem's formation, a manager may see new alternatives and possibilities. This type of intervention is very similar to those suggested by Watzlawick et al. (1974), some of which will be described later in this book.

4. Designing and reframing events. This type of intervention is aimed at facilitating the process of paradigmatic change by making it explicit. This intervention takes place during the fertilization, diffusion, and struggle for legitimacy stages. Reframing events are specially designed for the purpose of exploring various aspects of a new paradigm, or the impact of a new presupposition on the structures and processes of the organization.

Two exemplifying events are assessing operational presuppositions and scanning the environment. Assessing operational presuppositions entails looking for and testing basic concepts, presuppositions, or cause-and-effect explanations. Participants "step back" and examine the basic presuppositions they hold about what caused the present crisis. In scanning the environment, organization members consciously search the environment for signs of new paradigmatic concepts. If these concepts appear to be promising, they are incorporated into the organization's operations.

Delete Design Model

A different perspective is taken by Albert (1984), who developed an approach that consists of processes that help members to cope with the loss and death of the old paradigm and encourage them to be more open in the search for new directions. Albert's model is based on the premise that the possibility of change becomes bounded, not by the limits of man's rationality or by his inability to envision the future, but by his simple inability to extricate himself from his own past. It is focused on "letting go" processes and on processes such as denial, avoidance, resistance, and anger, typical of paradigmatic change.

The model is very complex and articulated; it is called the delete design model because it focuses on obliterating the past, not on adding to it. Only the basic principles of the model will be described:

1. Summarize the past. A summary is an abbreviated history of the past. If it is to create a sense of closure, it must summarize the meaning as well as the objective facts of the past, the hopes and dreams of the participants as well as their accomplishments.
2. Justify the change. Justification must state why this particular change is necessary or desirable, and why it is necessary or desirable now.

3. Create continuity between the past and the future. Emphasize the few valued elements of the past that will be preserved and will continue in the new arrangement.
4. Mourn the loss of what does not continue. It is never sufficient to deal with death by acknowledging its necessity, nor to argue that what has been deleted was not worth having.
5. Eulogize the past. Acknowledge, express, and celebrate the worth of what is left.

To summarize, the above three models are all based on the premise that paradigmatic change can be managed, and that the main task of the consultant and manager is to facilitate this process by raising members' consciousness to the context of the change (Burns & Nelson) or to the process of the change (Nicoll), and by helping members to let go of the old paradigm (Albert).

Strategic Planning and Change

Three approaches are presented here. The first is a general strategy suggested by Davis, the second is a strategy developed by Tichy, and the third is a model suggested by Barrett and Cammann.

Changing the Organizational Context

In an article on how to move organizations from a present state into a desired future state, Davis (1982) suggests taking what he calls the "retrospective strategy." This means discovering a future state and treating it as if it is the present state. Thus, "the present is the past of the future." Davis explains:

> The only way that an organization's leaders can get there [the desired future state] from here [the present state] is to lead from a place in time that assumes you are already there, and that is determined even though it hasn't happened yet. (1982, p. 73)

Davis claims that retrospective strategy is not "positive thinking" in which one has to invent a new future. Rather, it is a discovery of what exists. By using methods of environment scanning, auditing, and future scenarios, managers can pick up hints that may help them discover the future. Davis makes an analogy of his idea with the work of the archaeologist who wants to find the artifacts that give the answers before anyone else finds them. For the archaeologist ". . . the answers are already there; he does not have to create them. There is a key to the answer" (1982, p. 78).

The above strategy is based upon studies and theories of phenomenology of social scientists such as Herbert Mead, Gordon Alport, and Karl Weick. They hold that an action can become an object of attention only after it has occurred. While it is occurring, it cannot be noticed. Every planned act bears the temporal character of the past, every plan has the quality of an act that had already been accomplished (Weick 1979).

Davis' article, although dealing with transformation strategy, takes a theoretical perspective on how to move organizations to a desired future state. There are no descriptions of methods, nor examples of how to use this strategy.

Managing Strategic Change

Tichy's *Managing Strategic Change* (1983) is a detailed description of strategies and approaches for facilitating large-scale change. It is based on research, case studies, and personal observations of the author in facilitating wide-ranging changes in complex systems. Tichy defines "strategic change" as "non-routine, non-incremental, and discontinuous change which alters the **overall orientation** of the organization" (p. 17; emphasis added).

Tichy takes the management perspective, arguing that the task of managers is not only to manage and develop the organization, but also deliberately and intentionally to change its overall orientation (paradigmatic change). Under radical and rapid environmental and internal changes, the importance of managing this type of change is extremely important for the organization's survival and success.

Tichy argues that three different perspectives or, in our terminology, paradigms exist side by side in organization theory and practice, representing different ways to explain organizational reality:

1. The technical paradigm. It includes the Weberian bureaucracy, job design, technical systems, scientific and classical management, and contingency theories. This paradigm is largely restricted to organizing most effectively and getting work accomplished.

2. The political paradigm. It includes exchange theories, conflicts, power and coalition problems, and allocation of rewards. This paradigm limits much of its scope to political aspects.
3. The cultural paradigm. It includes the field of organizational development, humanistic psychology, human relations, cultural anthropology, and phenomenology. This paradigm restricts much of its scope to cultural aspects.

Tichy suggests integrating the above three perspectives into a more all-embracing, higher-level organizational paradigm. From this perspective, the organizational paradigm is the organizational ideology, and the alignment within and among three subsystems: the technical, the political, and the cultural. The organization's overall orientation consists of core values, which are beliefs about a desirable general mode of organizational conduct; the mission; and the strategy. This overall orientation determines the way the organization operates, and the nature of and the alignment within and among the technical, the political, and the cultural subsystems.

Strategic change typically starts with redefinition and reframing of the organization's purpose and mission, followed by changes in the three subsystems, and ending with the creation of new alignments within and between these three subsystems.

Tichy provides detailed strategies, models, interventions, and case studies exemplifying ways to manage strategic change. The main thrust of his book is its notion that second-order planned change involves a variety of change methods, some of which are traditional, left-brain, rational, and analytical, others are more right-brain oriented. Moreover, interventions aiming at facilitating a paradigmatic change must include changes not only in the organization's purpose but also in its three basic subsystems; otherwise, the change will not hold. From this perspective, second-order change interventions should aim at changing not only values, norms, attitudes, structures, and technology, but also the power structure.

Creating the Climate for Paradigm Shift

The model suggested by Barrett and Cammann (1984) is based on analyzing transformation efforts in a large, old steel company. Its main focus is on facilitating the very first stage of transformation, which is the transition from stability to openness to change, or what Kurt Levin terms "defreezing." The model postulates that in mature, stable organizations, the culture and paradigm preserve the order and inhibit change. More important, it is possible that the chief executive officer will feel the need for a paradigmatic shift, yet those who may be directly responsible for the changes to be made do not feel such a need.

Hence, the model suggests a set of operations that creates a need for change at lower levels of the system:

1. A series of presentations about the nature of the problems facing the organization; personnel meetings; small group discussions focusing on major changes in the environment that entail major changes in the organization
2. A series of management meetings that enable all managers to express freely their concerns and feelings, and to discuss possible solutions
3. A critical symbolic decision by top managers recognizing the seriousness of the situation and the need for drastic action
4. Creation of a standard — the senior managers convene for a few days to create a new mission for the organization that provides some general guidelines individuals can use to determine areas where change is necessary
5. The development of transition structures — creating task teams and coordination teams, creating internal facilitating groups: the task of the coordination team is to coordinate, monitor, and communicate with the task teams; the job of the task team is to examine areas where change might be needed, based on the new mission; the job of the facilitating team is to train managers in the skills of facilitating change.

The outcomes of the initial phase are a commitment to changing the mission and the culture of the organization, a model of the desired state to be accomplished, and an understanding of how the broader change will occur.

To summarize, strategic change is taking top managers' perspectives on paradigmatic change. It focuses mainly on changing the organization's mission. It employs principles and practices widely used in the field of planned change (such as small group discussions), but on a much larger scale. Strategic change focuses on the role of top managers in facilitating and managing transformation. The new mission is usually the product of the vision of the chief executive officer, and the main problem is defined as how to align managers and workers with this mission, and how to ensure their commitment to the change.

Future Envisioning

Focusing members' attention on the desired future rather than on the present situation is becoming a widely used method (Lippitt 1982; Peck 1983). This type of approach is embedded in, and based on, futurists' postulations that shared images of a desired future are able to shape thoughts, and guide actions and policies. The shared image thus "pulls" toward its fulfillment (Polack 1973; Markley & Harman 1982; Boulding 1976). From this perspective, organizations can be transformed by members having a new shared image of the desired state representing a new view, a new paradigm.

Wilner (1975) studied the role of imaginary visions in maintaining social order and mediating organizational and personal transformation. Her study shows that radical imaginary visions occur as a response to crisis situations, and have a transformative and potential curative power. Wilner reached the following conclusion:

> These visions are produced out of deep social crises of order; they are the product of individual imaginations that share in a collective experience of disorder and are often radically transformative and regenerative both for the individual psyches in which they occur and for the collectivities in which they find a communal resonance and assent; and further, they often lead to radical realignments in socio-political structures which have become inadequate and oppressive. (p. 5)

Studies on the futurists' perspectives will be discussed (see Chapter 12). In this section, the focus is on how managers and consultants can help members create or discover a shared imaginary vision of the desired future and to materialize it.

This type of intervention is typically a part of strategic planning or strategic change. Members gather for a few days and are involved in processes that help them elicit a shared metaphor or idea about new missions and purposes, and new points of view for the future. Various techniques are used, such as guided imagery, in which the consultant takes an active role; focused imagery, in which participants are instructed to focus their vision on specific subjects; and open imagery, in which participants are encouraged to evoke fantasies. Future envisioning is also used in organizational development; however, when second-order change is needed, future envisioning techniques are utilized to encourage members to go beyond the current paradigm.

Future envisioning approaches can be classified basically into two categories according to their way of dealing with the past and the present. Some approaches start the process with awareness of past and present realities, so as not to raise unrealistic expectations (Ackoff 1981; Brown & Weiner 1984; Boyce 1984). Others intentionally ignore the past and present, and encourage participants to give freedom to their imaginations, in order to go beyond the current paradigm (Lindman & Lippitt 1979; Mulligan & Kelly 1983).

Examples of future envisioning of the first type are those suggested by Boyce (1984) and Rutte (1984). These start with relaxation techniques and "going inside." Then participants, with eyes closed, are instructed to go backward and, through guided imagery, to "see" and "feel" various aspects of the organization and themselves in it. Participants are encouraged to explore and be aware of the current culture, purpose, and ideology of the organization; they then share their experiences in small groups, trying to find common themes.

The next step is to envision the desired future for the organization. With eyes closed, participants are guided to step into a future time (usually up to 20 years) and are asked to focus their images on different aspects of the desired organization. In some cases, they are told to step back and "see" how the image of the organization changes until it becomes the present image.

The next step is to draw or to write down what each individual has seen and to discuss it in small groups. Each group works on its differences and its common ground, trying to find shared imagery, metaphors, or symbolic presentation of the desired organization. Then each group visually and verbally presents what it saw to the larger group. The larger group then works on common themes or images, on conflicting themes or images, and their sources. The final "product" of the workshop is a shared vision of the desired future in terms of its basic nature and purpose, and the mission of the organization. This type of envisioning usually ends with the establishment of a planning committee, which translates the vision into real-world actions, plans, and programs.

An approach exemplifying the second type is the one used by Mulligan and Kelly (1983) for facilitating transformation. The technology is called *fantasies theme analysis*. Participants are encouraged to "daydream," to fantasize, to go beyond the current paradigm. The process takes place at the individual and the group levels. Through group interactions, shared fantasies emerge, are analyzed, and are accepted as guidelines for the future. The shared fantasies are then translated into more articulated sentences, a more operational program.

To summarize, futuring is a rapidly developing field. There are some who try to construct a future that will be a replica and continuation of the past: an improved past. Others try to extrapolate and predict in order to figure out how to "fit into" the future and "adjust to" what it will be like. These "transformers" see the future as a set of conditions that one can help to create and realize if one is clear about what is desired. Once members are clear about their desired future, goal-prioritizing procedures — procedures for assessing feasibilities, needed resources, strategies, and planning and implementing processes — are followed. There is some evidence that future envisioning, which focuses on the desired future, elicits significantly more creativity and energy for change than "problem analysis," management by objectives, prediction/extrapolation designs, and other frequently used approaches to long-range planning and change (Lippitt 1982). Futuring may be seen as a suitable approach to use in organizations where the old paradigm has died before the new paradigm has been born. Out of future envisioning the new may be born.

In this section three approaches were described. The first suggests focusing the change efforts directly on the organization's paradigm. The others focus the change efforts on the organization's mission and purpose, hoping that it will result in a paradigmatic change. The importance of the approach suggested by Tichy (1983) is in its emphasis on highly neglected, but crucial, dimensions: the political and the technical systems. All the suggested approaches are based on cases of facilitating second-order change, and they report positive results. Some of these results are still incomplete (discovering a new desired future does not ensure its implementation or its persistence).

EVALUATION

Change Manager Characteristics

The change managers, as they emerge from the above models and cases, are different from the organizational development practitioners, who traditionally have focused their attention on attitudes, norms, and values related to interpersonal relationships, truth, and love. Bennis

(1973), for example, described organizational development practitioners as follows:

> O.D. practitioners rely exclusively on two sources of influence: truth and love. Somehow the hope prevails that man is reasonable and caring, and that valid data coupled with an environment of trust and love will bring about the desired change . . . O.D. seems most appropriate under conditions of trust, love, and collaboration. (p. 78)

Some organizational development practitioners overrely on a purely cultural orientation. It limits their perception of the problems and hinders their attention to the context in which these problems exist and are defined as problems. Further, it curbs their use of other organizational dimensions, such as purpose and technical and political systems. Rather than focus on attitude changes, the new change managers work on the context in which attitudes are shaped. They encourage a search for and discovery of new ideas, ideals, and presuppositions. They challenge the old paradigm by helping people to be aware of its existence and of the choice they have in searching for a new one.

Although they use collaborative and participative methods, the new change managers are also "realistic." They tap the political system. They know that without changes in the power structure, without managing political campaign and conflicts, without networking and realignment, the change is doomed to fail. Moreover, they encourage technical and physical changes that provide a new internal environment that fits with the new paradigm.

Intervention Characteristics

The approaches presented in this chapter suggest various ways to facilitate paradigmatic change:

- By raising awareness of the process, or of the developmental stages of paradigmatic change (Nicoll)
- By raising awareness of the content of the current paradigm and of the existence of alternative paradigms (Burns & Nelson)
- By raising awareness of the necessity of paradigmatic change for the organization's survival (Barrett & Cammann)
- By facilitating the departure from the old paradigm (Albert)

- By facilitating the creation of a shared vision that actually represents a new paradigm (Lindman & Lippitt)
- By facilitating the alignment of members with the new vision and by facilitating their commitment to the change (Tichy).

Table 2.1 shows some of the differences in emphasis between typical organizational development interventions and paradigmatic change interventions.

Paradigmatic change appears to be a long and expensive process. All the case studies examined showed that it takes between three and ten years to plan, implement, and institutionalize the change. The time span depends not only on the organization's size and complexity, but also mainly on the internal and external conditions. Leadership, environmental threat, internal crisis, external opportunity, awareness of the need for change, and the possibility to implement the change by creating a new plant or subsystem — all these might significantly shorten the time and lower the costs.

Our investigation on the time and costs of paradigmatic change revealed that it usually demands the devotion of a steering team and task teams for as long as the change takes place. It takes about 10–15 percent of the work time of the steering group for at least the first few years. It also takes about 5–10 percent of the work time of the target team (change

TABLE 2.1
Distinguishing Between Organizational Development Interventions and Paradigmatic Change Interventions

Organizational Development Intervention	Paradigmatic Change Intervention
Does not challenge the current paradigm	Challenges and changes the current paradigm
Starts with diagnosing problems and searching for solutions	Starts with a new vision or a crisis in the old vision
Goal setting	Looking for a new purpose, core mission
Emphasis on cultural dimensions: values, attitudes, and norms	Emphasis on ideology, cultural, political, and technical dimensions
Agreement on solutions	Alignment of people and systems with a new purpose
Present orientation	Future orientation
Continuity with past	Starting a new future

Source: Prepared by the authors.

target) until the change is completed. The average costs of the change are about 5 percent of the annual budget or production volume of the change unit per year.

Organizational Characteristics

Leadership

The change efforts, as described in most cases, revealed that senior executives who managed paradigmatic change have some common characteristics:

1. They are "outsiders" who came to the system while it was in crisis, and already had new ideas about how the system ought to operate. These ideas actually represented a new paradigm.
2. They are not charismatic leaders with true believers, gurus, or authoritarian leaders demanding obedience and loyalty.
3. The "titles" their employees ascribe to them in these studies are facilitators, developers, diplomats, public relations experts, statesmen, and visionary leaders.
4. They attend to the people's needs; they are caring and respectful. They are willing to share power.
5. They focus the attention and consciousness of the members on the organization's purpose, but they also facilitate the "attunement" processes by means of which organization members can come to know, respect, and care for one another's needs and individual purposes.
6. They are not rational, analytical planners, but are driven by visions and intuition guided by strongly held intentions. They have the capability to communicate their visions, to open the organization to debate and conflicts, by networking and by reaching the critical mass needed for change. They are diplomats, not manipulators.
7. They use collaborative and participative methods. They open communication channels, and they attend to what people say, think, feel, and need.

This is not to say that this is "the only way" or "the best way" to manage second-order change. Perhaps it is the most democratic way. Those managers who are willing to use collaborative change methods are, in effect, people-oriented. It is, however, possible to transform organizations without using collaborative methods. "Heroes," "strong leaders," and "charismatic leaders" have done this, as Deal and Kennedy (1982) and Peters and Waterman (1982) have pointed out.

Type of Organization

Most of the cases on paradigmatic change deal with prisons, mental institutions, hospitals, schools, or what Goffman (1961) termed "total institutions." This might be accidental and it might not. Our search for answers to this issue brought us to suggest that ideological and total systems are more vulnerable to paradigmatic change than are other systems.

Ideological Systems

Social movements, ideological systems, or any system in which the paradigm is an end rather than a means to survive, are possibly better approached through paradigmatic change. In these systems, every new idea is treated as if it were challenging the whole world view. This makes the system sluggish in its adaptation and creates an ongoing discrepancy between the system and its environment. In order to protect its ideology, the system reinforces the stockade around itself and its ideas. It blocks out the anxiety by cutting off possibilities of change. Anxiety is escaped, but the system is imprisoned in its own stockade (May 1981, p. 202). In Holling's (1976) terms, the system is not resilient and is unable to absorb fluctuations. It tries to maintain stability and certainty in the short term while losing its ability to persist in the long term through variability and resilience to uncertainty.

Total Institutions

All-embracing systems such as prisons, mental hospitals, communes, and monasteries are vulnerable to paradigmatic change because of the complex interrelationships and interdependencies among their many components (Goffman 1961). These systems are sluggish in adaptation because they resist new ideas. Every new idea threatens an immediate effect on every aspect of the system (Niv 1980). The system protects itself from new ideas by closed boundaries, which might cause or lead to discrepancy and to a threshold beyond which the alternative is to undergo second-order change or to stop functioning. Like ideological systems, they are often not resilient. Often their resistance to transformation, their fear of a paradigmatic shift into the unknown, leads to their disintegration (Merry & Brown 1986).

Systems that are able to clearly define their boundaries; to separate themselves from other systems; to carefully select energy, matter, people, and information inputs; and to deliberately socialize their members may escape paradigmatic change for a long period of time. However, this strategy is hard to apply in the free and open modern world unless power or other authoritarian routes are taken.

Environmental Conditions

Environmental threat to the survival of the organization (Deal & Kennedy 1982; Warren 1984), new environmental needs and demands for new products and new services (Tichy 1977), and external opportunity such as federal grants for the new change (Tichy 1977; Sheldon 1979) may trigger a paradigmatic change and affect its success.

In the case described by Deal and Kennedy (1982), the government threatened to cut off financial support for a public metropolitan service organization unless the organization "passed into the 20th century." In the cases described by Tichy (1977) and Sheldon (1979), the government offered a large financial grant for a radical change. In all these cases there was a strong need for the new services and strong environmental support for the change. Lack of support for the change by those who were the customers or consumers might cause the failure of the change, as the case studies described by Gold and Miles (1980) and Owen (1983) pointed out.

Summary

The following propositions seem to be central in the theory and practice of paradigmatic change in organizations:

- If one wishes to change an organization, probably one will have to change the metarules, the underlying assumptions that shape and limit actions, processes, and structures.
- If one wants to facilitate paradigmatic change, one first needs a paradigmatic change in one's theoretical models, inquiry methods, and change approaches. This entails the creation of a new language.

- Paradigmatic change either is introduced into the system from outside (new management) or develops at the system periphery. It is, therefore, important to work with the periphery, for it is here (in many cases) that new ideas are first developed and accepted.
- It is possible that ideological systems are more amenable to transformation through a paradigm change approach.
- In some cases an old paradigm has died without a new one emerging. In these cases, approaches such as futuring need to be utilized to begin creating a new paradigm.

3

"High Performance" and "Excellence"

This chapter presents change approaches aimed at facilitating second-order change by introducing new "ideal types" of organizing already existing in a few extraordinary organizations. Recent work on "high performing" "excellent" systems has triggered new perspectives and new strategies for facilitating second-order change. These cases suggest that excellent organizations are different from other organizations. Furthermore, they are so profoundly different that they actually represent a whole new paradigm. In order for an organization to reach that state of being, it needs not "to do more of the same and better," but to do things in a completely different way and from a different perspective. The organization will have to change its paradigm.

The idea of applying Kuhn's theory of scientific revolutions at the organization level has already been discussed. The notion that organizations can be transformed to excellent systems represents a specific case of paradigmatic change. In this case the new paradigm already exists and even flourishes. Therefore, the task of the researcher is to discover the new paradigm, to describe and define its characteristics; the task of the manager is to find ways to apply it in the organization. For those who study excellent organizations, the desired future is not something vague and artificial that needs to be created, invented, or developed. Rather, this desired future already exists and is manifested in some extraordinary systems.

A CASE EXAMPLE: THE CASE OF KOLLMORGEN*

Kollmorgen is a diversified manufacturing company headquartered in Stamford, Connecticut. It markets printed circuit boards, periscopes, and electro-optical equipment. Sales were $230 million in 1981, having doubled every three years for the past ten years. Comprised of 13 virtually autonomous divisions, the company embraces a small-is-beautiful philosophy through decentralization.

Each president reports to a division board of five or six other division presidents and corporate officers, a structure that replicates the relationship between a corporate chief executive and a board of directors. Important decisions, such as capital expansion, and hiring and promotion of senior management, remain at the division level. Divisions are kept small (typically less than $50 million in sales and 500 employees) so that each employee may feel part of a family where his/her contribution matters.

When divisions grow past this point, they split. Although there are about 4,500 employees in Kollmorgen, the corporate staff numbers only 25. Kollmorgen's president claims that this organizational design is intended to expose all employees to the incentive and pressures of a free market. All employees share in their division's profits. Not only are the divisions run as freestanding businesses, but product teams within the divisions function very autonomously. They may share equipment and overhead support with other teams, but they set their own prices, determine their own sales goals, and manage their own production schedules. Incentives within product teams are high, for most new divisions emerge from successful ones.

Organizational innovation has recently extended to corporate management. A "partners group" of the division presidents and senior corporate officers has been formed by the president to bring freedom and equality into corporate policy making. Decisions are made by consensus, each partner having veto power over any major issue. In this atmosphere, honesty and trust are imperative.

A central theme in Kollmorgen's belief system is that people are basically honest and trustworthy, and that each wants to contribute to the organization. It is assumed that failure to behave accordingly signals the organization's failure to create an atmosphere conducive to such behavior. Kollmorgen's president states this explicitly in an article

---

*The case was taken from Kiefer and Senge (1984).

published in the 1979 Annual Report: ". . . an unspoken conviction that man is basically good, that each individual is the basic measure of worth, and that each, by pursuing his own good, will achieve the greatest good for the greatest number" (Kiefer & Senge 1984, p. 9).

That people are basically good and trustworthy is known as "Theory Y" (McGregor 1960); however, Kollmorgen's president adds to it a spiritual, visionary, and ethical dimension by saying that it is important to "share the spiritual benefits of our success with all people in the organization." He deeply believes that personal satisfaction lies not only in material rewards but also in the opportunity to pursue a lofty objective.

It might be appropriate to end this short review with the president's mission statement, which explicitly articulates his basic beliefs:

> . . . to fulfill its responsibility to Kollmorgen share holders and employees by creating and supporting an organization of strong and vital business divisions where a spirit of freedom, equality, mutual trust, respect, and even love prevails; and whose members strive together toward an exciting vision of economic, technical, and social greatness. (Kiefer & Senge 1984, p. 10)

The above example represents some of the characteristics of excellent systems as we will define, describe, and elaborate on them later in this chapter.

The excellence paradigm challenges some of the basic assumptions guiding organizational theory and research in relation to performance and change. Most of the research on organizations is problem-oriented. The purpose of the research is to throw light on the causes of unsatisfactory performance. The focus is on what is wrong or dysfunctional. The assumption is that one can extrapolate from the causes of ineffective performance to the causes of more effective performance. Emphasis is on studying the discrepancies between what is supposed to be happening in the organization and what is actually happening. What is supposed to be happening is taken as the standard for a desirable level of system functioning (Vaill 1978).

The approaches examined here took a different perspective. Rather than studying problematic organizations or problems in organizations, they focused on organizations that were highly successful in terms of financial criteria, innovations, and reputation. They studied their culture, structure, management, and other characteristics, and what made them the way they were. The next step was to develop learning and training programs, and to change methods for facilitating the transformation of "regular" systems into excellent ones.

The approaches to excellent organizations, and the retrospective analysis of these approaches, need to be guided not only by theoretical and practical factors, but by ethical factors as well.

Those who strive for "excellence" cannot escape the ethical or value judgment. What might be seen as "high performance" from one perspective might be seen as "compulsive pursuit of a socially useless, even destructive, objective" from another perspective. There is no real escape from this problem because the way one defines "excellence" depends on values. Hence, in this chapter, the analysis of approaches to excellent and high-performing organizations will be guided not only by theoretical and practical considerations, but by ethical ones as well.

THE DEFINITION OF EXCELLENT PERFORMANCE

The way one defines excellence is crucial, because it guides one's choice as to which organizations to study and, hence, affects one's findings. This definition is not value-free. Even the terms chosen to stand for excellence represent a value judgment. The studies on excellence basically represent two different ways to approach and to define the term. The first defines excellence in practical, measurable terms. The second defines it in more "soft" and valued terms, emphasizing ethical considerations.

Examples of definitions based on practical, measurable criteria are those used by Peters and Waterman (1982) in their study of the 64 best-run American companies, and by Kanter (1983) in her study of the 47 most successful and innovative companies in the United States. (It is interesting to note that although they are separate studies, more or less the same companies were involved.) The term used by Peters and Waterman is "excellence." For an organization to be defined as excellent, eight criteria were used, of which six were financial measures (asset growth, equity growth, wealth creation, average return on total capital, average return on equity, and average return on sales) and two were nonfinancial (reputation and innovation).

In order to qualify as top performer, a company must have been at the top of its industry on at least 4 out of 6 financial measures and in the other 2 measures for at least the last 20 years. Kanter used very similar measures and time periods but, while Peters and Waterman define "innovations" mainly in technical-operational terms, Kanter includes any kind of innovation. She defines innovation as the generation, acceptance, and implementation of new ideas, processes, products, or services (1983, p. 20). No comment is made about the nature or purpose of these innovations.

On the other hand, we find a different approach taken by others who explicitly integrate values and ethical consideration into their definitions of excellence. Kiefer and Stroh (1984) studied companies representing not only the highest performance in terms of financial measures, but also the highest human satisfaction. Kiefer and Senge (1984) added another important measure: the contribution of the company to its environment, to its community, and to the world. The term they used to stand for excellence is "metanoic organizations," which, in Greek, means systems capable of a fundamental shift of mind. These organizations operate with the conviction that they can create their futures and shape their destinies, and thus contribute to a better society.

Two more examples are the approaches of Ritscher (1983) and McKnight (1984). Ritscher uses the term "high performing, spirited organizations" to denote "high emphasis on ethics and integrity . . . spirited and empowered individuals" (p. 2). McKnight goes further and uses the term "spiritual organizations." He defines "spirituality" as an experience of something beyond our own boundaries, something that transcends our own ego. For McKnight, excellent organizations are those which, besides profit and innovations, have superordinate goals that raise the organization to a higher level of operation in which its employees and its environment benefit in terms of better life quality, development, and growth.

A broad, integrated definition of excellent organizations is provided by Vaill (1982), who has studied "excellence" since the mid-1970s. His definition seems to include most of the dimensions suggested by others, and adds important aspects such as quality of the product and fulfillment of noble ideas for the benefit of the organization's environment. The term used by Vaill for excellence is "high performing systems" (HPS). According to his definition, HPS are those organizations which meet the following criteria (1982, pp. 24–25):

- They are performing excellently against a known external standard. That is, they do more of something in a given time period, or do a set amount faster, than is usually done by their competitors.
- They are performing excellently against what is assumed to be their potential level of performance.

- They are performing excellently in relation to where they were at some earlier point in time.
- They are judged by professional and nonprofessional observers to be doing substantially better qualitatively than comparable systems.
- They are doing their business with significantly less resources than it is assumed are needed for what they do.
- They are perceived by other systems in their field as exemplars of high performance, and thus they become a source of ideas and inspiration for others.
- They are perceived to fulfill, at a high level, the ideals of the culture within which they exist, that is, they have "nobility."
- They are the only organizations that have been able to execute this work at all, even though it may seem that what is done is not so difficult or mysterious.

Although broad, this definition seems to meet the criteria of internal logic, integrity, and consistency; it is a practical definition. It also taps the ethical aspects by adding the quality dimension (no. 4) and the cultural ideals dimension (no. 7). But the ethical aspect remains open to the interpretation of the reader. What culture, what values, what quality of a product is important? There is probably no simple answer to the ethical aspect of high-performance and excellent systems. However, those who want to achieve "excellence" have to make explicit the values and the ethics that guide their definitions and their choices.

PERSPECTIVES ON "EXCELLENCE" (IDEAL TYPES)

High-Performance

Vaill studied a variety of systems, such as top colleges, marching bands, a Coast Guard unit, hospital units, military units, drug rehabilitation agencies, stock brokerages, and small businesses, all of which have the criteria of high performance. His findings can be summarized as follows:

1. HPS are clear on their broad purposes and on short-term objectives for fulfilling these purposes. They know why they exist and what they are trying to do. Members have strikingly congruent ideas.

2. There is widely shared, deep commitment to these purposes. There is high motivation and a high level of energy that is focused toward achieving the organization's purpose.
3. Teamwork in HPS is focused on the task. The distinction between "task" and "maintenance" tends to dissolve because members' behavior is integrated in the system's operations. Satisfaction and motivation are derived from task performance and sense of purpose, not from maintenance processes.
4. There are firm beliefs in the "correct form of organization," and a considerable effort is devoted to attaining and maintaining this form.
5. Strong and clear leadership is not ambivalent. Initiative is highly valued. Leadership style varies widely from HPS to HPS, but is remarkably consistent within given systems. Hence leaders are reliable and predictable.
6. HPS are fertile sources of inventions and new methods within the scope of the task they have defined and within the form they have chosen. They are relatively conservative about new methods and inventions that take them outside the task boundaries and structural forms they have traditionally practiced.
7. HPS are clearly bounded from their environments; much energy is devoted to maintaining these boundaries. There is a strong consciousness that "we are different."
8. HPS avoid external control; they "scrounge" resources from the environment nonapologetically. They produce what they want by their own standards. Thus they often frustrate other systems or the larger system of which they are a part.
9. There is an organic "fit" among the system's various elements and practices.

Metanoic

A similar approach to high-performing, excellent systems is described by Kiefer and Stroh (1984). The term used to describe those systems is "metanoic organization," which in Greek means "capable of a fundamental shift of mind" (*meta,* "transcending"; *noia,* "mind") or, simply stated, these organizations operate with the conviction that they can create their future and shape their destiny; they are capable of inspired performance. The authors studied four high-performing, high-tech corporations. Their findings support some of the propositions offered by Vaill.

Organizations capable of inspired performance appear to have the following elements:

1. A deep sense of purpose, often expressed as a vision of what the organization stands for or strives to create.
2. Alignment of individuals around this vision.
3. An emphasis on personal performance and an environment that empowers the individual, a deep commitment to employees' personal well-being and growth. Personal power means an individual's ability to produce meaningful results; it is viewed as the key to increasing both the organization's power and personal satisfaction.
4. Effective structures that take systematic aspects into account. In order to manifest a vision of personal worth and responsibility, they often create decentralized structures and small, semi-autonomous groups, and eliminate multiple levels of management.
5. A capacity to integrate reason and intuition. Organization leaders use intuition extensively to create the organization's vision and future direction. They also use it to understand and design structures that translate individual energy into collective results.
6. "Metanoia." The organization members, particularly the leadership, recognize that in some deep way they are the organization. They know they are responsible for the quality of their personal lives and of the organization, and they believe they can shape their destiny together.

Excellence

Peters and Waterman's (1982) study of America's best-run companies provides eight attributes that characterize excellent corporations:

1. A bias for action, for getting on with it. The standard operating procedure is "Do it, fix it, try it." There is a strong inclination to experiment and a belief that there is a solution for every problem.
2. Closeness to the customer. These companies learn from the people they serve. They provide unparalleled quality, service, and reliability.

Many of the innovations are gotten from customers, and result from listening intently and regularly.

3. Autonomy and entrepreneurship. They foster many leaders and many innovators throughout the organization. They encourage using imagination in all spheres, trial and error, innovation, taking risks, and supporting successful attempts.

4. Productivity through people. The excellent companies treat the rank and file as the source of quality and productivity gain. They respect every individual.

5. Value driven. They have clear, shared values that constitute the philosophy of the company about how matters should be handled.

6. Sticking to their knitting. With few exceptions, the odds for excellent performance seem strongly to favor those companies that stay reasonably close to businesses they already know.

7. Simple form, lean staff. Elegantly simple structure. Top-level staffs are lean.

8. Simultaneous loose-tight properties. The excellent companies are both centralized and decentralized. They have pushed autonomy down to the shop floor. On the other hand, they are fanatic centralists around the few core values they hold clearly.

Innovative

A study of the most successful companies in America was conducted by Kanter (1983). She discovered that one of the most important variables related to excellence was the rate of innovation in the company. Innovations were strongly related to the following elements:

- Decentralization of structure and power. Balance between circulation and focusing of power, local autonomy, team work, broad job charters, and decentralization of resources.
- Values and norms that favor change and individual initiative instead of stability and tradition. Employees feel energized through autonomy and involvement in innovations and change. Climate of pride and family spirit.
- Rewards. Positive incentives for initiative. Incentives are visibility of success and the chance to do more challenging work. Job security.
- Open communication. Horizontal and vertical. Mobility of workers across jobs. Free information flow.

Humanistic

Perhaps one of the most inclusive descriptions of the ideal-type organization of the near future is provided by Harris (1983). This model is based on observations made in the microelectronics industry, from an open-systems theory and humanistic psychology perspective. Harris termed it "humanistic capitalism." The model can be summarized by the following three dimensions:

1. Organizational culture — futuristic, fast-moving, information-rich, kinetic organization. A modern human system with transient units, mobile personnel, and continuous reorganization. Role assignments are more temporary and less rigid or precise. Expertise, talents, and professional disciplines converge in task accomplishment. Organizational arrangements are fluid and participative to accommodate changing roles, relationships, and structures. Characterized by task forces and project teams, disposable divisions and ad hoc units. Self-renewing and adapting enterprise in a continually dynamic environment.

2. Power and authority — horizontal dispersement, with a shift of decisions laterally or to lower levels of responsibility. More emphasis on the authority of competence and a team approach. More sharing of decision making and seeking diverse input, including from workers and consumers. Organizational communication is more circular and lateral, demanding fast information flow by computerized systems. Requires complex problem solving to meet increasingly nonroutine, novel, and unexpected problems or challenges. Organizational focus on human resource development and people maintenance.

3. Synergistic personnel — associative persons skilled in collaboration and cooperation. Varied, competent people, including women and minorities with responsibilities, who are self-energizers and self-actualizers. Seeking primarily challenges for personal and professional development, these are mobile cosmopolitans. Executives and managers are seen as coordinators and consultants who often work on mixed, temporary teams. They operate in complex settings within a responsibility matrix requiring flexibility and varied functional skills. Skilled in human relations and group dynamics, these knowledge workers and technicians are capable of quick, intense work relationships and disengagements. Agents of planned change, they find transience can be liberating. They are advocates of quality, profitable service and cooperation among labor-management-government-consumer.

Adaptive

For DeGreen (1982) the ideal type of organization is the one capable of long-term survival and growth in a possibly hostile environment, and in the face of sudden, rapid, unexpected environmental changes; an organization that can deal successfully with the unexpected and with the ever growing complexity of its environment and of itself. The main elements of this ideal type are resilient structure — flexible structure capable of absorbing large-scale, unexpected changes; forecasting, sensing, and monitoring mechanisms; problem-solving, decision-making, and learning mechanisms. Figure 3.1 shows the general model as suggested by DeGreen (1982, p. 296).

To summarize, six ideal type models of excellence have been described. Table 3.1 shows the approaches and the main elements emphasized in each model.

TABLE 3.1
Ideal Organizing

Writer	Term	Emphasis
Vaill (1978, 1982)	"high performance"	describing HPS
Kiefer & Stroh (1984)	"metanoic"	vision & purpose
Peters & Waterman (1982)	"excellence"	structures & procedures
Kanter (1983)	"innovative"	innovations
Harris (1984)	"humanistic capitalism"	culture
DeGreen (1982)	"adaptive"	monitoring & sensing

Source: Prepared by the authors.

Vaill's main efforts were first to call attention to the existence of extraordinary performance. Basically he describes what high performance is, not what makes it. The others followed him, tried to find basic elements that might affect excellence. Each of them emphasized different elements. An integrated framework based on these studies is suggested.

The findings on the characteristics of high-performing, excellent organizations can be summarized according to five basic dimensions: purpose, culture, individuals, the system and its environment, and management and communication. Hence, a high-performing, excellent organization has the following dimensions:

1. Purpose
   • Has a clearly stated vision and purpose.

Figure 3.1. Generalized Top-Level Block Diagram of an Adaptive Organization.

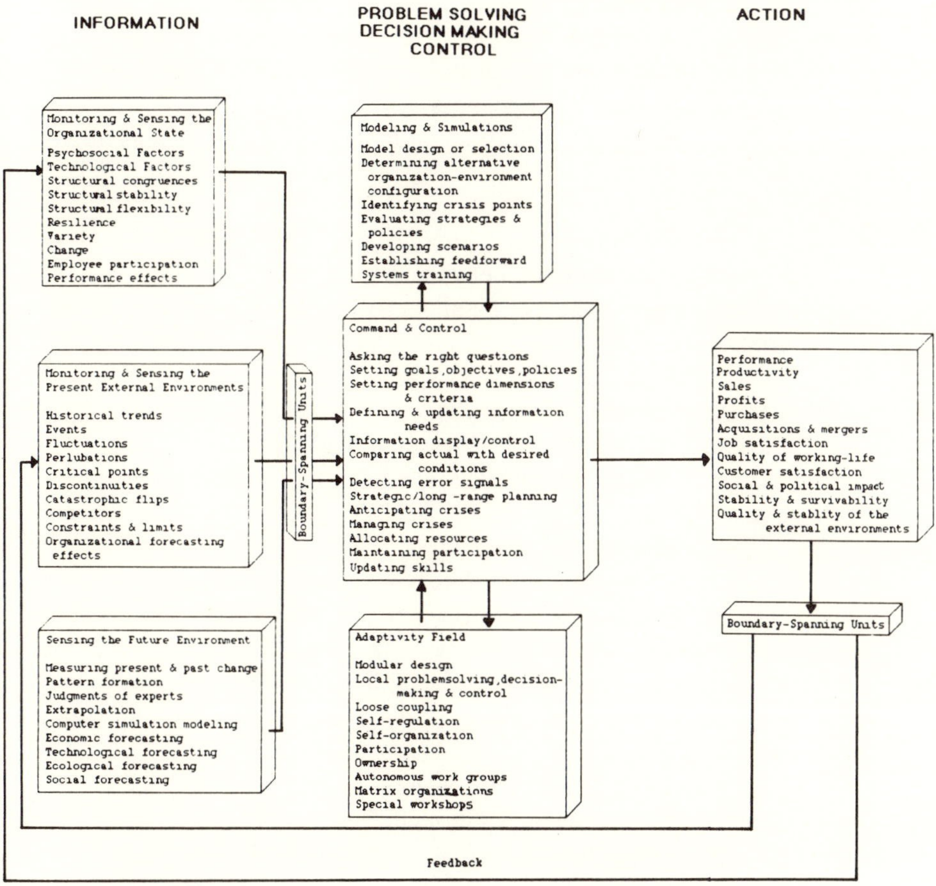

INFORMATION PROBLEM SOLVING ACTION
DECISION MAKING
CONTROL

```
Monitoring & Sensing the
Organizational State

Psychosocial Factors
Technological Factors
Structural congruences
Structural stability
Structural flexibility
Resilience
Variety
Change
Employee participation
Performance effects
```

```
Modeling & Simulations

Model design or selection
Determining alternative
  organization-environment
  configuration
Identifying crisis points
Evaluating strategies &
  policies
Developing scenarios
Establishing feedforward
Systems training
```

```
Monitoring & Sensing the
Present External Environments

Historical trends
Events
Fluctuations
Perturbations
Critical points
Discontinuities
Catastrophic flips
Competitors
Constraints & limits
Organizational forecasting
  effects
```

```
Boundary-Spanning Units
```

```
Command & Control

Asking the right questions
Setting goals,objectives,policies
Setting performance dimensions
  & criteria
Defining & updating information
  needs
Information display/control
Comparing actual with desired
  conditions
Detecting error signals
Strategic/long -range planning
Anticipating crises
Managing crises
Allocating resources
Maintaining participation
Updating skills
```

```
Performance
Productivity
Sales
Profits
Purchases
Acquisitions & mergers
Job satisfaction
Quality of working-life
Customer satisfaction
Social & political impact
Stability & survivability
Quality & stability of the
  external environments
```

```
Sensing the Future Environment

Measuring present & past change
Pattern formation
Judgments of experts
Extrapolation
Computer simulation modeling
Economic forecasting
Technological forecasting
Ecological forecasting
Social forecasting
```

```
Adaptivity Field

Modular design
Local problemsolving,decision-
  making & control
Loose coupling
Self-regulation
Self-organization
Participation
Ownership
Autonomous work groups
Matrix organizations
Special workshops
```

```
Boundary-Spanning Units
```

Feedback

Note: Similar structure recurs at various lower levels of the organization.

Source: DeGreen 1982.

- Has a strong, collective alignment with that vision and purpose
- Is deeply committed to service
- Is dedicated to quality and excellence
- Carries this dedication to excellence down to the smallest details
- Has a strong emphasis on action and on achieving results.

2. Culture
   - Strong culture, strong values; they are visible and shared by all
   - Consciously shapes its culture to support its purpose
   - Emphasizes teamwork

- Places high emphasis on ethics and integrity
- Places high value on keeping agreements and commitments
- Encourages and practices effective two-way communication
- Supports innovation and ideas for change, tolerates mistakes
- Supports honesty and openness
- Encourages people to talk about their feelings as well as about facts.

3. Individuals
- Treats individuals as empowered, trusted, and competent
- Ensures that individuals feel valued and special
- Is dedicated to the personal and professional growth of its employees
- Energizes members with work spirit
- Respects individual differences
- Ensures that individuals feel secure in their jobs
- Is a place where individuals feel whole, that work is part of their lives.

4. The system and its environment
- Has strong consciousness of its boundaries and its uniqueness
- Has an action-oriented concern for its natural and human environment
- Has real, human communication with the outside community
- Emphasizes the contribution of its products or operations to the benefit of humankind
- Maintains close contact with customers and clients (feedback)
- Senses and monitors its environment
- Has strong consciousness of the quality of the environment
- Forecasts the future.

5. Management, structure, and communication
- Delegates authority as low in the power structure as possible
- Makes extensive use of collaborative decision making
- Assigns jobs to individuals and teams and then "gets out of the way"
- Practices straight two-way communication with employees
- Uses positive reinforcement extensively and effectively
- Has a narrow, simple structure that supports action and results
- Keeps hierarchy to a minimum
- Practices extensive, informal communication throughout the organization

- Uses intuition and nonanalytic management approaches as well as analytic ones
- Has strong leadership that combines loose and tight properties.

What elevates specific organizations above all the others of their kind has to do with people, values, purpose, communication, and teamwork, what can be called the soft side of the organization. Harder, more tangible organization aspects, such as cost accounting or cash flow analysis, and even analytic, rational management systems, such as management by objectives, auditing, and matrix structures, while all important, are not related to high performance.

LEADERSHIP AND EXCELLENCE

How did these high-performing, excellent companies become the way they are? What is the major element that made the transition possible? The studies on high-performing systems all provide the same answer. Peters and Waterman put it in a precise and decisive way: ". . . what we found was that associated with almost every excellent company was a strong leader (or two) who seemed to have had a lot to do with making the company excellent in the first place" (1982, p. 28).

The notion that transforming organizations into excellent ones is closely related to "strong leadership" and management behavior receives support from other studies on excellent companies. Tichy (1983) calls these transformers "charismatic leaders," Deal and Kennedy (1982) call them "heroes," Kanter (1983) uses the term "change masters," and Vaill (1982) uses the terms "purposing leadership" and "strong and clear leadership."

Peters and Waterman (1982) devote two chapters of their book to the examination of the characteristics of leaders who made their systems the way they are. Their findings are that these leaders are not typical analytical, rational managers, but that they are intuitive, creative, people-oriented, visionary, and purposeful. The researchers argue that the rational, analytical model of leadership includes the following shortcomings:

1. It has a built-in bias. It leads to obsession with cost and quantitative elements, not with qualitative elements or values

2. It leads to an abstract, heartless philosophy. The rationalist approach takes the living element out of situations that should exist above all
3. It does not value experimentation and abhors mistakes. This leads to overcomplexity and inflexibility
4. It causes denigration of the importance of values
5. There is little place in the rationalist world for internal competition.

The basic dimension of high-performing leadership is called "transforming leadership," defined as follows: "leadership that builds on man's need for meaning, leadership that creates institutional purpose . . . he is the value-shaper, the exemplar, the maker of meanings . . . he is the true artist, the true pathfinder" (Peters & Waterman 1982, p. 82).

Transforming leadership represents a unique balance among three managerial elements: (1) the pragmatic, analytic, and rational element; (2) the maintenance and people-oriented element; (3) the purposeful, visionary, and creative element (Peters & Waterman 1982, p. 81).

Like that of Peters and Waterman, Vaill's work on high-performing systems provides the same conclusions. That is, high performance is strongly related to "strong leadership," and the main element in this leadership is what he calls "purposing," a term that stands for finding a purpose for the organization and "inducing clarity, consensus, and commitment regarding the organization's basic purpose (1982, p. 29). In his work, Vaill has discovered that top managers of high-performing systems devote an extraordinary amount of time to the task of purposing. They also have strong feelings about the attainment of the systems' purposes. And, finally, they focus their attention on key issues and variables relating to the purposing.

Vaill argues that purposing is a learned behavior. He suggests establishing learning programs in which top managers will be able to understand the importance of purposing and to acquire skills of purposing management.

Deal and Kennedy (1982), in their study of the relation between "corporate culture" and "high performance," also emphasize management behavior as a major element of transformation. They go further still by arguing that "heroic management" is the appropriate term to describe behavior related to excellence. They describe the characteristics of those heroes vividly:

> Heroes are neither rational managers who do strategic planning, write memos, and devise flow charts, nor are they charismatic leaders. . . . They are motivators, magicians, and saviors. They have unshakable character and style.

They do things everyone else wants to do but is afraid to try. Heroes are symbolic figures whose deeds are out of the ordinary, but not too far out. (Deal & Kennedy 1982, p. 76)

Deal and Kennedy suggest that the following characteristics pertain to transforming leaders:

- They are highly visible, credible, and consistent in support of the values they espouse.
- They are masters of communication.
- They use symbolic actions such as rites, rituals, and ceremonies to reinforce their values.
- They motivate employees by providing positive reinforcement.
- They provide a lasting human climate within the system.
- They know how to succeed and to make change attainable and part of human capacity.
- They provide positive role models for workers to follow.
- They set high standards of performance.
- They encourage creativity, innovation, and trial and error.

Kanter (1983) lists five essential skills shared by managers who work in excellent companies:

1. They thrive on novelty. Like kaleidoscopes, change masters know how to "twist and shake up" their habitual mind-sets to create new patterns of thought. They work as "cross-fertilizing agents" who comb the organization for new sources of data. They provide the right environment for the emergence of kaleidoscope thinking.
2. They inspire co-workers with a clear vision and a sense of direction. They instinctively know how to articulate change with faith and conviction.
3. Change masters build coalitions of support within the organization. They form alliances to shape their visions into working realities.
4. They work in teams. They encourage democratic decision making on projects.
5. They promote self-esteem among employees. They encourage open communication.

Like Peters and Waterman, Kanter argues that "change masters" do not act according to the industrial-age model of the analytical, rational, and authoritarian manager.

Bass (1985) points out that first-order change involves what he terms "transactional leadership," and second-order change or achieving excellence involves what he terms "transformational leadership."

Transactional leaders recognize what actions subordinates must take to achieve outcomes. They clarify these role and task requirements for the subordinates so that they are confident in exerting necessary efforts. They also recognize subordinates' needs and wants, and clarify how they will be satisfied if necessary efforts are made.

Transformational leaders motivate subordinates to do more than they were originally expected to do, and to engage with high spirit in transforming the organization and/or achieving excellence in performance. Transformational leaders have the following capabilities and characteristics:

1. They raise members' level of consciousness about the importance and value of designated outcomes and ways of reaching these outcomes.
2. They get members to transcend their own self-interests for the sake of their team, organization, and the larger society.
3. They raise members' need level (Maslow hierarchy model) from the need for security to the need for recognition and self-actualization.
4. They are charismatic leaders. They arouse enthusiasm, faith, loyalty, pride, and trust in themselves and their aims.
5. They are people-oriented. They maintain a developmental and individualistic orientation toward their subordinates.
6. Intellectual stimulation. They enhance the problem-solving and creativity capabilities of their associates.

Ackerman (1984), Harrison (1984), and Kiefer and Stroh (1984) have pointed to the possibility that transforming organizations may be related to a more humane leadership style. Harrison terms this style "stewardship." He explains:

> The new leader is seen as having a caring, respectful, and positive attitude toward people, and a willingness to share power. He or she is more open and non-defensive regarding his/her own faults and vulnerabilities than former leaders, and less likely to use fear, domination, or militant charisma than heretofore. The picture is one of a personally secure and mature individual who can articulate the values and high principles which give organizational life meaning, but who is more humble and receptive than we normally expect visionary leaders to be. (1984, p. 103)

Harrison, and Kiefer and Stroh argue that the important achievement of transformation leadership is alignment and attunement. Alignment occurs when organization members act as parts of an integrated whole, each finding the opportunity to express his or her true purpose through the organization's purpose. Attunement is a resonance of harmony among the parts of the system, and between the parts and the whole.

To summarize, transforming organizations may be related basically to two leadership styles. The first is the strong, charismatic leader; the second is the more humane leader. There is nothing new in the notion that major changes are usually made by strong, charismatic leaders. However, this process usually involves the loss of power and responsibility by lower echelons, and the results may be destructive (Reason 1984). Some recent studies suggest finding a more balanced style and attending to leadership elements that can be learned. Three leadership dimensions appear to be important for transforming organizations to excellent systems: (1) purposing, (2) innovation, and (3) people orientation.

1. Purposing creates institutional purpose; provides meaning; involves pathfinding and visioning; induces clarity, consensus, and commitment regarding the organization's purpose; and inspires employees with clear vision and a sense of direction.

2. Innovation and creativity involve taking risks; encouraging creativity, innovation, and trial and error; thriving on novelty; valuing experimentation; using intuition; and setting high standards of performance.

3. People orientation consists of working through teams, promoting self-esteem among workers, attending to qualitative elements of products and procedures, attending to feelings and to people's needs, empowering and sharing power, open communication, positive reinforcement, and providing a lasting humane climate.

APPROACHES FOR TRANSFORMING ORGANIZATIONS TO EXCELLENT SYSTEMS

The emphasis on the role top executives play in transforming organizations into excellent ones naturally leads to approaches that focus on "reeducating" managers. Most of the approaches to excellence are in fact training programs and workshops for top executives. However, some practitioners and managers are already developing approaches and methods that facilitate organization transformation to excellent systems. The purpose of this section is to describe and analyze some of these briefly.

The approaches for transforming organizations to excellent ones can be categorized according to their main content or purpose. There are at least three types of approaches:

1. Those which focus on changing the organization's mission, purpose.
2. Those which focus on educating managers for managerial excellence.
3. Those which focus on performance and on elements that hinder or facilitate high performance at the individual, group, and organizational levels.

Purposing

An outline for a training program for top managers is suggested by Vaill (1982). "Purposing" is the term he proposes to describe management activities that were found to be related to high performance. The term refers to "that continuous stream of actions by an organization's formal leadership that has the effect of inducing clarity, consensus, and commitment regarding the organization's basic purpose" (p. 29).

From high-performing systems Vaill has identified seven functions of purposing:

1. Purposing occurs in relation to the expectations of those who own or charter the system. The content of what HPS leaders talk about and do is seen to have these key outside forces as reference points.
2. Purposing is seen in the articulation of the grounds for basic strategic decisions.
3. Purposing is seen in the leader's accounts of the meaning of the system's daily activity.
4. Purposing is evident in decisions *not* to do things.
5. Purposing differentiates the organization from other superficially similar organizations. It provides its unique identity.
6. Purposing is the expression of what the leadership wants.
7. Purposing in some sense entails the mythologizing of oneself and the organization.

Purposing occurs through the investment of large amounts of microtime and macrotime, the expression and experience of very strong feelings about the attainment of purposes and the importance of the system, and the attainment of understanding of the key variables for system success. Transforming organizations to HPS is related to leadership that has integrated these three factors at a very high level of intensity and clarity.

The approach suggested by Tichy and Ulrich (1984) also concentrates on management behavior and purposing. They suggest four phases and describe management activities necessary for organization revitalization:

1. Felt need for change. Being sensitive and receptive to dissatisfaction with the status quo. Being able to identify triggers for change and sensing felt needs for change require environmental scanning capabilities and projecting future environmental conditions that the company may face. Having the skill of identifying and responding to stakeholders and adapting to different stakeholders.

2. Creation of a vision. Providing the organization with a vision of a desired future state. Having a vision is the core responsibility of the leader. It must be congruent with the leader's philosophy and style. At General Motors, after several years of committee work, a vision of the future was drafted that included a mission statement and eight objectives for the company. This vision was consistent with the leadership philosophy and style of Roger Smith. An important skill in developing a vision is being able to define a firm's distinctive competence.

3. Mobilizing of commitment. The process of evolving commitment and mobilizing support requires a great deal of dialogue and exchange. It must go well beyond a few days' retreat. During this phase, key individuals must be involved in setting goals that are visible and can be reinforced by success. Leaders must be aware of the critical importance of getting subordinates to accept the vision, and to see how the vision and future will meet their needs. The leader will have to act as a role model for subordinates. He or she will embody the attitudes and behaviors that subordinates should work to attain.

4. Institutionalization. Transformational leaders need to transform their vision into reality, their missions into actions, their philosophies into practice. Alterations in communication, decision-making, and problem-solving systems are tools through which transitions are shared so that visions become practice. At a deeper level, institutionalization requires shaping and reinforcing a new culture that fits with the new system. The human resources systems of selection, development, appraisal, and reward are also major levers for achieving this phase.

Educating Managers for "Managerial Excellence"

This is perhaps the most common approach. Consultants develop training programs and workshops in which participants learn about the characteristics of "excellence" and learn to apply them to their organizations.

A typical example is the handbook developed by Ritscher (1983), based on the eight marks of excellence presented in the study of Peters and Waterman (1982). Ritscher translates the elements characterizing excellent organizations into actions, behaviors, and directions that should be learned by top managers. For example, under the title "conduct a vision and purpose meeting," Ritscher suggests a top management team meeting in which the purpose is "to develop a collaborative statement of vision and purpose that is accurate, succinct, and compelling" (p. 23). The author suggests the way in which the meeting should be conducted.

Another example is working on the element "commit to service" ("close to the customer"). Ritscher suggests actions and directions to managers that might enhance the organization's commitment to its customers. The examples are the following:

- Employ customer feedback forms or other ways of getting feedback directly from the customers.
- Ask people "How can we improve service," and then follow through.
- Tell stories that carry the message, "To us service is important," (1983, p. 27).

Ritscher has developed workshops and training programs for top managers based on the elements characterizing high-performing systems — for example, a workshop in which a management team works together on generating a new vision and purpose for the organization, then learns ways to infuse them throughout the organization and to align members with them. The workshops and training program cover almost all the elements characterizing high performance.

The book, *Managing for Excellence,* written by Bradford and Cohen (1984) is also a "guide to developing high performance in contemporary organizations." Its basic premise is that those who want to succeed in changing their organizations to excellent ones need to learn four basic skills: (1) building a shared responsibility team, (2) continuously developing subordinates, (3) building a common department vision, and

(4) establishing "over-arching" goals, meaning challenging, feasible goals that reflect the core purpose of the department and have larger significance.

Ritscher's handbook provides guidelines and action steps for middle managers, explaining how to apply the above four components in their departments. An important notion of this book is the claim that the management style characterizing excellence is not the "heroic style" but what is called the "developer style," consisting of the four components. This claim is based on assessment of training programs for middle managers. Bradford and Cohen provide some examples of managers who participated in their program and changed their departments to excellent ones.

The importance of the study by Harris (1983) is its comprehensiveness. He describes in detail all the organizational dimensions that need to be transformed and the content of the change (or how each dimension should appear after being transformed). His study is actually a guidebook for senior managers on how to transform their organizations to meet the challenges of the future. Eleven dimensions are involved:

1. Changing the corporate philosophy, the ideals and ideas that the organization lives by and that makes it distinctive
2. Transforming organizational identity and space. Creating uniqueness in physical settings, in culture, and in quality of work
3. Changing purposes and standards. Goals and policies should be based on "humanistic capitalism"
4. Transforming organizational values and norms. From Theory X to Theory Y
5. Transforming corporate look and style. Creating a healthy, stimulating environment, and mentally and physically healthy individuals
6. Revolutionizing corporate processes and activities. Matrix structure, teamwork, management that places emphasis on innovation, renewal, and change
7. Transforming organizational communication. Using modern technology to enhance open communication and participation
8. Changing career development patterns. Human resource development, learning, and training as ongoing processes. Education for changing roles, leadership development
9. Transforming organizational relationships. Team participation, trust, openness, authenticity, helpfulness

10. Transforming organizational recognition and rewards. Employers take care of both health needs and ego needs of their workers
11. Developing organizational potential. Developing transformational leadership and strategies, actualizing employee potential.

Focusing on Individual and Organizational Performance, and Elements That Hinder and Facilitate High Performance

These approaches are complex, multilevel, and multidimensional. They include a model guiding the process of change and a variety of change methods. It is typical of these approaches to incorporate fitness or well-being of individuals, groups, and the whole organization. Two examples are provided here.

Coke and Mierau (1984) developed a change model based on the premise that the paradigm of excellence involves two basic components: individual well-being and organizational well-being. The main variables that affect the optimization of these two components are described in Figure 3.2.

The model guides assessment techniques, training programs, workshops, and interventions assumed to result in high performance. Its advantage is that it deals with excellence from a multidimensional perspective. High performance is related not only to the product or to financial output, but also to individual well-being (mental, physical), to the work ethic, and to organizational well-being ("soul," "mission").

Figure 3.2. Subsystem Stress Pyramids

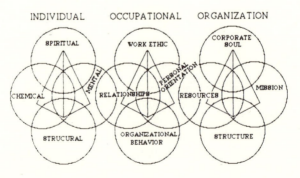

Source: Coke and Mierau (1984).

The second example is the model and approach developed by Adams (1984). The process of change is based on a practical model aimed at "achieving excellence in personal performance." The basic premise of Adams is that high-performing systems need to attract and to include members who are able to evoke and maintain their own "personal peak performance" (PPP). The model consists of three interrelated dimensions and their elements, as shown in Figure 3.3.

PPP is manifested in words such as "energized," "focused," "enthusiasm," "exhilarated," "inner calm," "attuned," "confident," "powerful," "alert," and "flowing." These experiences are most readily evoked and maintained when the six elements listed under PPP in Figure 3.3 are present. These six elements are not innate, and anyone can learn them.

PPP is related to the person's well-being: physical, mental, emotional, and spiritual. These elements, too, can be learned. The third dimension relating to both PPP and well-being is the personal belief system. On the one hand, beliefs help one to focus and to relate to the world. On the other, they provide the boundaries of one's sensitivity, by cutting many alternatives. Adams helps people become aware of the three dimensions and enhance their PPP. He then works on the collective belief system as reflected in the organization myths, legends, traditions, shared

Figure 3.3   Some Key Considerations in Achieving and Maintaining Personal Peak Performance

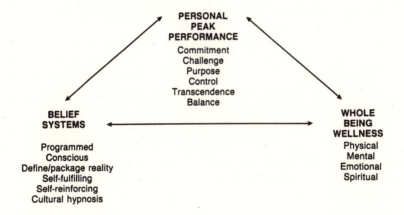

Source: Adams (1984a).

habits, and unwritten rules that, if they remain untouched, may "hypnotize" the system members.

The above models, training programs, and approaches are a few examples representing the rapidly developing field of transformation and excellence. The perspective taken is the management perspective. The main focus of intervention is on management reeducation and training. Managers are introduced to models of excellence, and behavioral aspects are then learned. Change is managed by the management team, while the consultant is mainly a trainer and reeducator. There is already some empirical evidence that this type of approach may facilitate change in culture and in performance.

EVALUATION

The purpose of this section is to define and make explicit some of the basic propositions existing implicitly in some of the approaches described in this chapter, and to examine the evidence that confirms or disconfirms them.

Proposition 1

We are in a state of paradigmatic change at the individual, organizational, and social levels. The new paradigm is already here and is manifested in high-performing, excellent, or metanoic systems. This proposition is derived from Kuhn's theory on scientific revolution. According to this theory, the new paradigm emerges while the old one is still in existence. Characteristics of emerging paradigms may be roughly predicted in at least two ways: (1) on the basis of anomalies in and/or deficiencies of the present paradigm; (2) on the basis of emerging values, premises, world views, language, metaphors.

The studies of excellent systems point to the possibility that the new paradigm of organizations is already here. Markley and Harman's study (1982) on culture transformation points to the possibility that a new paradigm is emerging "because of increasingly intense human systems problems that lie beyond the ability of traditional approach to resolve" (p. 223). The works of futurists such as Ferguson (1980) point in the same direction. Organizational transformation's rapid development as a change paradigm supports this view. The fact that books such as *Theory Z, In Search of Excellence,* and *Corporate Culture* were, for a long time, best sellers also suggests that many are yearning for that new paradigm.

However, whether these few "metanoic" systems are "exceptional ones" or "early harbingers" is hard to know. Moreover, Sheldon's study on the process of paradigm change in health institutions shows that a paradigm may exist and even die without the existence of a new one (Sheldon 1980). Studies on "alternative education systems," for example, have shown that two paradigms can exist side by side without one replacing the other (Broad 1977; Flaxman & Homestead 1978).

Hence, whether we are already witnessing the emergence of new organizational paradigms, or have just examined exceptional ones, is a matter of value bias. We probably will not be able to answer this question until the domination of a new paradigm is obvious.

Proposition 2

The death of the old paradigm and the birth of the new one is always toward growth, toward a better and higher level of organizing from the individual, organizational, and social perspective. This proposition is derived from the theories of Jantsch (1976) and Land (1973), among others. Many scholars assume that organizations tend to transform into a system of higher complexity with higher adaptation capability. However, transformation can be toward a state that is less satisfactory, even toward disintegration (Prigogine 1984; Merry & Brown 1986). The possibility that paradigm change can be negative, at least from some perspectives, is sometimes avoided by organizational transformation practitioners. Their writings are often characterized by optimism and good faith.

There are, for example, at least three negative aspects in excellent companies. The first is shared values. Clapp (1983) examined some of the companies studied by Peters and Waterman (1982), and found that the "values shared by all" are those of the top managers and that, in many cases, they disguise, or create an illusion of, a benign family. The same is true with policy that is determined solely by managers that employees are expected to fulfill.

Another negative side effect of HPS is their effect on top managers. The studies point to the fact that leaders of these systems work very hard. They do not respect time and place. They work day and night, at their offices, at their homes, and wherever they happen to be. They work evenings, weekends, and vacation periods. Vaill (1982), for example, found that "Their consciousness is dominated by systems, issues, and events. They see the rest of life often, in terms of the system's jargon, technology, and culture" (p. 32). The time devoted to their families and to social activities is very little. No wonder some of the excellent organizations are characterized by "burned-out" managers (Kanter 1983, p. 392).

Harrison (1984) studied what he calls the inhumanities of excellent systems and reached the following conclusion:

> They burn people out; they take over their private lives; they ostracize or expel those who do not share their purposes; and they are frequently ruthless in their dealings with those outside the magic circle. . . . It seems to me no accident that many of our most exciting tales of high performing . . . are either literally or metaphorically "war stories." War is the ultimate expression of unbridled will in the pursuit of "noble" ends. (p. 100)

Thus, even "excellent" systems have their inhumanities.

Proposition 3

Performance in terms of profit and growth is the most important measure of excellence. This implicit proposition is typical of some studies that take only a management perspective on performance. This approach is strongly opposed by those who suggest taking into consideration ethical and moral dimensions, such as individual growth and ecological conservation. Katz and Kahn (1978) point out that effectivity must include the organization's contribution to its higher-level systems.

One of the most vigorous attacks on the market-oriented, nonethical perspective is that by Ramos (1981), who analyzed the current paradigm of organization theory and called for establishing a whole new paradigm that will incorporate moral considerations. He explains:

> The old theory implies that production is only a technical matter. However, the fundamental assumption of the new science of organizations is that production is both a technical and moral issue. Production is not only a mechanomorphic activity; it is also an outcome of men's creative enjoyment of themselves. In a sense, men produce themselves while they produce things. In other words, production should be undertaken not only to provide enough

goods for man to live a healthy life, but to provide the conditions for him to actualize his nature and enjoy doing so. Thus, the production of commodities must be managed ethically, because as an infinite consumer man does not endure, but exhausts his very being. Moreover, production is also a moral issue because of its impact upon nature at large. Nature is a living system which can only endure as long as one does not violate the biophysical constraints superimposed upon its restorative processes. (p. 171)

Proposition 4

Charismatic leadership, transformation, and ethics. Some scientists describe transformational leaders as charismatic and as heroes. However, charismatic leaders and true believers may transform social systems to highly negative forms from the perspective of freedom, self-responsibility, and ethics.

In a study on the change in authority patterns in American organizations, Heller (1984) states that periods of crisis, uncertainty, and transition provide convenient circumstances for the emergence of messianic movements and charismatic leaders promising stability, simplistic solutions, and "back to the good old ways" of doing things. She points out the possibility that this authority pattern is emerging in organizations.

There is another direction: leadership with people, not over people. Most of the managers of excellent systems are not charismatic, but empowering and nurturing. Many scholars are intrigued by this issue. Lawrence (1979), for example, argues that transforming organizations entails transforming authority patterns toward personal responsibility and empowerment. Harrison (1984), analyzing the issue, comes to the conclusion that the most fundamental aspect of paradigmatic change is the change in our consciousness, and this cannot be forced or led by charismatic leadership, but by what he describes as "stewardship."

Strong, charismatic transformational leadership raises the question of morals and ethics. Transformational leadership is moral if it deals with true needs and is based on informed choice. The moral transformational leader is guided by such universal ethical principles as respect for human dignity and equal rights. Moral leadership should mobilize and direct support for "more general and comprehensive values that express followers' more fundamental and enduring needs," writes Burns (1978). Burns adds that moral leadership helps followers to see the real conflict between competing values, the inconsistencies between espoused values and behavior, the need for realignment of values, and the need for changes in behavior or transformation of institutions.

The well-being of organizational life might be better served in the long run by moral leadership. That is, transformation that results in the fulfillment of real, authentic needs will prove to be more beneficial to the organization than transformation that deals with manufactured needs and group delusions.

Proposition 5

By conforming to the marks of excellence (such as "close to the customer") an excellent organization will emerge. There is not yet sufficient evidence to support this proposition. Tichy and Ulrich (1984) point out that a number of chief executive officers have taken the eight characteristics of the excellent companies and are blindly trying to impose them on their organizations without first examining their appropriateness. There is also a problem in implementing nonconcrete elements such as spirit and style. Owen (1984), for example, argues as follows:

> . . .these eight marks of excellence are really characteristics of organizations that **have been** excellent; they do not in themselves guarantee excellence in the present moment. Indeed, one might implement all of them and end up miles from what excellence is all about. And this is because excellence is not a *thing* but rather a *condition of becoming.* It is not a concrete entity, but rather a matter of style and elegance of spirit. (p. 7; emphasis added)

Much work has been done on achieving organizational excellence. Unless we try to facilitate the transformation of systems into excellent ones by using the knowledge we already have, we will not know how much it is or is not possible.

4

Changing the Organizational Myths

This chapter describes an approach that focuses on cultural elements, such as myths and rituals, as a vehicle for facilitating transformation. The use of myths and other symbolic elements as a vehicle for change has spread rapidly. In recent years, more and more studies and articles on this subject have been published. Annual conferences are held (such as the Organizational Folklore Conference, Santa Monica, California, March 1983, sponsored by U.C.L.A.), and myths seem to play an important part in the field of transformation (for example, Barbee 1983; Kropovsky 1983; Owen 1983a; Stephens et al. 1983).

A CASE EXAMPLE: THE STORY OF EVMA*

This is a brief summary of change effort conducted in a large, complex, medical organization, the Eastern Virginia Medical Authority (EVMA). EVMA is a health service center situated in Tidewater Virginia. Its aim is to provide all the health services to a community of 1.3 million residents divided into seven municipalities or regions. EVMA consists of a medical school with a graduate school, mental health center, rehabilitation institute, 28 local hospitals, and 7 institutions of higher education. It is a community-based organization.

EVMA represents a radical idea: to transform the traditional health care system based on local competitive institutions into a regional,

---

*The case was taken from Owen 1983b.

unified, high-standard, low-cost health care system that includes the full range of health treatment. Moreover, the aim is to make this system self-sufficient and a lever for developing medical education so that the medical staff can be recruited locally.

The idea started as the vision of a small group of key people in Tidewater who had gathered every week since 1966 to discuss ways of transforming the old system into a new one. In 1973, the medical school was established and a change was legislated that enabled the medical authority to be established. Since 1973, more and more local institutions have joined the authority. The vision of a few seemed to have become reality.

Yet the performance and operation of EVMA were plagued with many problems, and in 1982 the organization was considered to be in a crisis situation. A new manager was appointed, and he called Owen in to help him revitalize the organization. The main problems of the organization were the following:

- There was no consensus as to the nature, the purpose, or the mission of the organization. This disagreement caused conflicts inside the system.
- Local hospitals and other institutions were suspicious about the purpose of EVMA.
- It was difficult to keep all the institutions together.
- The overall performance of the organization was poor.
- The consumers of the service were suspicious about the purpose of the organization.
- There was not sufficient public support, both financially and morally.
- The seven municipalities continued to struggle over power and authority, which caused more problems in keeping the organization unified.

The above problems were detected by a team consisting of the new president and the consultant. Their first meetings were devoted to creating trust, to locating the basic problems, to learning the history of the organization, and to examining different approaches to cope with the problems. They concluded that the purpose and the ideology of the new organization were not clear and not mutually agreed upon; hence there were conflicts and very little public support for the organization.

Process of Change

The approach employed followed two interrelated tracks: strategic planning and organizational myth diagnosis.

Strategic Planning

A formal planning group was created that included 44 people representing the 7 municipalities, the institutions, and the professional groups. This group met once a week for nine months and passed through four basic phases of deliberation:

1. Development of mission ideology and purpose for the whole organization
2. Identification of the role and the responsibility of the central authority
3. Identification of the health care needs of the region
4. Outlines of possible approaches and appropriate institutional roles that may be performed by any of the several local institutions.

Organizational Myths Diagnosis

The first track was accompanied by a process of diagnosing the organizational stories, metaphors, and myths in order to help the top management group and the planning group understand the cultural context in which the organization operated, and to provide some strategic options that they may pursue in order to bring change to the organization.

The consultant observed the organization and listened to what people said about it. He interviewed many people in the organization, representing all the different professions, levels, and institutions. He also spoke with people representing agencies connected with the organization, customers, and the founders of the organization. More than 100 people were interviewed.

The central purpose of these interviews was to find the stories, metaphors, and myths of EVMA. The questions used for discovering these cultural elements were simple ones like What is EVMA? What is its story or history? What should it be? The interviews exposed the consultant to conflicting metaphors and myths; the first one was entitled "EVMA the Omnivore"; the second, "EVMA the Unifier."

"EVMA the Omnivore" described the organization in very negative terms, using frightening metaphors and stories with catastrophic endings.

The central theme described the organization as spreading a cancer by capriciously and destructively devouring and taking over every local institution, and by strangling competition and private initiative.

"EVMA the Unifier" described the organization in very positive terms. It was a story of a small group of dedicated people who conceived the idea of establishing regional cooperation, in the form of a self-sufficient health system, based on local professional people, for the benefit of all, at a low cost. EVMA was an ideal creation of a courageous few against overwhelming odds. They invested their time, energy, and money to fulfill a dream.

Which myth represents "reality"? What people believed became truth in their eyes. The two myths were used a vehicles to facilitate the change. The strategy was to enhance and accentuate the positive myth and to remove or at least to diminish the influence of the negative one.

The consultant brought his "findings" to the top management team and to the planning group. The top management team analyzed the two myths, their meanings, and how they affected the operation of the organization. Then steps were decided upon to accentuate the positive aspects and to remove the negative. The findings strongly influenced the team to decide and to agree upon the strategy of the organization, its nature, its orientation, and to make it explicit and acceptable to the management and members.

The findings were discussed in the planning group. While top management decided upon the general orientation, mission, purpose, and nature of the organization, the planning team worked on more detailed issues of how to implement the ideas in day-to-day operation. Strong emphasis was given to cooperation between local institutions. Their authority and functions were defined. The needs of every area were examined and the means were allocated accordingly. The structure of the whole organization was defined and agreed upon. The decision-making process was changed to fit the nature of the organization.

The results of the intervention showed marked improvement in the functioning of the organization, and, most important, the original idea of the EVMA received support and approval from its local institutions and workers. The mission and purpose of the institution was clarified and agreed upon.

To summarize, the transition from a traditional medical system to a public, regional, self-sufficient, and all-embracing system represents a second-order change. It entailed changes in the basic assumption underlying the system's operations, in its ideology, structure, operations, and decision-making process. The intervention conducted by Owen helped the organization to institutionalize the change. In other words, the intervention was made because it was difficult for top managers to institutionalize the radical change — the transition from a small, local health center to a large, complex system.

The transition from one form of organized health service to a completely different form was managed by a group of powerful citizens who had a vision in the 1960s and worked hard to implement this vision. Their dedication, political awareness, and ability to raise money made it possible. But the establishment of a new system does not automatically ensure that the change will persist. Structural change does not automatically entail attitude change. This was the role of the consultant: to help the organization implement the vision, to institutionalize it, and to change attitudes and behaviors so that the change would persist.

The use of myth analysis and organizational myth as done by Owen seems to be a useful, practical, and relatively simple method for dealing with the identity of the system. It encouraged top managers and the core group to deal with the very nature of the system in a way that did not provoke a threat. The intervention helped to facilitate a second-order change that was already on its way.

In the following sections an effort will be made to summarize, classify, and analyze the information on myths and transformation. The first part of this chapter deals with the definition of myths, with their role in organizational life, and with how they are created, maintained, and changed. The second part deals with practical aspects of myths and transformation, with approaches that use myths as a tool for transformation.

The studies and cases examined here define organizational culture not as norms, values, and beliefs, but as the symbolic language and action of the organization. Some studies approach the organizational culture from an anthropological perspective, rather than from a sociological one. A typical anthropological approach to organizational culture and its relationship to myths and transformation is provided by Jones et al. (1983). They define culture as follows:

> ... the stories and ceremonies, rituals, and play which evolve from it and in turn help to form it. In times of organizational stress, in times of transition, in times of transformation, story telling, celebration, and ritualistic behavior may assume special importance.... Narrating, celebration, creativity, and play are basic needs of human beings and aspects of an organization's culture can *transform* the organization. (pp. 177-78; emphasis added)

The above quotation captures the main ideas related to organizational culture, myth, and transformation.

ORGANIZATIONAL MYTHS AND RITUALS: DEFINITION

The concept "organizational myth" is used differently by various authorities, and a distinction between two basic perceptions should be made. The traditional way of approaching organizational myth was to emphasize its disconnection from reality and its dysfunction for the organization's adaptation, performance, and survival. The new way to approach organizational myth is quite the opposite. The emphasis is on its representation of reality as perceived by members, and its role in the process of adaptation and change.

A typical definition of myth as dysfunctional beliefs is provided by Bradford and Harvey (1970): "An organizational myth is an ill-founded and untested belief which powerfully affects the way in which organization members behave and respond" (p. 2). The authors see myths as dysfunctional because they are used by an organization's members as defenses in order not to accept responsibility.

Bradford and Harvey describe four characteristics of myths: (1) They frequently develop from events that occurred in the past; (2) they are assumed but seldom tested; (3) the individuals who believe in them have information that could disprove them; and (4) they permit their holders to be passive, dependent, and ultimately irresponsible in coping with the organization's problems.

Another example of using the concept "myth" as misrepresentation of reality is the study of Westerlund and Sjostrand (1979), who studied organizational myths held by organizational practitioners. They describe and analyze many myths held by practitioners that were "handed down from one generation to another," and were never empirically tested and supported. These myths have been brought into being to protect managers and practitioners from awareness of the uncertainty in organizational processes.

Hedberg (1981) distinguishes between two kinds of myths; "myth" and "fantasy": "The term myth emphasizes the multiple origins that theories of action may have. Some are born out of observations from reality, others are sheer fantasies" (p. 12). Hence, fantasy is related to wishful thinking and is detached from reality, while myth is born out of reality.

Merry (1983) distinguishes between "myth" and "delusion." Organization delusions, unlike myths, are ". . . distortions of organizational reality by an organization's members to keep on living in an unbearable, seemingly unchangeable organizational situation" (p. 172). According to this definition, delusions are organizational fantasies that arise from the organization's present situation (crisis) and that distort this reality so that people do not confront the "unbearable." Hence, myths defined as fantasies, delusions, illusions, or dreams emphasize their negative role for organizational adaptation, performance, and change.

Some emphasize the role of organizational myth in the process of the organization's adaptation, performance, and transformation. Myths are perceived not as beliefs detached from reality or as a distortion of it, but as reality perceived by the organization's members. In their study on organizational myth and its relation to "qualitative change," Boje, Fedor, and Rowland (1982) write: "Myth-making is an adaptive mechanism whereby groups in an organization maintain logical frameworks within which to attribute meaning to activities and events" (p. 18).

Organizational myth, as defined by these authors, is one way in which elements of organizational culture are conceptually organized into a system of relevant logic. This logic then becomes the basis for legitimizing present and future behavior. A myth is constructed to exemplify why the given practices and procedures are the "only way" the organization can function effectively. People are not entirely rational; most are rational in the way they "bound" their world to make it "seem rational." Myths are a form of "bounding," permitting meaningful organizational behavior to occur while "glossing over excessive complexity, turbulence, or ambiguity."

Stephens, Eisen, and Ensign (1983) argue that myth is the next step beyond belief structures. It takes hard and soft "facts" that people have attempted to measure, codify, or understand, and places them in a broader context of values, attitudes, and larger purpose. This leads to ways of understanding created from and based on the belief structures, ways that, as they become more pervasive in the culture, take on the quality of myth. They define myth as follows:

> The myth is the story that we tell ourselves which explains the nature of our reality. It is a whole picture which is constructed out of the particular pieces of our attitudes and beliefs. Myth becomes our touchstone to what is "real" and what is "important." . . . These are the "truths" to which we look when trying to decide how we should conduct our lives, what we should actually do, and how we should think and feel about it. (p. 211)

A study of organizational myths and their relation to organizational transformation was conducted by Owen (1983b, 1983c). He examined the role and nature of myths in human systems. To the above definition, Owen adds the future as an important dimension of myths: "Myth is a body of likely stories which emerge from the life of an organization, through which the organizational past, present, and potential is understood" (1983c, p. 36).

Stories and tales become myths as they are assembled in a pattern that the organization finds to be a meaningful description of itself. Myths are useful vehicles for maintaining the organization's life. As the story is told, new members are informed what the organization is all about. Old members are guided in their daily conduct because purpose is given and values are articulated. The story recounts not only what has been, but what is hoped for.

Owen went further by claiming that the organizational myth is the manifestation of the deep-rooted identity of the organization, a profound truth that can be expressed only through symbolic stories:

> Myth-making is what you do when you have something to say that is so profoundly true and basically available that you have virtually no alternative but to tell a story. Myth, therefore, is *the story*, the **only story** — the **truth**. (1983c, p. 36; emphasis added)

People find it difficult to express in words and sentences what the organization is all about. By telling a story, a metaphor is created that symbolizes what the organization is and is not. Owen explains it thus:

> The central purpose for which myth exists is to make the ineffable effable, to speak what cannot be spoken, to bring to expression that which cannot be expressed. . . . **Myth is the word from the depths of being itself.** (1983c, p. 37; emphasis added)

Mythos includes saying, which is the myth, and doing, which is the symbolic action connected to the story — and is the ritual. Ritual is acted-out myth. It is the nonverbal communication of what the story is all about. It enhances the story by providing symbolic actions and procedures. Hence myth and ritual are perceived as one, inseparable entity. Therefore, some use the term "mythos"; others, "mythuals."

To summarize, myths are "truths" as perceived by their holders. They arise from the organization's life and are not an "empirical reality." Whether they are functional or dysfunctional depends on the perspective taken: functional for whom? functional to what purpose? Heroic stories about the past may help members to cope with the difficulties of the present despite the fact that they are exaggerations, or even distortions, of the "truth." Instead of talking about functional and dysfunctional myths, it may be more useful to study the role myths play in the organization's life.

THE ROLE OF MYTHS IN THE ORGANIZATION'S LIFE

The roles myths play in the daily life of organizations have been discussed and classified. Boje et al. (1982) suggests classifying myths according to the two roles they play: one group of myths concerns standards of desirability; the other concerns cause-and-effect relationship. Myths concerning standards of desirability are those which create and legitimize past, present, or future actions and consequences, and those which maintain and conceal political interests and value systems. Myths concerning cause-and-effect relationship are those which help explain and create cause-and-effect relationships under conditions of incomplete knowledge, and those which rationalize the complexity and turbulence of activities and events in order to facilitate predictable action taking.

These four categories enable us to consider and analyze the function of myths in organizations and their role in organizational change.

Myths that Create, Maintain, and Legitimize Past, Present, and Future Actions and Consequences

Besides anchoring the present in the past and providing legitimacy, myths may be important creators of organizational futures, and hence may be utilized for facilitating second-order change. Some examples are provided here. B. R. Clark (1972) reports how entrepreneurs and reformers have pushed aside old structures in favor of the image of the future they intend to create. Sproul and Weiner (1976) document how this type of process was of prime importance in the creation of the National Institute of Education. King (1979) describes how "future expectations" explain the results of many interventions.

Polak (1973) notes that when the dominant images of a culture are anticipated, they "head" social change. They have a "magnetic pull" toward the anticipated future. By their attractiveness and legitimacy they reinforce each movement that takes the society toward them, and thus they influence the decisions that will bring them to realization.

A similar theory and explanations for revolutionary changes during the history of mankind are provided by Markley and Harman (1982). They analyze the process of evolutions and revolutions in the history of mankind, and claim that all revolutions were anticipated by guiding images of man in the universe. Evolutionary periods terminate by crisis in which a new image of the future and the role of man in a different society emerge and are accepted. This leads to a revolutionary change that fulfills this image.

Myths that Maintain and Conceal Political Interests

This function of myths is of great importance for the diagnostic phase and for locating organizational problems. Pfeffer (1981) describes how myths can be used by the dominant coalition to camouflage its power. Actual power groups often use the rationalizing function of a myth to justify actions that may otherwise appear to be selfish or unethical (Selznick 1976).

While power groups have the ability to maintain and impose their own myths on others, the myth provides the legitimization of this power. The myth that domestic car buyers would not settle for a compact car inhibited new resource allocations in the U.S. auto industry. The lack of much success with a few compact cars served to support this idea. Only when the evidence became overwhelming and crisis followed did the automakers reexamine the "big car" myth.

Myths that Help Explain and Create Cause-and-Effect Relationships

Under conditions of incomplete knowledge, myths function to support decisions and acts by explaining cause-and-effect relationships. The myth functions as a provider of meaning. Women's groups, for example, argued that men have perpetuated a myth about female unreliability in order to exclude them from better and higher-paying jobs. The myth was that most women work until they marry, and that a woman's career is naturally secondary to her family. By providing a rationale for not promoting women, a self-fulfilling prophecy developed.

Not surprisingly, many women chose to leave the labor force when they married. The data then supported the dominant myth.

Myths that Rationalize Complexity and Turbulence to Allow for Taking Predictable Action

Myths of this type provide the illusion of rational actions and decisions, and create predictability in the face of random, complex, and turbulent processes. Managers and consultants are predisposed to see every action as a result of an a priori goal. They tend to bind causes to effects and rational intentions to actions. Even if an action is unintended, "latent" goals will be searched for to explain its origin (Kamens 1977; Meyer, 1979; Sproul and Weiner 1976). Myths provide these goals.

Mintzberg (1975) notes that many executives outwardly adopt the planning, organizing, directing, and controlling model of management while in fact they make decisions hastily. Managers are bombarded with competing, contradictory demands from their superiors, subordinates, and peers. Their typical reaction to subordinates' demands for change is rejection, which is rationalized by the importance of "tradition" or "past success." Essentially, the myth provides the manager with a ready-made rationale to avoid change.

Owen (1983b) proposes some other roles of organizational myths:

1. Definition. Myths provide identity to those who hold them and define the group. They provide boundaries between "we" and "they."
2. Initiate new members. Until an individual participates in the myths of the organization, he or she is not really a member. Myths serve as a socializing mechanism.
3. Sustain the group. Myths function as cohesive glue and sustain the group, particularly in times of crisis. Organizational myths include stories about bad times and heroes, and provide encouragement for coping with crisis.
4. Challenge the group. Organizational myths not only recount the past, but also point to where the organization should go. They embody the dreams or visions of individuals and groups.
5. Value preserving. Myths create a narrative world through which the values are communicated and preserved.

To summarize, there are two basic perspectives about the role of myths. Most studies emphasize their role in maintaining the present state. A few studies deal with their role in changing the present state. From the planned-change viewpoint, the first perspective may explain why and how organizations resist change, while the second perspective may provide the theoretical model for using myths as a vehicle for planned change.

THE LIFE CYCLE OF ORGANIZATIONAL MYTHS

Studies on myth making show that myths tend to rise and fall, allowing new myths to come into being. Hedberg and Johnson (1977) propose that myths change cyclically: "A ruling myth is challenged when it no longer can provide convincing strategies; it is also challenged by the arrival of competing myths" (p. 12). According to this study, the decision-making process is largely sustained and guided by existing myths. When the circumstances under which decisions are made change, the myths must change in order to provide new guidance for the decision-making process.

Boje et al. (1982) and Owen (1983c) go further, arguing that the process of organization transformation includes the transformation of organizational myths. They describe the myth-making life cycle as a

Table 4.1.
Myth Life Cycle

Myth Stage	Company Situation	Myth Development
Development	Rapid growth; high profit-ability; no real competition	Myth is successfully guiding decision making and strategy
Maturation	Company's growth is slowing; competition becomes prominent	Myth and company identity completely intertwined
Decline	Environment changes; competition becomes substantial; profit falls; mission is a hindrance to action	Some units stick to the old myth; some begin to develop competing myths for renewal
Reformulation	Company situation has deteriorated to the point that drastic change is needed	Myth shifts to include new quality

Source: Boje et al. (1982).

function of environmental changes and organizational change. Table 4.1 shows this process.

Hence, myths, together with their organizations, rise, develop, mature, decline, and are reformulated. They sustain and are sustained by dominant coalitions, organizational success, and environmental support. Boje et al. (1982) accept the theory that for facilitating revolutionary change, sufficient tension, crisis, and dissatisfaction must exist in the organization. Therefore, only when the organizational myths are in decline, and new myths are beginning to be formulated, can one intervene between myths held by dominant coalitions and countermyths held by other groups. This tension may be utilized for managing change.

Owen describes four ways in which myths deteriorate, die, or change. These four ways are organized according to their function from the organization's point of view. The first is the most dysfunctional way for myths to die; the last, the most functional.

1. Attrition. This situation occurs when organization members become so afraid of the future that they adhere to every fine detail of the old myth, until its vitality is dissipated.
2. Environmental change. When the organization's environment changes drastically, there is a need for new myths to support, explain, and sustain a revolutionary change. In this situation the old myth degenerates to the level of idle talk.
3. Rebellion. The death of a myth may occur when the organization's storytellers break the old story and either invent a new story or substantially modify the old myth.
4. Self-administration. In this situation, an internal critique is built into the myth that does not allow the participants in the myth "to rest easily." It is always calling attention to new needs and changes in reality. The myth itself provides a mechanism for its renewal.

It should be noted here that myths do not always die; sometimes they just take on another form. Under circumstances such as turbulent environment and crisis, myths may turn into fantasies (disconnection from reality), as Hedberg (1981) points out, or into delusions (distortion of reality) as Merry (1983) states, or into nostalgia (living in the past). The myths about the big car, held by the dominant coalitions in the U.S. auto industry, was not changed to a myth about the small car, despite the dramatic changes in the environment (gas prices).

MYTHS AND ORGANIZATIONAL TRANSFORMATION

Why choose organizational myths as a vehicle for organizational transformation? What makes myths and rituals so profound and useful for facilitating transformation? At least seven assumptions were found relevant for addressing the above questions.

Myth as a Vehicle for Attitudes and Behavioral Change

A group from U.C.L.A. (Jones et al. 1983) whose research concerns organizational symbolism and transformation makes the following claim: "Any organization can be transformed. The costs are negligible. The results are dramatic, immediate, and of tremendous consequence" (p. 176).

This provocative claim is based on the assumption that transforming an organization requires reorientation to such concepts as fundamental needs, capabilities, and forms of behavior. The human animal uses symbols. Language itself is symbolic, and storytelling employs language in especially powerful and evocative ways. Rituals and myths are forms of human communication that shape understanding of and attitudes toward the organization, and thus affect behavior within it.

It is relatively easy to start with myth change because "human beings need to narrate"; it is "part of the process of accomplishing tasks." Myths provide the context under which people operate, as well as a time context for comparing past and present attitudes and behaviors. Most people not only need to have a story but also like to tell it.

The point emphasized by Jones et al. (1983) is that myths are strongly related to attitudes and behaviors, and that they are usually visible — people enjoy telling them; therefore, myth is a useful vehicle for a change in attitudes and behavior. The group also suggests a transformation approach that will be presented in the next section.

Myth as a Vehicle for Values and Behavioral Change

Organizational myths shape the world of the organization by articulating the values and modes of behavior relating to them. They determine the nature of truth, describe and prescribe the meaning and course of life in the organization. By adhering to myths, one actually enters the world of good and bad, right and wrong, the world of meaning (Owen 1983c).

Hence, myth is a vivid way by which values are expressed and communicated, so that members can identify with these values and therefore behave accordingly. By eliminating specific myths and by enhancing and revitalizing others, one can shape value and behavior.

Myth as a Vehicle for Defining Boundaries

McWhinney (1982; 1984) and Smith (1982) claim that organizational transformation is possible only when the organization is aware of what it is or is not, or where its boundaries are. Smith, for example, writes:

> In order for an entity to be able to change itself, it must first have a conception of itself as an entity-as-a-whole, separate from other entities in its ecosystem, and be able to draw coherent distinctions between what is its own behavior, and what is the behavior of other entities in its ecosystem. (p. 345)

McWhinney refers to the same phenomenon but calls it "individuation." Myths are a powerful way of expressing the nature of the organization, and what makes it different and unique.

Myths as an Expression of Periods of Change

Owen, Nold (1983), and Jones et al. (1983) suggest that myths "record" the process of transformation, its creation, its heroes and villains. Myths not only communicate the values and purposes related to periods of crisis and change, but also log the successive transformations that have taken place, and thus define the nature of transformation as it is understood in that organization.

Jones et al. (1983) write about the function myths play in the process of transformation: ". . . they [myths] can strongly influence the groups' understanding and acceptance of change. In fact, they not only publicize transformations, they help bring them about, to give them credence and make them last" (p. 177).

Myths as a Vehicle for Generating and Mobilizing Energy for Change

Myths may be powerful tools for generating energy for action and transformation. Owen showed how the myth of "black is beautiful" served Carmichael as a tool for unifying blacks and mobilizing their energy toward their struggle for equal rights. Ackerman (1983) and Barbee (1983) developed models that describe organizations as energy fields and myths as energy sources for transformation.

Organizations as Metaphors

Organizations are sometimes regarded as nonconcrete entities. Some describe organizations as an "energy flow" (Ackerman 1983); others, as "relationship entities" (Smith 1982). If organizations do not exist in a concrete form, the only way to talk about them is metaphorically or by telling their stories. Then the nature of our understanding of organizations will depend on the metaphors we use — that is, the way we experience, see, and understand organizations depends primarily on the characteristics of the myth or metaphors we choose to use, for "how we talk, shapes what we talk about." Smith thus writes about the power of metaphors in relation to second-order change: "If we want to change relationships, we can do this by changing the metaphors used to describe those relationships" (1982, p. 330).

If we start to think about organizations as "loosely-coupled systems" (Weick 1979), this myth shapes not only our understanding of organizations but also our behavior in dealing with them.

Myth as a Vehicle for Transforming "Organizational Identity"

Last, but not least, second-order change is a change in the organization's identity. It is a deep change that entails changes in basic assumptions underlying the organization, changes in values, attitudes, perceptions, and behaviors (Margulis 1977; Owen 1983c).

By tapping the organizationl myth, one actually taps the organizational identity in a relatively nonthreatening way. Most of an organization's members apparently like to talk about its heroes, its history, its metaphors. They often are willing to examine the meaning and role of myths (Mulligan & Kelly 1983). Therefore, myth appears to be a useful vehicle for reaching deep organizational levels and for changing them in a relatively nonthreatening way.

INTERVENTION STRATEGIES, APPROACHES, AND TECHNOLOGIES

In the previous sections theoretical aspects of organizational myths in relation to organization transformation were discussed. In this section an attempt will be made to describe briefly and to analyze a sample of change methods, some of which are only tentative suggestions while others are interventions already used in "real-life situations." The change methods will be described according to the following classification: training programs, assessment methods, intervention methods.

Training Programs

The term "training program" refers to learning programs and workshops in which participants from different organizations learn new skills, knowledge, and behavior. Such a program is suggested by Jones et al. (1983). The following is a brief description of a training program termed "culture sensitivity training," suggested by Jones et al. for manager training and for facilitating organizational transformation.

Phase 1. The managers learn what organizational culture is, what its components are, its processes, and its role and function in organizational performance and adaptation. The emphasis is on symbolic elements such as myths, rituals, ceremonies, rites, celebrations, and language. Participants are exposed to case studies exemplifying the role of the above elements in the process of adaptation and change.

Phase 2. The managers are encouraged to share with the group stories, rituals, metaphors, and games from their organization. A group discussion follows to clarify the role, the function, and the meaning of these elements in the organization's life.

Phase 3. The managers learn to assess their organizations by using myths and rituals. They share their case studies and examples myths and rituals, and what they mean for the organization. Group members assess their organizations with the help of the facilitators.

Phase 4. The managers choose targets for change and collect data relevant to the change. They present the changes and the actions for implementing them in the group. Cultural elements such as myths, rituals, and metaphors that may be used for enhancing, facilitating, and implementing the changes are discussed and chosen. Action steps are planned with the help of the trainers.

Phase 5. The managers implement the changes in their organizations together with the trainers, who now become external consultants.

The above training program deepens the understanding and awareness of managers of the role of symbolic elements in their organizations, and may be a lever that helps managers to initiate and implement second-order change. However, there is no evidence that transformation is an immediate process with negligible costs.

Assessment Methods

Organizational myths are powerful and useful vehicles for understanding the identity of the system and the way it operates. Boje et al. (1983) suggest that the transformation process be started by identifying myths and rituals that support or hinder existing operations, procedures, and strategies. They claim that since individuals within organizations rely upon myths as an unquestioned basis for interpretation and decision making, it may not be appropriate to question them directly about these assumptions. The myths that underlie the perceptions of reality will be too deeply imbedded in the cognitive framework to be discerned by introspection concerning "hard" data. Hence, understanding is possible through using anthropological methods such as participant observations and ethnographic analysis techniques. The assessment must uncover two major subjects important for the intervention: the myth life cycle and the dominant coalition.

Boje et al. accept the theory that for facilitating second-order change, sufficient tension, crisis, and dissatisfaction must exist in the organization. Hence, only when the basic organizational myth is in decline and a new one is beginning to formulate, can one intervene to facilitate revolutionary change. This condition is not sufficient. For intervention to be successful, the organization's dominant coalition must be involved in the process and take ownership of it.

The analysis of myths may reveal the power structure; it enables one to see how decisions are made, which group tries to impose a certain myth on the other, and where the real power lies. Boje et al. provide examples from the U.S. auto industry, where dominant coalitions held different myths about the "desired car" preferred by Americans. The victory of the old myth held by dominant coalitions hindered needed transformation, and the industry deteriorated until a severe crisis occurred.

The study of Boje et al. is theoretical and conceptual. However, their suggestions were used to facilitate organizational transformation. Owen developed their ideas and built a structured method for analyzing organizational myths. He does not use myth assessment as a stage before the intervention, but as an integrated part of the intervention itself. Moreover, his method has already been tried out in transformation projects.

Owen grouped myths according to their content, function, and form. He developed the following classification, which guided his analysis:

1. Myth content, which includes the following:
   - Creation stories. How did it all get started? What does it seem to be?
   - Consummation stories. Where does it all seem to be heading? How will we know when we arrive there?
   - Crisis stories. How the system adapted to changes.
   - Value stories. Stories about heroes or villains in which the central concern is appropriate behavior.
   - Rebel stories. Stories about persons with new or different ideas.
2. Myth form, which includes the following:
   - Stories. Usually short stories (10–15 minutes) with special sounds, metaphors, symbols, punchlines, jokes.
   - Rituals. Activities that assume symbolic meaning.
3. Myth function, which includes the following:
   - Define the group. Myth has a boundary-setting function.
   - Initiate new members. Follow new employees and listen to what they are told.
   - Sustain the group. Myths help organizations cope with hard times. Through myths, members can refer to past experiences when heroes and members successfully coped with crisis.

- Challenge the group. Myths tell not only about the past, but also about dreams and visions.

The above classification provides a model for assessment. Owen developed a technique called the mythograph that organizes the myths as shown in Figure 4.1.

The methods used by Owen are very similar to those suggested by Boje et al. (1982). They include "open interviews," "participant observations," "nonparticipant observations," and what Owen calls "hanging out." The interviews take about one hour, and the questions are open-ended; they function as stimuli for telling the story. The basic questions are "What is this place?" "What should it be?" "How did all this start?" A story, once told, does not make a myth. The consultant must look for groups of similar stories repeatedly told that collectively create the field of mythos within which the organization operates.

"Hanging out" means participating in the work flow and being present in times and at places where rituals occur. Coffee breaks and staff meetings are typical places for rituals to occur. The data are collected, summarized, and put into the mythograph. A positive situation would be every single box saying the same thing. But that rarely occurs. The advantage of the mythograph is that it enables one to deal with the levels and kinds of mythic dissonance or consonance. Different and contradicting myths held by different groups or levels channel energy in different directions. The consultant may share his findings with the chief executive officer or with a "steering committee," or he may teach internal groups to do the analysis themselves. The myth analysis is used for facilitating transformation by eliminating those which hinder the change or by creating new alignment among myths, or generating a whole new story.

Figure 4.1. Mythograph

A. Organizational goals as stated by C.E.O.
B. The official history
C. Tales from the tribal scribes
D. Myths and rituals in the organization

Level	Sector I	Sector II	Sector III
Exec.			
Mid.			
Tech.			

Source: Owen (1983b).

Owen provides two examples of how he used the above method to facilitate organizational transformation, one of which was presented and analyzed at the beginning of this chapter.

Intervention Methods

Intervention methods include change efforts conducted by the organization's members, or some of them, with the help of a consultant. The first four interventions provided here are tentative interventions suggested by Boje et al. (1982).

1. Demythifying. The practitioner trains the organization members in the principles of the behavioral sciences, and develops skills for analyzing and counteracting common organizational myths. This intervention is very similar to that suggested by Jones et al. (1983) as a training program for managers.
2. Myth exchange. The first step for the practitioner is to demonstrate the existence of different systems of logic and filters for viewing reality. Organization members must learn to identify different organizational myths as alternative views of reality. The second step is the technique of "transpection," through which the person attempts to bracket his/her own mythical thinking and to reason in terms of the logics held by others, so that he or she can see reality as others see it. The last step is having A explain to B how he/she sees B's world. Exchanging myths entails the ability to communicate what is seen in the logical categories of both the original and the new myth.
3. Myth balancing. In this intervention, the focus is not on shattering people's deeply held myths, but on providing them with a fruitful way of thinking about their experiences. Rather than picking one or the other opposing view, intervention should provide participants with a balanced view of reality, that is, allow for the incorporation of existing beliefs by way of modification and balance, rather than rejection.
4. Myth enrichment. In periods of crisis the myth-making system needs to be enriched or revived in order to help actors cope with hard times. The intervention is aimed at finding meaningful interpretations and enriching feelings of purpose, direction, and meaning. This also involves uncovering the dysfunctional or negative aspects of existing myths and replacing them with positive, functional ones.

Stephens, Eisen, and Ensign (1983) suggest an intervention based on confronting small myths with large myths. According to their study, myths operate on different levels. For each level there exists a higher level, each myth existing within a larger context. The small myth asserts what is everyday, tangible, practical, and explicit. The large myth encompasses an overall pattern, a background, and is usually abstract and implicit.

In times of crisis or transition these two levels of myth are in conflict, and dissonance occurs. The dissonance becomes either a revolutionary catalyst for change or a regressive one. People can retreat to a lower order of integration (rely on their small myth, ignoring the large one), or they can change to a higher degree of integration by finding a new myth structure in which both levels are congruent. Individuals in organizations can identify small and large myths, choose which ones to focus on and to align with. The intervention includes a deep and long awareness process. It starts with work at the individual level, in which participants are encouraged to identify their small myth and the large myth that provides the context for it.

This process is made possible by encouraging participants to bring forward stories, symbols, and metaphors, through which they identify small and large myths. They learn to recognize and identify conflicting world views, paradoxes, and ambiguities. Then they are encouraged to choose one or a few world views to guide the organization's mission and operation, and to align it with their small myth. This process is done in three phases at three levels. The first phase is focused on the individual level, the second on the group level, and the third on the organizational level. This intervention has been used in "real life" situations.

There is also an approach that focuses on organizational metaphors. Metaphorical statements (such as teachers' metaphors: "We are in the front line") are actually the tips of the icebergs of condensed meaning — the organizational myth. The consultants using this approach worked with groups and top managers. They employed various techniques (such as guided imagery) to encourage the participants to share images and metaphors related to their organization's operation. These metaphors were then used to challenge the organization's basic assumptions, accepted truths, strategies, and way of thinking.

The purpose of this method is to break the barriers to innovation, creativity, and transformation. The final stage of this process is to reveal new insights, to visualize meaningful new imagery and metaphors, and to create a new framework of meaning for the organization. The techniques used may include graphics, creative writing, semantics, focusing, hypnosis, listening to music or poems, and watching pictures and slides. This approach has already been used for working with the organization's members.

The intervention suggested by Owen, as reported here, was taken from two case studies published by him. Owen works with a "core team" consisting of top managers and representatives from all the organizational units. The core team is responsible for the change efforts. The work with this group includes the following phases:

1. Self-assessment of organizational myths. Participants work in subgroups according to their units, and are encouraged to bring forward the myths of their units and of other units. The different myths are shared and analyzed in the group.
2. Establishing a mythical flow pattern. The group creates an alignment among myths that enhances the achievement of the organization's mission, high performance, and satisfaction.

Figure 4.2. Mythical Flow Pattern

Source: Owen 1983c.

3. Remything — developing a new story. The purpose of this phase is to develop a new story for the organization, to create a new myth concerning the future, the direction, the new vision for the organization.

The techniques used by Owen to discuss organizational myth are telling stories and anecdotes, visioning, listening to stories of the old days, and generating images by exposing the organization's members to artifacts that symbolize some aspects of the organization's purpose (such as the first product, the first machines, pictures). The purpose of the intervention is to create a new story, a new vision agreed upon by all, which will lead the organization in a new direction. Owen is one of the few who work with large corporations on organizational transformation by using organizational myth as a vehicle for facilitating the change. He stresses the crucial importance of creating a bridge to the old myth so that the new myth is seen as encompassing it and not eradicating it.

To summarize, the main focus of the above assessment, training, and intervention methods is on the symbolic language (myths) and action (rituals) of people in organizations. They focus on patterns of symbolic language and action. These patterns are taken from the organization's subconscious and are raised to the conscious level. They are then used as a vehicle for deep awareness of their meaning and as a manifestation of the organization identity. The awareness of the role that myths play in an organization's life enables people to understand how belief systems shape their behavior, and allows them to be aware of alternatives.

In the current "state of the art" there are some practical assessment and intervention methods. There are also some ideas and suggestions for change approaches. There is evidence suggesting that second-order change may be facilitated by using myths and rituals. There are at least two reported case studies in which an effort was made to facilitate organizational transformation by using myths.

EVALUATION

Change Agent Characteristics

The change agent emerging from the above studies and writings is quite different from the traditional one. The traditional change agent often takes the analytical-deductive orientation to change. He or she is occupied with rational, logical models and schemes leading to his understanding the organization's problems, and where and how to intervene in order to solve these problems. This is a logical, step-by-step process. The diagnosis is an exhaustive, data-gathering phase based on analytical models, attempting to gather "objective data" for locating specific problems, cause-and-effect relations. The diagnosis guides the location, the mode, and the process of the intervention.

The change agent, as he or she emerges from the above studies, is more anthropologically oriented. He or she uses methods like open-ended personal interviews, nonparticipant and participant observation, unobtrusive measures, and other ethnomethodological methods. He or she is more open to emerging organizational patterns. He or she uses the senses to perceive how the system works, what makes it work, and what makes this specific system different from others. The mode of inquiry is inductive and holistic rather than deductive and analytic.

This type of change agent does not distinguish between diagnosing and changing. The intervention is not necessarily guided or determined by a preceding diagnostic phase. In the case of EVMA, for example, the diagnosis was used as a complementary act to the effort for change. The intervention creates new dynamics; thus accompanying it with diagnosis can provide new energy to the process, as the case of EVMA showed.

The traditional change agent often uses a traditional problem-solving model. This model implies a step-by-step process in which problems are first located and analyzed, and then alternative ways of solving them are examined and determined. The "new" change agent does not look for problems or dysfunctions but for patterns of behavior and symbolic patterns that provide meaning to that behavior. His or her approach to change is "pattern exchange," not a problem-solving process.

Although the above two types of change agents are not mutually exclusive but complementary, they can be better understood by comparing them, using the criteria shown in Table 4.2.

The tactic used by Owen to work with organizational myths was to take the route of indirect manipulation of the operative myths. This was possible in two different ways. The first way was to identify the elements of myth that were the closest to supporting the proposed change and to supply, develop, and enhance them. The second way was to identify another myth current within the group that matched the organizational need more closely and seek to institute the proposed change through this myth.

Table 4.2.
Comparison of Traditional and Organizational Transformation Consultation Modes

Criterion	Traditional Consultant	Organizational Transformation Consultant
Scientific mode	rational, analytic, deductive	inductive, holistic, intuitive
Emphasis	problems and dysfunctions	patterns and functions
Change process	problem solving	pattern exchange
Diagnostic tools	models, surveys, questionnaires	ethnomethodological approaches
Intervention mode	structured, organized, step-by-step	open, emerging, mixed

Source: Provided by the authors.

Intervention Characteristics

Some traditional interventions usually focus on changing "some significant aspects of an organizational culture" (Burke 1981, p. 9). Culture is commonly defined in terms of what is shaped in the organization members' minds. From this perspective, culture consists of norms, values, and beliefs; culture is the set of important understandings (often unstated) that members have in common.

Organizational transformation takes a different approach to organizational culture and its role in organizational planned change. In organizational transformation, as it emerges from this chapter, culture is defined in terms of what is directly observable concerning the organization's members. From this perspective, culture consists of patterns of behavior, language and stories, and the use of material objects. The main purpose of organizational transformation intervention is not just to change some significant cultural aspects but to use those aspects (such as myths and rituals) as a vehicle for facilitating second-order change — that is, to facilitate change in the organization's world view, mission and purpose, functional processes, and culture.

Organizational Conditions

Organizational conditions found to be favorable for successful change efforts were the following:

1. Inconsistencies among cultural elements. The existence of contradictory myths was a source for tension, conflict, and crisis. This inconsistency, as Owen and Tichy hypothesized, may be used for facilitating second-order change.
2. Organizational crisis. The combination of organizational crisis and new manager triggered the change process in EVMA, as it did in some of the previous case studies. This finding provides support for the hypothesis that for second-order change to occur, sufficient tension and crisis have to be present in the system. This condition is necessary, but not sufficient. The process may start and be managed successfully when new, usually outside, top managers take the lead.

The Environment

One of the main sources of the crisis in EVMA was the lack of support by suspicious consumers concerning the purpose of the system. As in the case of the alternative public school (Gold & Miles 1981), where the parents did not support the change, here those who were supposed to be the consumers of the services refused to use them. These findings support the hypothesis that for successful second-order change in public service institutions to occur, there has to be support of the potential consumers.

Outcomes

The ultimate outcome of Owen's intervention in EVMA was the institutionalization of the original vision. This finding, as reported by Owen, is based on verbal feedback from those members who worked closely with the consultant and on personal observation.

SOME FINAL THOUGHTS ON ORGANIZATIONAL MYTHS AND CHANGES

Different terms are used to describe the "superstructure" of the organizational belief system. The term used by a person may reveal his or her basic view of the nature or role of this superstructure. Thus, one can find the terms "myths," "illusions," "delusions," "daydreams," "hallucinations," "fantasies," and even terms taken from therapy, such as "projections" and "introjections." All the above terms represent specific aspects of organizational behavior related to the superstructure of the belief system.

The context in which the organization's belief system is shaped is therefore very complex. Its complexity can be shown by taking just two relevant dimensions related to the superstructure: time and reality (functions, operations, and behaviors tested empirically). Putting these elements on a two-dimensional table, the structure shown in Figure 4.3 emerges.

An organization's members may collectively distort their past by glorifying it (nostalgia); or they may distort their present reality in order

Figure 4.3.   The Myth-making Field

Relation to Reality	Time		
	Past	*Present*	*Future*
Invention	mythology	fantasy	vision
Distortion	nostalgia	delusions	wishful thinking
Facts	history	reality	anticipation

Source: Prepared by the authors.

to avoid awareness of the need for change (delusions); or they may translate future trends in a way that will enhance the present belief system (wishful thinking). When an organization's members examine their belief systems in relation to reality, and change the basic assumptions underlying these belief systems according to empirical evidence, then the superstructure represents reality. The superstructure related to past reality may be history; the one related to present facts may be reality; and the one related to the future may be anticipation.

The creation of a whole new past can be called "mythology." The creation of a new reality in the present can be called fantasy; and the creation of a whole new future detached from present trends can be called a vision. Thus, what members say about their organization may represent "reality" as perceived by the narrators.

Myth and Dysfunction

The debate about the function or dysfunction of myths for the organization's survival raises the question Functional or dysfunctional for whom? What may be functional from the organization's perspective may be dysfunctional from the group or individual perspective, and vice versa. Organizational myths possibly are neither inherently positive nor negative. They are facts of organizational existence that have a large range of roles within the organization's daily life. From the perspective of change in the organization, they are important factors to be considered, analyzed, and potentially altered or incorporated into the efforts for change.

Myth and Ethics

Myth making is a powerful way to generate energy, to motivate people, to unify them, toward achieving organizational goals. "A strong myth," which is a visible, shared-by-all myth, supported by rituals and symbols, may be not only a barrier to change but also a barrier to individual expression. Moreover, a myth can easily blind or block the individual's awareness of his or her actions and their consequences.

Adolf Hitler represents the best (or worst) example of a leader who used myths for his own ends. His creation of the Third Reich and his rise to power began with the articulation of the myth of "blood, iron, and race." The stories taken from the heroic past were followed and empowered by rituals, symbols, and symbolic terms. The myths provided a strong belief system that imposed total conformity of the individual. The very fact that strong myths can motivate people to act inhumanely by tapping the unconscious, and by blocking the conscious and the conscience as well, must be taken into consideration by top managers and organizational practitioners while dealing with this issue.

5

Reframing

This chapter describes an approach that focuses on changing an organization's members' perceptions of reality by encouraging them to experience a new perspective on the problem at hand. This type of approach results in changes of perceptions, relationships, and behavior, but not necessarily in structures. Reframing processes, like scientific revolutions, do not change the empirical reality or the empirical facts; rather, this is a process of discovering new and even higher logical frameworks and of looking at the world from a new perspective. As one is occupied with a new perspective, his or her perception of reality is changed — and, hence, attitudes and behavior are changed. Following this, at a later stage "reality" itself may change.

A CASE EXAMPLE: THE PROBLEM OF THE
SECOND GENERATION LEAVING THE KIBBUTZ

This is a short description of reframing intervention developed by one of the authors and his colleagues at the organizational development institute of the kibbutz movement in Israel (Levy 1979). The intervention was made in three small kibbutzim, and showed positive results in terms of changes in perceptions, relationships, behaviors, and procedures. The intervention was designed specifically to help small kibbutzim to cope with the problem of youngsters leaving the kibbutz.

About 50–60 percent of the children born on the kibbutz leave. For some kibbutzim the percentage is even higher. This phenomenon is perceived by many, especially by those who established the kibbutz, as a serious problem that threatens its future. The first generation perceives the kibbutz as a value system with a specific mission and a high level of moral living. It expects the youngsters to stay on the kibbutz and to ensure its continuation.

In many kibbutzim, leaving is perceived in negative terms: as an act of betrayal, as immoral, and as an expression of failure of the whole community to educate and socialize its youngsters. In these kibbutzim, those who leave feel uneasy when visiting their parents, and some do it secretly. Their parents also feel uneasy and may even have guilt feelings. Paradoxically, the more the kibbutz tries to deal with the problem, the more conflicts, stress, and bitterness arise, and the more youngsters tend to leave.

The traditional way of coping with this problem was to take the problem-solving process and the first-order change approach. The problem was first diagnosed; elements that might hinder staying or facilitate leaving were looked for and defined. A task team was then established to suggest solutions. For example, among the "causes" of leaving were lack of sufficient kibbutz education, lack of appropriate housing for youngsters, and lack of activities and facilities.

Therefore, the solutions were "doing more of the same": additional classes on kibbutz were added and housing was improved. Youngsters received more and more privileges that others did not have; energy and resources were spent on this issue. Yet, the result was a blind alley and the problem was complicated even more. Youngsters perceived themselves as children deserving attention and privileges, and as in a position of power. The middle-aged generation felt deprived because resources and privileges were given to those who had not yet contributed substantially to the kibbutz. And, most important, the percentage of youngsters leaving did not drop.

We were consulted by such a kibbutz. We studied the solutions attempted hitherto and their results, and concluded that the problem was the attempted solutions, which were embedded in and shaped by a logical framework that we wanted to challenge, or at least make explicit. Our strategy was based on the ideas of Watzlawick and Fisch (1974). That is, we wanted youngsters and parents to view the relationship between themselves from a different perspective based on a wider logical framework.

We noticed that there were not big differences between kibbutzim in the percentage of those leaving, and that this phenomenon is typical of various small communities, villages, and cities. Our assumption was that in the kibbutz, too, it is natural for many to want to escape from their image and to live away from their parents. Furthermore, not everyone "fits" into communal life, and those who do not, might have presented a problem had they stayed on the kibbutz. We noticed the double-bind messages youngsters got from their parents: "Be responsible, independent, and choose your own way of living, but choose what we choose for you."

Some initial attempts to explain our view logically resulted in a debate, highly charged with emotion and ideological arguments. At this point, we decided to attempt some of the reframing methods for intervention. A workshop was designed for youngsters and ther parents. The kibbutz was divided into mixed groups of youngsters and parents with about 18 members each; each group had 2 two-day sessions. The workshops were based on structured experiences in which participants had to move, to role-play, to play, to visualize and express feelings, and to process their experiences.

The intervention included two weekend workshops. The first started with an icebreaker and a movie was shown, presenting problematic relationships between parents and their son who was about to leave. The movie ended with the decision of the son to stay on the kibbutz, because he wanted to take care of his parents and not shame them with his decision. We then asked participants to role-play the situation and speak about their experiences. Other sessions we designed and used included the following:

- Parents tied the youngsters and themselves together with a rope. Participants expressed their feelings while tied.
- Parents kept the youngsters in the room while the youngsters were instructed to leave.
- Subgroups had to reframe the concept of "leaving" into its opposite and give it a positive connotation ("independence," "going out to life"); then they were asked to generate ideas for facilitating the quest of all the youngsters in the kibbutz to leave.
- In mixed small groups, participants were instructed to "brainstorm" and provide ideas for the best way to fail in absorbing the young generation.
- Participants were encouraged to experience double-bind messages (such as "Choose what I chose"; "At age 21 I expect you to know what's good for you").

- Youngsters were instructed to role-play staying in the kibbutz to make their parents proud and feel accepted.
- In a "fishbowl," parents and youngsters talked to each other about their feelings and anxieties, assuming that all the youngsters had already left.

This intervention was applied to three small kibbutzim. In all three cases, it resulted in reframing the problem from "youngsters leaving the kibbutz" to "how to ensure the survival and growth of the kibbutz." What was previously perceived as a problem was now perceived as a natural process that could perhaps be changed but not avoided. Further, it immediately lowered the tension in the kibbutz and changed attitudes toward those who had already left. Moreover, the direction taken now was to establish the climate and procedures that encouraged those who had left to visit the kibbutz and participate in its holiday festivities, as is commonly done in most families.

The kibbutz now focused its attention and efforts on ensuring its growth by opening its gates to "outsiders." A task team was appointed to be in charge of the kibbutz's growth. Once the climate changed, it affected the leaving rate. Some who had already left and wanted to return were able to do so without guilty feelings. The fact that energy was now spent on possible practical solutions revitalized the kibbutz. It was rescued from a vicious circle by taking a new perspective on the issue based on a different logical framework.*

Reframing, like most transformation interventions, is aimed at raising members' awareness of the existence of alternative realities that they may choose to accept. It does not deal with the implementation of second-order changes. It is typically an intense, short intervention, focused on the first stages of the process of second-order change in a seemingly illogical way.

The theoretical link between organizational transformation and reframing was made explicit in the work of Smith (1982; 1984), who argued that every transformation of human systems involves some aspects of reframing. However, reframing is not often used by managers and organizational consultants for facilitating second-order change. It is widely used by family and group therapists for facilitating radical changes

---

*For further information on the subject see A. Levy, "The Second Generation: Why Do They Leave the Kibbutz?" *Kibbutz Studies Bulletin* (English), November 1980, pp. 8–13.

in perceptions, attitudes, and behaviors. Some consultants have begun using reframing interventions in organizational settings, and report positive results (Nicoll 1980; Watzlawick & Fisch 1974); others have worked with organizations at the individual level and also report positive results (Bandler & Grinder 1982). Many leaders who have transformed their organizations have inadvertently used some reframing processes.

REFRAMING: DESCRIPTION AND DEFINITION

Reframing is a pivotal element in the creative process, the problem-solving process, and communication processes, all of which are part of the process of organizational second-order planned change.

In the creative process domain, de Bono (1971) distinguished between vertical and lateral thinking. Vertical thinking begins with a simple concept and proceeds with the concept until a solution is reached. "Lateral" refers to thinking that generates different ways of perceiving a problem before seeking a solution. J. L. Adams (1974) describes the structure of our frames of meaning and how our beliefs, perceptions, emotions, intellect, rationality, and culture block our awareness of alternative frames of meaning.

In general communication theory, there is an axiom that a signal has meaning only in terms of the frame or context in which it appears. Further, the context in which a phenomenon is perceived creates its meaning. Once the context is changed, the same signal receives a different meaning. Thus a broken leg is perceived as a disaster for the athlete and as a relief for the soldier who has to go into battle (J. Miller 1978).

In family therapy, reframing is widely used for facilitating changes in family members' roles, relationships, and behavior. Minuchin and Fishman (1981) argue that human beings are framers of reality. They have shared beliefs of what is significant reality in tradition, religion, history, language, and structural arrangements. People bring to therapy their own frame of reality, as they define it. They ask the consultant to help them solve their problems within the reality that they have framed. Trying to solve their problems within the old frame of reality means preserving the context in which the problem occurred.

Minuchin and Fishman argue that real change (second-order change) starts with the clash between two framings of reality. The family framing is relevant for the continuity and maintenance of the system more or less as it is; the consultant framing is related to the goal of moving the system toward a new, totally different reality.

In organizational change theory, Smith (1982) argues that second-order change entails changing the organizational context that provides meaning to the organization's operations:

> If we wish to change the entity we need to change the meanings the entity attaches to its and others' experiences. . . . The most potent way to do this is to alter the relationships [between the entity and its context] from whence meaning emerges. (p. 358)

Organizational context is the metarules that shape the organization's rules and actions, and provide meaning for them. Smith argues, in regard to these metarules, that we can neither state nor form an image of them. We can merely evoke them in others, and they cannot be explicated just through logic. Knowing them is mainly a matter of perception. Therefore, comprehending these governing rules is not a matter of reassessing, thinking logically, or remembering; it is a matter of emotional insight or perception.

In problem-solving theory, Watzlawick and Fisch (1974) studied the nature of resolutions that change the context of the situation in which the problem is formed. They defined this type of resolution as second-order change. They found that second-order change resolutions are, in many cases, illogical, even unexplained and paradoxical. This is so because second-order change requires a shift to one logical level above what is to be expressed or explained. A metalanguage that is not necessarily available has to be used. Regarding second-order change resolutions, Watzlawick and Fisch said: "In each case the decisive action is applied (willingly or unwillingly) to the attempted *solution* — specifically to that which is being done to deal with the difficulty — and not to the difficulty itself" (p. 18; emphasis added).

A commander received an order to clear a city square by firing at rioting rebels. He commanded his soldiers to take up firing positions, their rifles leveled at the crowd, and as a ghastly silence descended, he drew his sword and shouted: "Mesdames, m'sieurs, I have orders to fire at the carnaille [rebels]. But as I see a great number of honest, respectable citizens before me, I request that they leave so that I can safely shoot the carnaille." The square was empty in a few minutes.

The officer could have opposed hostility with hostility (more of the same) and thus solved the problem. But in the wider context, this change would not be a change at all; it would have further inflamed the existing turmoil. Through his intervention, the officer effected a second-order change — he took the situation outside the frame that until that moment contained both him and the crowd. He reframed it in a way that was acceptable to everyone involved, and with this reframing both the original threat and its threatened "solution" could safely be abandoned.

Watzlawick and Fisch's ideas about the nature of second-order change may be summarized as follows:

1. Second-order change is applied to what in the first-order change perspective appears to be a solution. This is because in the second-order change perspective this solution reveals itself as the cornerstone of the problem whose solution is attempted.
2. While first-order change always appears to be based on common sense (for instance, applying "more of the same" techniques), second-order change usually appears to be weird, unexpected, and lacking in common sense; there is a puzzling, paradoxical element in the process of change.
3. Applying second-order change techniques to the "solution" means that the situation is dealt with "here and now." These techniques deal with effects and not with their presumed causes; the crucial question is "what," not "why."
4. The use of second-order change techniques lifts the situation out of the paradox-engendering trap created by the self-reflexiveness of the attempted solution and places it in a different frame.
5. Second-order change is introduced into the system from the outside; it amounts to a change of the premises governing the system as a whole.

For defining "reframing," the definitions provided by Watzlawick and Fisch and by Bandler and Grinder are helpful. Watzlawick and Fisch define reframing as follows:

> To reframe, then, means to change the conceptual and/or emotional setting or viewpoint in relation to which a situation is experienced and to place it in another frame which fits the "facts" of the same concrete situation equally well or even better, and thereby changes its entire meaning. (1974, p. 95)

Bandler and Grinder (1982) added to the above definition the behavioral aspect of change: "The meaning that any event has depends upon the 'frame' in which we perceive it. When we change the frame we change the meaning. . . . When the meaning changes the person's responses and behaviors also change" (p. 1).

These two definitions are useful in understanding the concept "reframing." By "reframing" we mean using techniques that either force or enable participants to go beyond their current frame of reference (or paradigm), to have new perspectives on the current situation, and to choose a new perspective to adhere to. In reframing, there is a radical, sudden change in perception and behavior, a jump to a different logical level, while the situation itself (the "facts") may remain quite unchanged — indeed, even unchangeable. What turns out to be changed as a result of reframing is, first of all, the meaning attributed to the situation, and therefore its consequences, but not its concrete facts.

TRANSFORMATION, LEADERSHIP, AND REFRAMING

Scholars attribute to transformational leadership the capacity to provide new vision, to communicate this vision, to align members to it, and to mobilize energy for institutionalizing this vision (Tichy & Ulrich 1984). Transformation leadership has the capacity to step beyond the current belief system that defines the nature of a problem and shapes its solutions. It has the capacity not to be caught in vicious circles, in repetitive failing solutions, and does not despair in periods of crisis and chaos. It can revitalize declining organizations by reframing.

The notion that organizational transformation involves leadership that is capable of reframing second-order problems (problems that can be solved only by second-order solutions or change) is based on the examination of studies and case studies on success and failure in organizational transformation. Two examples are provided. The first is a case study that is an insight into how the president of Antioch College succeeded in transforming a small, liberal arts college at Yellow Springs, Ohio, into a unique, inventive, and prospective national university (Warren 1984).

Antioch College was in a deep crisis, its survival in jeopardy, when its president decided to transform the system instead of trying to maintain it. In his efforts to transform the system, he displayed two major behavioral patterns that may be seen as part of the practice of reframing. The first is the ability not to be caught in the current logical framework and in repetitive first-order solutions, and to keep an open mind to alternative logical frameworks or higher levels of perspective. Warren describes the president's behavior during the stage of crisis and chaos:

> While others were in shock, he was in control. While many were denying the facts of institutional difficulty, he was asserting them. While many were angry with the distress and prospects for change, he was enthusiastic about the promise they held. ... While an increasing number slipped into depression, he exhibited exceptional energy and purpose. And finally, while many resigned themselves to the collapse of the institution and looked elsewhere for new jobs, he asserted a new optimism about the future of Antioch. (p. 105)

The second behavioral pattern is the ability to use the crisis for reframing the problem and to provide a new direction for solving the problem, based on a totally different logical framework. Warren called this principle "capitalizing on the crisis." In a time of crisis, when others were looking to meet the payroll and to pay creditors, the president of Antioch was considering new directions for the college. Confronted with possible bankruptcy, he spoke of the changing face of higher education: "He suggested that the future of the institution rested importantly in urban centers with older, married, full-time employed students. This declaration by the president represented a radical shift from the orientation of the college" (Warren 1984, p. 104). The president of Antioch reframed the problem from how to maintain the system to how to transform it into a totally new system. He thus saved the system from demise.

The second example is the study of Bibeault (1982) on how to revitalize organizations in decline and deep crisis. In studying the reasons for organizational decline, he found that 52 percent of these reasons were internally generated problems and 15 percent were internal problems triggered by external factors, all within the management's control. Only 9 percent of the reasons were external factors beyond management's control (p. 25). Bibeault therefore attributed organizational decline and crisis mainly to management's behavior.

Further, Bibeault examined factors of bad management, mostly related to organizational decline. Three factors were indicated:

1. Functional blindness. The tendency of managers to ignore warning signals and to assert that the problems are temporary and may be solved by traditional measures. In other words, "Most ailing organizations have developed a functional blindness to their own defects. They are not suffering because they cannot solve their

problems but because they cannot **see** their problems" (p. 17; emphasis added).

2. Narrow outlook. Organizational decline is related to the inability of managers to look at problems from different perspectives horizontally (finance, production, people, environmental perspectives) and vertically (higher-level and broader perspectives).

3. Displacement activity. Doing what one knows best repeatedly instead of doing what should be done.

The ability of an organization's members to observe problems from a higher-level logical framework, or "metasystem" level, can be learned. Argyris and Schon (1978) argue that an organization's members can learn to cope with major problems by examining the basic assumption that shapes these problems. They call this "double-loop learning." Jantsch (1980) argues that as we learn more about evolution, we create organizations capable of "self-transcendence." Self-transcending organizations are those which have the capability of observing themselves from a metalevel and transcending to a higher level. Smith (1984) makes the link between the reframing practice as suggested by Watzlawick and Fisch and the notion of the self-transcending system suggested by Jantsch. He writes:

> The concept of reframing is very helpful for the task of thinking about organizational self-transcendence. . . . For a human system to be autopoietic (adapt proactively to its environment) it must be able to be self-transcendent. That means moving out of its own construction of reality and entering into dialogue with multiple realities it can create by reframing its own and others' experiences in as many different frameworks as possible. (p. 292)

Thus Smith links the process of transformation, which is needed for organizational adaptation, and the process of reframing, which is the ability of the organization to move out of its own "construction of reality."

THE PRACTICE OF REFRAMING

Explicit conceptualizations of reframing and its use for facilitating second-order changes have been made by a number of therapists who understand that problem behavior makes sense when viewed only in the context in which it occurs. Most of these therapists work with families, groups, and organizations, but at the individual level. Among them are Watzlawick, Fisch and the Mental Research Institute group in Palo Alto (Fisch et al. 1983); Halley and Hoffman (1967); and Salvador Minuchin and the group at the Philadelphia Child Guidance Clinic (Minuchin & Fishman 1981). These therapists have designed specific reframing interventions such as "content reframing" and "paradoxical injunctions," some of which will be described later in this section.

To the above groups one must add therapists such as Satir (1967), who uses a great deal of reframing in her work with families, from simple redefinitions to more elaborate reframing via psychodrama in her "parts parties" and "family reconstructions." Whitaker (1976) reframes with nearly everything he says to the families he works with. Symptoms become reframed as accomplishments or skills, "sanity" becomes craziness, and "craziness" becomes sanity. Bandler and Grinder (1982) developed a structural programmed reframing method called "six-step reframing."

Some of the above therapists argue explicitly that reframing techniques may be applied to facilitate second-order change in organizations because organizations operate under specific frames of reference (paradigms) and actually are like extended families. There is already some evidence about using reframing principles to facilitate organizational second-order change (Nicoll 1980; Burns & Nelson 1983). In the following paragraphs some reframing techniques will be described and analyzed.

Short-Term Intervention and Second-Order Resolution

Watzlawick and Fisch (1974) suggest formulating and applying a four-step procedure:

1. A clear definition of the problem in concrete terms; this permits the crucial separation of problems from pseudo problems.
2. An investigation of the solutions attempted so far; problems are created and maintained by wrong attempts at solving a difficulty. A careful exploration of these attempted solutions not only shows what kind of change should *not* be attempted, but also reveals what maintains the situation that is to be changed.
3. A clear definition of the concrete change to be achieved; utopian goals can become problems by themselves.

4. The formulation and implementation of a plan to produce this change. The plan is based on the reframing principles: the target of change is the attempted solution, and the tactic chosen must be translated into the person's own "reality."

Reframing

Minuchin and Fishman (1981) suggest three reframing techniques: enactment, focusing, and intensity.

In enactment, the consultant helps the system's members to interact with each other, and to experience their reality as they define it. The consultant then recognizes the data, changes their meaning, introduces other elements, and suggests alternative ways of transacting that become actualized in the system. In focusing, the consultant, having selected elements that seem relevant to change, organizes the data of the system's transactions around a theme that gives them new meaning. In intensity, the consultant heightens the impact of the therapeutic message. The system's members experience their dysfunctional transactions intensely — that is, how they occur, and how pervasive they are in different system levels. Then a system's members experience a new reality, where the symptoms of the old reality are challenged (p. 77).

Paradoxical Interventions

One more reframing technique commonly used in family and group therapy is the paradoxical intervention. A paradoxical intervention is one that, if followed, will accomplish the opposite of what was seemingly intended. Its success depends on the system's members' defying the consultant's instructions or following them to the point of absurdity and then recoiling. The target of the systematic paradox is this hidden interaction that expresses itself in a symptom.

A description of a paradoxical intervention is provided by Papp (1981). She suggests three major techniques or steps used in designing and applying a systematic paradox: (1) redefining, (2) prescribing, and (3) restructuring.

1. The purpose of redefining is to change the group's perception of the problem. The symptom is redefined from being a foreign element

outside the system to being an essential part of it. Behavior that maintains the symptom is defined as benignly motivated to preserve group stability. Anger is defined as caring, suffering as self-sacrifice, and so on. Rather than trying to change the system directly, the consultant supports it, respecting the inner emotional logic on which it runs.

2. Having been defined positively, the symptom-producing cycle of interaction is then prescribed as an inevitable conclusion of the group's own logic. When the cycle that produced the symptom is consciously enacted, it loses its power to produce a symptom. The secret rules of the game are made explicit, and the group must take responsibility for its own actions. The group "is led through a state in which it is confronted by itself and forced to argue against the demands of its own truth." (p. 246).

3. Whenever the group shows signs of changing, the consultant restrains them. As the group recoils from this prescription and presses for change, the consultant regulates its pace. He or she constantly enumerates the consequences of the change and anticipates the new difficulties that will arise, predicting how they will affect the system, and cautiously allows the system to change in spite of it.

Another technique used in paradoxical intervention is "reversals." A reversal is an intervention in which the consultant directs someone in the system or the entire group to reverse his/her attitude or behavior in regard to a crucial issue in the hope that it will elicit a paradoxical response from other system members, from the individual, or from the group. Reversals are useful when some of the system's members are cooperative and will follow direct advice while other members resist it.

A well-known therapist using paradoxical and reversal interventions in family therapy is Palazzoli (1978). He defines the purpose of his interventions as a radical reshuffling of the system. A typical paradoxical intervention consists of steps in which the consultants enter the system as members, avoiding any critical attitude or judgment. They then prescribe paradoxical roles to each person in the family system; the identified patient becomes the family leader, the parents become children, and the therapists become the parents. This type of paradoxical restructuring of the system leads to a radical shift in perception and behavior. The therapists "shake the family out of its destructive clinch, as it were, and try to give all members a new chance to pursue their own individuation and separation" (p. 14).

To summarize, the above interventions are predesigned, structured, and sophisticated. They are seemingly illogical and demand skill, intuition, and creativity from the consultant. They are widely used for facilitating second-order change at the group and family levels. They seem to be helpful when the whole family is present in the therapeutic session and when first-order changes have not worked. They may also be applied in organizational settings, as some of the above therapists suggest and as has been shown in the first few attempts to use them, by the authors and others.

EVALUATION

Change Agent Characteristics

The manager, therapist, or consultant, as he or she emerges from the above interventions and case study, is a highly skilled professional. He or she plans, designs, and constructs very sophisticated interventions. Yet, he or she is not only an engineer but also an architect and an artist. Creative thinking, imagination, intuition, and spontaneity are used to design and facilitate the change.

The manager typically attempts to introduce his or her own logical framework or to nudge the system into a framework different from the one it now holds. He or she studies the problem from three main perspectives. The first is how the problem is manifested in the present — that is, what its symptoms are and how members experience it now. The second is the attempted solutions and their results. The third is what other frames can be taken so that a breakthrough in solving the problem can be made. These three perspectives provide the information on which the intervention design is based.

Intervention Characteristics

The reframing interventions share some common characteristics:

1. They attempt to change the participants' perceptions of reality by helping them to view the problem from a different logical framework based on different presuppositions.
2. They are seemingly illogical and irrational.

3. They are focused on symptoms and/or attempted solutions, not on supposed causes. The intervention is concerned with what happens and how it happens, not with why it happens.
4. They are "here and now"-oriented.
5. They are planned, structured, and directed by the manager or consultant.
6. They are usually short and intensive.
7. Participants have little, if any, influence on the intervention design, purpose, and direction.
8. The interventions are very experiential; participants must use their bodies and senses, to move and to role-play.
9. When done by a consultant, he or she introduces his or her logical framework. In this case the change is introduced from outside.

Organizational Characteristics: Type of Problem

As in the case study, the problem of youngsters leaving their parents or leaving rural communities has evidently existed for a long time and a solution has not been found to change this; thus there is reason to assume that there is no ultimate solution. On some kibbutzim, however, members have convinced themselves that the dropout rate can be radically changed. This conviction, rather than the dropout rate, creates untold problems — mainly through increasing polarization between generations.

The attempted solutions had increased the polarization in the system, and thus a small problem turned into a big one. More and more members began to "realize" that more needed to be done. "More of the same" was their recipe for change, and that solution was the problem. In a chapter entitled "The Utopian Syndrome," Watzlawick and Fisch (1974) suggested the following:

> Practically there exist many situations in which reality can be changed to conform to a premise. But there are probably as many situations in which nothing can be done about the actual state of things. . . . Thus it is the premise that things **should be** a certain way which is the problem and which requires change, and not the way things **are**. (pp. 60–61; emphasis added)

Watzlawick and Fisch argue that without the "Utopian premise," the actuality of the situation may be quite bearable. So what is involved here is a mishandling of change: First-order change is attempted where only second-order change can lead to a solution.

Characteristics of the Outcome

Reframing interventions typically change people's perceptions of reality, which results in changes of basic premises about this reality. The outcome is changes in behavior related to the treated problem. Thus, the outcome of reframing intervention seems to be a "jump" to a new state consisting of new premises about, and new perceptions of, the treated problem and new behaviors related to the problem. There is also a new "fit" of these three components. However, the reality itself (such as youngsters leaving the kibbutz) remains unchanged.

To summarize, reframing interventions are widely used in family and group therapy. Those who use these types of interventions argue that they can be applied to organizational settings; there are already some examples showing that reframing interventions may help an organization's members to cope with second-order problems. The basic strategy taken here is to push the system to an extreme, beyond its elastic limits; to bring it to a critical point, a threshold, where a new perspective or new logic is suddenly achieved. From a theoretical perspective, many reframing interventions are based on positive feedback and amplifying fluctuation. Instead of allowing the system to move through all the different developmental stages on its way to demise or revitalization (crisis, chaos, back to basics), the consultant or manager, by using reframing techniques, pushes the system to a point where members can view their own behavior from a "higher" logical framework. This strategy fits with Prigogine's (1984) theory on order through fluctuations (see Chapter 12) and provides some evidence supporting his basic ideas.

From management's perspective, transformational leadership seems capable of viewing a present situation — as bad as it is — from a "metalevel" logical framework. It is capable of creating or discovering alternative realities, or what Davis (1982) calls "contexts," and of reframing problems. These capabilities, as suggested in this chapter, can be learned. Some models of learning seem to be compatible with this proposition (for instance, Argyris & Schon 1978).

It is important to note the differences between strategic change approaches suggested by Burns and Nelson (1983), Davis (1982), and Tichy (1983), and reframing approaches suggested by Minuchin and Fishman (1981) and Watzlawick and Fisch (1974). Table 5.1 shows some of these differences.

As shown in Table 5.1, reframing interventions are usually short and focused on attempted solutions, repetitive dysfunctional behavior, and

Table 5.1.
Differences Between Strategic Change and Reframing Interventions

Characteristic	*Intervention*	
	Strategic Change Interventions	*Reframing and Paradox Interventions*
Time orientation	future	present
Focus on	mission	symptoms
Change agent	facilitator	programmer
Profession is	craft	art
Senses	vision	perception
Duration of intervention	long	short
Intervention	logical	paradoxical
Intervention is aimed at	finding new direction	solving problems

Source: Prepared by the authors.

symptoms. They utilize sophisticated technologies; hence, the intervention seems to be more art than craft. Strategic change interventions are quite different. They take long and focus on changing the organization's mission, purpose, and belief system. The intervention is craft, not art.

For many managers used to a collaborative approach to consulting, a reframing approach may raise problems. This is definitely a one-sided approach in which the client is told what to do. There is no attempt to collaborate or share power in the diagnostic and intervention stages.

This raises the issue of learning how to change. Many change projects attempt not only to change the organization, but also to help it learn how to develop and change itself. Reframing, at this stage of its development, makes no claims of helping the organization learn how to change itself on its own.

A major problem of reframing organizations is to find ways to get a large collective of people to reframe their reality. The technology to do this with many people has not yet been sufficiently developed. Nevertheless, this approach holds much promise, and development efforts might profit from the experience already accumulating in the systemic family therapies and pioneering attempts to apply this to organizations.

6

Rechanneling Energy

Organizational transformation has been described as channeling, focusing, and applying energy for the purpose of revitalization. A survey of recent textbooks on management and organizations reveals that the existence of energy in social systems is not yet recognized. When energy does appear, it is in the form of a fuel source such as gas: Books with a systems approach to organizations do include energy. Energy, with matter and information, is seen as flowing between the organization and its environment.

A number of organizational practitioners do recognize the existence of energy in organizations. Beer (1981) connects energy to human effort and motivation as one of the important kinds of energy in organizations. Steele and Jenks (1977) build their consulting approach on energy as one of the most important elements of organizational life. Levinson (1972) diagnoses the energy levels of organizations.

What is organizational energy? The concept stands for the level of spirit, morale, enthusiasm, motivation, pace, and volume of performance. It captures the vitality or stamina of the organizational life. Organizational energy can be viewed from several perspectives: (1) as a source or potential for action, (2) as an outcome of organization life, (3) as an accomplishment of tasks and objectives. This chapter provides managers and practitioners with ideas and approaches that can help them to infuse new energy into their organizations or to rechannel energy for the purpose of revitalization and transformation.

A CASE EXAMPLE: THE TRANSFORMATION OF THE CITY COLLEGE*

Background

The city college was an old, small, undeveloped education system operating in storefronts and offices scattered around the center of town. Yet, during the last 20 years the town had undergone industrialization and growth. City residents and the city council felt that the present system could not fulfill the new needs of the city. The problem was that the city included three ethnic groups, each of which thought that the college should serve quite diverse practical and symbolic functions, and should rebuild in its neighborhood. Moreover, there was no clear idea about the characteristics of the new system.

For example, the white and the old populations wanted an education system for the senior adults to complete degree programs and for adult education. The blacks saw the college as facilitating the first years of education prior to going on to the university. For ten years the leadership of the city struggled with the issue without finding a solution. In this situation the city department of education decided to use external consultants to help establish the new college. After learning the issue, the consultants decided to establish a group of 60 people who represented the city council, the college functional groups, and the interest groups. This group was labeled the "core group," and its task was to provide the city council with a model of the new college and its location.

THE INTERVENTION

The intervention consisted of three sequential workshops, each two to three days long.

The first workshop was focused entirely on the individual level. The purposes were to separate the participants from the immediate issue, to illuminate the concept of open systems, to facilitate the integration of each individual, and to build the group identity. The participants learned to view themselves as open systems, and to examine their input and throughput processes, their environment and its influence. The learning was basically experimental, and included values, perceptions, and the ideal type of college of each participant.

---

*The case was taken from McWhinney 1982.

The exercises provided the facilitators with some insight into the positions that people held regarding education, community relations, and architecture. It also created the "individuation" necessary to allow subsequent integration or, to put it in McWhinney's words: "Until the individuals know their own mind, and have articulated them, they are restrained to joining with others" (1982, p. 86).

The second workshop was carried out a few weeks later. About half of the participants decided not to continue, and thus the core group consisted of 30 participants. The purpose of this workshop was to create an ideal model for the new college. The participants shared stories about the creation of the old college, critical events in its history, and what it meant to them. Then they went through visioning exercises, guided images exercises, and experiential exercises. Individuals had to visualize their ideal college, its mission, and its basic characteristics. Then they had to experience their model, to be their model, and to act like their model. They had to pass through awareness processes about the roots and the sources of their model.

The purpose of the exercise, besides creating an image of the new college, was to enable the participants to be aware of the influence of their own ethnicity, culture, and background on the image, and to be able to change their models according to educational needs of today and tomorrow, not of the past. Subgroups worked on the different models. Again individuals had to be subsystems of their models and to experience the buildings, the parking lot, the admissions office, and so on. The models were created by drawing, by modeling in clay, or by building with oak boxes; these were then shared in the large group.

The group searched for common characteristics. From the different exercises a common image emerged; the group decided to call it "cluster college." The dominant image at the end of this workshop was one of confluence and differentiation: "a clustering confluence" — separate groupings of departments with their own academic and social facilities, but with central features that would produce confluence. The group reached consensus on the purpose, mission, and basic physical and academic characteristics of the college without arguing or voting.

At the end of the second workshop, participants received a study by a private firm on the advantages and disadvantages of three possible sites for the college. A group meeting was held to learn the study but not to decide on the site.

The third workshop was held a few weeks later, after the participants communicated the ideas of the new college to their interest or professional groups. The energy and enthusiasm of the core group was very high, and each member felt that the main problem now was financial support. During the few weeks that had passed since the end of the second workshop, participants had succeeded in persuading individuals and business firms to provide financial support for the new college.

The third workshop focused on elaborating the ideal model, to make it compatible with the present and future educational needs, and to decide upon the site for the new college. It was a classic opportunity for a rational problem-solving process. Again the consultants used conscious processes in which the group had to work as individuals and small groups to articulate the image into a site design that could be submitted to the community college board. The main exercise was held in subgroups; each subgroup had to experience one of the dimensions of the ideal college, to be that subsystem, and to be aware of the needs it should fulfill, its basic construction or principle. Then each subgroup had to draw or build or describe its work and share it in the large group.

At the end of this workshop, it became clear that the present site of the college would not be suitable for most of the needs expressed, and thus it was dropped as a contender. The energy was focused on the emergent resolution — the top of the hill site — almost as though the other alternatives had never been seriously supported. This site, although it was the most expensive alternative, nevertheless was the most appropriate place for the shared model to be. There was no formal vote, no rational explanation of the alternatives. The agreement emerged as a natural process.

After the final workshop, a small team worked on the model and handed it to the education department. The city council then decided to establish a professional team to implement the new model. This phase was conducted without the help of the consultants.

Low energy is one of the major blocks to the renewal of a deteriorating organization, especially a neurotic organization. Having dissipated much of its energy on dysfunctioning, the organization has none left to invest in change efforts. The communication breakdown, internal conflicts, ineffectiveness, repetitive crisis, failures of change projects, the negative selection of high-energy people who leave the organization, the breakdown in leadership, the inability to maintain accepted norms of behavior, individual frustration, the decrease in income and reserve resources — all these and other factors have drained the organization's energy bank (Merry & Brown 1986).

APPROACHES FOR ENERGIZING AND RECHANNELING ENERGY

Transforming the organization involves a transformation of its energy level. Without an unblocking of the energy flow, a revitalization of the energy level will not occur. Rechanneling the energy, freeing and enlivening its flow, is both a transformation and an approach to transformation.

Some of the ways that have been developed to rechannel and vitalize organizational energy are the following:

- Managing in the flow state
- Creating new structures, such as the fusion team, networks, vertical linking, and a transitional structure
- Reformulating the organization's core process
- Creating alignment around common meaning and values
- Using Gestalt therapy approaches.

Managing in the Flow State

Ackerman (1984) has proposed an approach to transformation that she calls "managing in the flow state." She describes organizations as "dynamic energy fields" always in flow, and sees management as managing the energy flow. This flow state is seen in Figure 6.1.

The organization can be viewed through an energy model of concentric circles. At the core is the organization's purpose — its reason for being. This is what gives meaning and direction to the energy flow and the form. The second ring depicts the sources of energy, such as people, relationships, myth and ritual, polarities, symbols, values, and goals. The third ring details the channels through which energy flows, such as communication channels, meetings, work flow, scheduling, review systems, and decision making. The outer ring describes the fields that are created by energy in the organization. They include the organization's culture, its leadership style, and morale. Surrounding the organization are forces such as suppliers, customers, unions, the government, and the economy.

Many organizations deal with form. Their model of organization is one of parts that need to be congruent. When things go wrong, the parts need to be fixed so that they fit together better in order to return the

Figure 6.1. The Organization as Energy Field

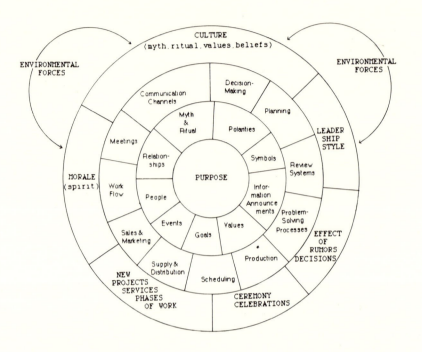

Source: Adams 1984a.

organization to its status quo. Managers are taught to problem-solve and maintain control over the parts.

Ackerman suggests paying less attention to form and control, and instead focusing attention on what is happening in the organization, what is blocking the flow, what is assisting the fit, what is needed in the long range. This is a view of organizations as dynamic energy constantly changing and moving. She proposes that management style can be a major factor in blocking or freeing the flow of energy in the organization. She differentiates three styles. Fear management is overcontrolling, self-oriented, has a win/lose mentality, creates obstacles and barriers, and constrains and blocks the energy flow. Solid state management, the traditional mode, works with the system, ensures fit between parts, and is results-oriented. Flow state management works with the energy flow of the system, dissolves obstacles, changes structure to suit energy needs, encourages others to take responsibility, is oriented to process, embraces polarities, seeks meaning in the organization's purpose, empowers others, and works from an apprehension of the totality.

Ackerman describes the flow state manager as seeing the organization as offering an abundance of opportunities, valuing calculated risks and continual learning, valuing structures, and able to change them. He or she knows how to bond people together by a common purpose, needs and values all stakeholders in the organization, is able to appreciate the meaning in all events, is open to conflicts and differences, sees the synthesis of polarities, is not attached to self-action and power, is able to change according to needs, focuses on empowering others, is able to manage ambiguity, has a sense of timing, knows how to bring change by the use of critical mass, and is able to nurture his or her inner self.

Implementing changes in the organization to transform to the flow state might involve the following:

- Training people to scan the organization to see where to open blocks in energy channels
- Management seeing the organization as form and energy, and examining how they fit the different management styles
- Identifying the key sources of energy in the organization and how to use them
- developing a strategy to build a critical mass.

Ackerman attempts to delineate transformational technologies:

> Some of the technologies being used today to facilitate transformation include visioning, creating/identifying the context for change, aligning form and energy toward the achievement of vision, myth and ritual, building a critical mass, networking, creating collective intention revealing and shifting people's belief systems, and designing organic structures like the Fusion Team. (1983, p. 4)

Creating New Structures

Rechanneling energy in the organization involves organizing form so that it does not constrict and block energy. It also involves creating structures that encourage energy flow, align the flow, and revitalize the creation of new energy sources. Some of the approaches to doing this involve the development of new forms of structure in the organization.

Three of these forms that are suggested as vehicles for transformation are (1) the fusion team, (2) networks, (3) vertical linking.

The Fusion Team

A fusion team guides and oversees the coming together of a large group of people to perform a complex or innovative task. It is a form of large group management that oversees the creative process as balancing the needs of people with the requirements of the budget and the timetable. The fusion team usually consists of nine volunteer members committed to implementing a major change. Leadership is emerging and contingent upon needs. Ackerman and Whitney describe the fusion team as "a form of group management set up to orchestrate a large scale project, by balancing the needs of people with the needs of the project and the working process" (1984, p. 150). The application base of the fusion team is small so far, but it has been used most effectively and encouragingly by Burns and Nelson (1983) in an army setting. It was also used effectively in the planning and implementation of the Organizational Development Network 1984 convention in Los Angeles.

The fusion team works by allowing decentralized, unique contributions to emerge, by empowering individual autonomy, by encouraging synergy, and by giving expression to the multitude of needs found in the most complex organizations and projects.

> Once established, the fusion team becomes the visible management group. Fusion team members become caretakers of the process, keeping the group's vision and the context for its work clear and consistently in front of group members. It is an organic body, changing shape, membership and focus depending upon what the larger group needs in order to accomplish its task. (Ackerman & Whitney 1984, p. 150)

The fusion team reflects these values: the pursuit of excellence, enabling people to develop their potential, taking care of members' needs, trust in the individual, balance of task and maintenance, flexibility, and shared leadership. A fusion team can be used whenever a large group of people is brought together to accomplish a project over a period of time. Examples of use of a fusion team are in implementing a major organizational change, running a conference, creative problem solving, and developing a product such as a plan, a book, or an event.

Membership in the fusion team is voluntary and changes over time. Leadership within the team varies according to what needs to be done, often changes hands and is shared. It is a "leaderful" group. Division of labor within the group is on a voluntary basis.

Within the larger group the fusion team's members stimulate, link, and transform energy. They act as liaison between various subgroups in the larger group. They create a control center through which all information flows. They are responsible for planning and facilitating the larger group's meetings. The fusion team is the energy manager of the larger group, monitoring and stimulating levels of positive energy.

Networking

Networking is a system of information exchange among an interrelated group of individuals with needs for similar kinds of information and knowledge. Successful networks go beyond the transfer of data; they lead to creation and exchange of knowledge (Carrillo et al. 1984). Information exchanges between emergent networks of people have almost always been behind major social changes. Very few systems have voluntarily executed radical changes or chosen to cease to exist. In most cases, major changes are "driven" by networks of dedicated people. Hence, by encouraging networking, managers or consultants may facilitate the diffusion of new ideas and their legitimization. Adams (1983) writes:

> . . . fundamental change in the basic context of, or "reality" of any given system is difficult to impossible when operating from within that context of reality. Fundamental changes can occur only when a critical mass of people are able to see and accept another "reality," and this most often takes place in the form of informal emerging networks of people sharing a common vision. (p. 7)

Adams has suggested a network-based model for working with resistance to the organizational change. In most organizations there will be about 10–15 percent immediate accepters of the new transformation vision, 20–25 percent will be early adapters, 25 percent will be late adapters, 20–25 percent will be skeptical, and 10–15 percent will be hard-core resisters. Adams suggests that instead of confronting the hard-core resisters, the earliest efforts should be to identify the strong supporters and help them network with one another. They later can plan how to network with early adapters, without alienating the resisters. The next stage can be networking with late adapters, and so on.

Social transformation can be seen as a process of networks of networks. Processes of networking seem to be developing in various countries, and possibly these loose networks of like-minded people with a humanistic/holistic view of life and society may be the forerunners of transformation to a more enlightened social order (Ferguson 1980). Networks of like-minded people in similar organizations may also serve as agents of transformation of these organizations. The women's movement may be seen in this light.

Computer networks of innovative individuals and organizations are another possible vehicle of transformation. A number of such networks for conferencing, exchanging innovative ideas, and dealing with organizational transformation have been established within the last few years. The Meta Network is an example of this genre. It sees itself as "closing the gap between the human condition and the human potential," and, among other subjects, conferences on organization transformation. The spread of the microcomputer opens new horizons for networking.

Networks consist of interdependent actors that can be individuals or collectivities. They are voluntarily bounded for common purposes of mutual interest; membership is categorically open, and always nonhierarchical (probably collegial). They depend upon visible and verifiable rewards, and exist outside single organizational boundaries. This description by Ross Speck at the 1983 organizational development conference would preclude internal networks within an organization. It might be advisable at this stage not to accept the last part of Speck's description, and to include in the term "network" networks within a single organization, as suggested by Adams. Thus organizational transformation may be catalyzed by the flow of information, knowledge, ideas, innovations, and common interests between people in different organizations, and also by like-minded people networking within their own organizations.

Vertical Linking

Hawley (1982) has suggested an approach called "vertical linking." He builds on his experience as a consultant in using this approach in the transformation of a number of organizations. He describes vertical linking as a process by which organization members at all levels jointly undertake to vitalize the organization.

The organization enlists employees from many levels to gather information about problems and strengths in its work climate. This information is fed back to management. Following this, large portions of the organization's work force are enlisted to participate in solving the problems. Vertical linking involves a large enough section of the work force (20–60 percent at some points) to bring changes in the organization's work life.

The process consists of six steps:

1. Start-up
2. Sensing, Collecting information
3. Feedback and action planning by upper management
4. Verification of key issues with employees
5. Response action program, Key issues are addressed by task forces and special work groups
6. Solidification of improved behaviors.

The major innovation of the approach is the large number of organization members involved in the project.

A Transitional Structure

Another structural approach is the creation of a transitional structure parallel to the existing structure. Barrett and Cammann (1984) suggest that this structure consists of a steering team, a coordinator team, task forces, and a communication network that links these teams. The purpose of this structure is to manage the process of change.

Adizes (1979) approaches change with a similar transitional structural strategy. The formal organization structure is viewed as unable to bring about transformation. It deals with the everyday activities of producing results and administration — both on a short-term basis. Whenever one attempts to introduce entrepreneurial and integrative projects (both oriented to long-term change) into the formal structure, it will stifle them. The pressure of everyday management, problem solving, and administration will overcome the need to invest time, energy, and other reosurces in creative, innovative, integrative, long-term change projects.

Change and transformation need to be brought about by creating a special structure coexisting with the functioning formal structure. This transitional, parallel structure consists of ad hoc synergistic teams that are created specifically to deal with issues that could not be handled by regular management and its committees. These teams consist of the people who have authority, power, and influence in dealing with a special issue. They are trained to deal with issues, and when they have completed their mission — within a short, defined time period — they are disbanded. The activities of these teams — the creation and training of new teams — are coordinated by a special management team.

The Adizes approach includes a stage of redefining the organization's core mission. An activity such as this could lead to an organizational transformation. A special longer-lived team is created for this purpose. This team changes its membership, size, and form throughout its life cycle of redefining mission.

The approach of developing a transitional parallel structure has been used in regular organizational development change projects. Such an approach was tried at General Motors, and some consultants see this "collateral organization" as a new change strategy in organizational development. It remains to be seen if transformational change necessitates a transitional parallel structure as the carrier of the change effort.

Reformulating the Core Process

McWhinney has developed what he calls an "alchemic" approach to organizational transformation. He describes it thus:

> The alchemic mode is an uncovering of what is, a raising to awareness of the relation of the individual to society, of individuals to technology and of society (or the organization) to the technology. It is a process of continuing redefinition of the environment and of identification of direction. It is also a process of **creating reality** and exploring within that created reality so that what is, is what has been created. (1982, p. 77; emphasis added)

McWhinney sees the purpose of alchemic procedures as awareness, which is achieved in the full development of the individual and the community, and their relationship to the created environment. This is done by taking what is and transforming it through clarification and redefinition. This transformation of awareness leads to practical results: efficiency, conflict resolution, opportunity creation, and energy for production. The focus is on choice making and not on problem solving. The aliveness of the system, the involvement of its members, their awareness, and the transformation of their way of being are the measures of achievement: "The alchemic procedures work interactively in a spiral of awaring, creating and acting, repeated at progressively deeper and broader levels, working always with the triple awareness of the individual, the group (organization or community) and the transforming work" (McWhinney 1982, p. 77).

The alchemic approach makes wide use of the technology of open systems planning, which leads to a reformulation of the statement describing the organization's core processes. The organization's constituents, who have labored collectively to create the new statement, align themselves around it.

Describing McWhinney's approach as "open systems planning" or as an attempt to reformulate the organization's "raison de vivre" — its core process — does not give credit to the depth and richness of the approach. A whole world of innovative ideas, original approaches, and deep understandings is enfolded in the alchemic mode. A major problem of communicating them is that they approach transformation from within the context of a new paradigm and use a whole array of new concepts that mean little to one who has not experienced them.

In practical terms the work can be seen as repetitive recycling and deepening of a four-phase process. The first phase is one of separation from everyday environment and concerns; the second is a process of individuation; the third deals with formulating the organization's core process; the fourth is one of planning and setting constraints.

The first phase is one of cleansing by separation of the participants from their everyday environment and concerns. The concerns are defused by a process of catharsis.

The second phase is one of individuation, which involves a deep process of self-awareness and definition of boundaries between the self and the organization. This is a strengthening process in which people's belonging to the organization is based on autonomy as individual persons, without confusing the individual and the organization. People become more aware of themselves and more centered. Various approaches and techniques are used to enhance this process. These might include a process in which individuals relive and relate to peak experiences they have had in the organizational context; a process such as finishing the sentence: "I am . . ." ten times, and then working on this; a process in which people create a mandala of their "puppets." People identify aspects of themselves that they bring out when they deal with important people in their environment. They name these people, then describe their behavior and the circumstances that activate their own "puppets."

The third phase begins with a similar cleansing process at the organizational level to clear away incidental problems of the moment. This is followed by a series of experiences aimed at uncovering and making explicit the central transforming process of the organization. This "core process" is a deeper version of "what business are you in?"

McWhinney describes it as "the integration of the being and transforming aspects of the organization." While this is, from one aspect, an internal core process, it always contains a mission beyond the organization itself. This process is generally facilitated with an open systems planning strategy. The participants map out in a graphic form all the organization's stakeholders, statements of what they expect from the organization, and the organization's responses to these expectations. This could be followed by a process of re-creating a lifeline history of the organization with markings of major events. Another process might involve identifying the major values that must characterize a process of resolution. This could be done by graphically depicting the stakeholders with statements the organization would ideally have them make. From these statements, themes of major organizational values may be drawn.

Based on these activities, the participants can attempt to formulate an expression of the organization's core process. This is a "right-brain" process, working on the level of metaphor and intuition, and not done in a rational, linear, analytical mode. The product may be a graphic design or a statement around which all participants align themselves as expressing the essence of the core process of their organization.

The fourth phase is one of planning. This is a process of constraint setting — that is, defining the reality that constrains and limits the space of solutions. When the list of constraints is completed, it forms a charter for the search for a resolution. It is the basic document which defines the governance of the domains in which a legitimate solution is to be found.

As McWhinney describes it, this alchemic process is not a one-time event. It is a life's work continually cleansing, continually deepening the individuation and the self observator power of the philosopher's stone and the clarity with which the organization operates out of its core process.

Decisions, in the usual sense of the word, have little meaning in the alchemic approach. By going to deeper levels of the complex issue, levels of values and core processes; by work on individuation and mutual trust; by increasing awareness of different styles of problem resolution that stem from different world views, issues come to resolution. This is not a process of problem solving or decision making, but one of issue resolution. In this process, alternatives are freely evoked and discussed, and there is a movement to resolution by confluence.

The alchemic mode draws on many insights from Eastern and mystic approaches, such as the works of Gurdijieff, Ouspensky, the Sufis, Zen, and Tao. It draws much from general systems theory, especially in its later form, such as cybernetics II. The works of Jung and Maslow, and many ideas from Janstch find their expression in McWhinney's practice.

Aligning Around a Common Vision

Kiefer and Stroh (1984), Ritscher (1983), and McKnight (1984) see the creation of a commonly held vision as a major element in energizing organizations so they become spirited organizations. Kiefer and Stroh (1984) put vision and purpose at the head of their list of variables influencing an organization's effectiveness. They advocate a new rule for organizational development practitioners as visionary leaders, or as cocreators of a new organizational vision who act with others in the organization to bring that vision into existence.

In this view, instead of current problems and present circumstances being dealt with, they are seen as indicators of how far the organization has gone in the creative process. The consultant's vision will be the new paradigm to accelerate and energize the transformation process. The consultant, together with leaders from the organization, can teach people how to build a new organization and not just cope with the old one.

The approach may involve engaging the organization members in the process of visioning, working to integrate complementary visions and helping the organization members discover their common purpose. People can be supported to believe that they can create the vision that they value and can take personal responsibility for both their vision and existing circumstances. This active view of the consultant's role in transformation contrasts sharply with the view of others who see the consultant's role only in terms of midwifing a process that is already taking effect.

For Ritscher (1983), excellent systems are those that are characterized by spirited empowered individuals and spirituality. Ritscher defines spirituality as follows: "the spiritual is an experience of something beyond our own boundaries, something that transcends our own ego. It is an experience that we are a part of something that is more than just ourselves" (p. 1).

Yet spirituality can be defined more pragmatically, in terms of how it is manifested in daily life or in the work place. From this perspective, spirituality consists of five qualities: integrity, affection, empowerment, openness, and effectiveness. Ritscher argues that high-performing systems manifest these five qualities collectively. Hence, spirited systems do the following:

1. Treat individuals as empowered, trusted, and competent
2. Ensure that individuals feel valued and special
3. Show dedication to the personal and professional growth of their employees
4. Support honesty and openness
5. Encourage employees to talk about their feelings as well as about facts
6. Stand for something beyond profit and efficiency, and align employees around this vision.

A very similar perspective is provided by McKnight (1984). He defines spirituality as "an animating life force, an energy that inspires one toward certain ends or purposes that go beyond one's self" (p. 5). McKnight found that employees perform most energetically, creatively, and enthusiastically when they believe they are contributing to a purpose that is outside or larger than themselves. The same is true at the organization level. Organizations that stand for something beyond their own immediate needs (profit, efficiency), and align their policy, procedures, structures, culture, and management to support their vision, are high-performing. Hence the contribution of McKnight's study is to introduce one more important element characterizing high performance: high spirit, enthusiasm, or high energy.

Perhaps some of the most thorough research on the concept "spirit" was conducted by Connelly (1984). This research into "work spirit" explores the dynamics, operation, origins, and uses of this energy, spark, or vitality. Research findings reveal that there are seven signs of work spirit:

1. Enormous energy — often one is described as "being on a roll"
2. A positive, open state of mind — one has a Buddha-like attitude of allowing and "If life hands you a lemon, make lemonade"
3. A sense of purpose and vision — a person with work spirit really knows what he or she is about, and wants to contribute to the.world
4. A full sense of self — one is operating intellectually, emotionally, physically, and spiritually, often far beyond one's earlier expectations
5. Participation in creation and nurturing — people with work spirit understand that they are creators, have impact on things around them, and nurture the growth of others

6. The risking (sensing) living moment — in those touchstone moments, a person with work spirit is on the line, sensorily aware of his or her surroundings, and vital in the moment
7. A sense of higher order and oneness — people with work spirit see the whole picture, what's important, and how each person and aspect fits into the universe, the wholeness of things.

Work spirit is seen as a resource for organizations, as a source of energy and aliveness. Fostering work spirit is related to the alignment of the individual's energy with the overall purpose and mission of the organization. Drawbacks of work spirit are related to discrepancies between what is vital and important to the individual, and what is important to the activities and directions of the organization.

Kiefer and Stroh (1984) have incorporated the new paradigm of excellence into programs for leadership and team development. One program is an advanced seminar for senior executives designed to develop the abilities that leaders of excellent systems have to incorporate:

1. To create and to communicate a personal and organizational vision to which they are wholeheartedly committed
2. To catalyze alignment around a common vision
3. To revitalize and to be committed to the vision in the face of obstacles
4. To understand an organization as a complex system whose structure may enable or thwart realization of the vision
5. To empower themselves and be the sort of people whose presence empowers others
6. To develop intuition as a complement to reason.

The second program is a workshop for functional groups that want to excel in achieving a common task or purpose. This program deepens the alignment of group members around a common purpose, develops their personal effectiveness, and enables them to create structures that translate their individual energies into collective results. The program includes techniques of agreeing on a common purpose that identifies strategic objectives necessary to achieve the purpose and processes designed to deepen alignment, to instill personal responsibility, and to empower group members individually and collectively.

Assessment of the two programs conducted over two years after the programs (before-after assessment) reports increased sales of more than 50 percent per year and 50 percent reductions in time invested in new product development. There was also significant improvement in working relationships, work satisfaction, and decision-making and problem-solving effectiveness. Kiefer and Stroh concluded that "the new paradigm works, and clearly merits further experiments and applications" (1984, p. 183).

Using Gestalt Therapy Approaches

Gestalt therapy may be a way of unblocking the energy flow of organizations in need of a transformation. It has become known as a very effective therapeutic approach to individuals. Basically, however, Gestalt therapy is a human systems approach. From a methodological viewpoint, this means that the concepts and propositions of Gestalt therapy may be applied homologously to other, higher levels of human systems. In effect, it is possible to use them to understand phenomena in groups, organizations, communities, and nations.

Merry and Brown (1986) have pointed out the similarities between the neurotic behavior of individuals and the neurotic behavior of organizations and their subsystems. Among other characteristics, they have drawn attention to the low-energy climate found in declining organizations. In such organizations the neurotic functioning has drained all the energy out of the system, leaving none for integration and self-organization.

The excitement energy of the system can be blocked by sensory or emotional desensitization. Sensory desensitization is possible by blocking awareness. Some of the common ways of doing this are denial of the existence of unsatisfied needs, diminution of their intensity and their spread, and devaluation of their importance.

Two of the common methods of emotional desensitization are blocking emotional expression and blocking personal expression. If the emotional excitement in the organization cannot flow freely, the organization may desensitize itself to all but the most overwhelming kind of emotional response. The organization climate may be insensitive to the whole gamut of the affective domain. The other common phenomenon is that of an organization blocking all personal expression. This is often found in bureaucratic organizations or departments where people are seen as role bearers and not as individuals. The depersonalizing aspects of bureaucracy, when carried to the extreme, can drain all energy, motivation, and excitement out of a system. This also occurs in an extremely task-oriented work team or organization that ignores all aspects of human functioning other than those directly related to the job.

A major need in organizational transformation is to mobilize the organizational energy necessary for the transformative process. In some cases, however, when the organization is most in need of energy, motivation, and voluntary effort, it is most depleted of these. An organization in crisis that has thrashed around ineffectively for years, in a firefighting mode and in a climate of conflict and demotivation, has enormous difficulty finding the reserve energy resources essential for pulling itself out of the mire into which it is sinking.

Gestalt therapy may be of help in finding ways to unclog the blocked energy channels and revitalize the system. The Gestalt therapy approach may take various directions:

1. As a conceptual framework and diagnostic model for understanding what is happening in the organization and how to go about changing it
2. As a way to manage and interact in organizations
3. As a style for a consultant to use in working with organizations
4. As a source of new ideas about how to intervene in organizations
5. As the focus for training workshops for key individuals in the organization.

As a conceptual framework, de Vries and Miller (1982) showed how neurotic-style leadership affects organizational pathology. Possibly the major source on the relationship between organizational dysfunction and organizational transformation is the work on the neurotic behavior of organizations by Merry and Brown (1986). It contains a plethora of concepts and theories needed to understand and diagnose organizational pathology, especially in its manifestations that have similarities to the neurotic behavior of individuals. Merry and Brown suggest that when neurotic organizational behavior has reached a deep maladaptive level at which the organization is in a state of decline, possibly the only way out, banning demise, is an organizational transformation.

As a way of effective management, Herman and Kornich (1977) propose a Gestalt therapy approach to management that they call "authentic" management. They point out that managers who try to suit their style to an ideal type, such as human relations, pay heavily. They advocate focusing on recognition and mobilization of individual strength and power; intensification of problem behavior until a change occurs;

seeing conflict as a vitalizing force; emphasis on enhancing individual autonomy and competence; increased awareness of present behavior and completing unfinished business. These and other Gestalt therapy concepts serve as guidelines for authentic management.

Karp's (1976) work on collaboration gives support to McWhinney's approach (detailed in this chapter), which begins transformation with a process of individuation. Karp suggests that successful collaboration can be based only on recognition of the power that resides in the individual and his or her right to be himself or herself.

Applications of Gestalt approaches to management behavior and training were suggested by Fraser (1984), who shows how Gestalt techniques can help managers to cope with blockages to internal and external awareness, to creative problem solving, to communication, to self-expression, and to energy. He points out a number of blockages, including generalizing, having rigid expectations, blocking out internal and external awareness, catastrophizing, sticking to obsolete rules, and getting into a vicious circle of conflict. These and many other blockages can be dealt with by Gestalt approaches, such as focusing on "I" rather than on "one," focusing on "what" and "how" rather than on "why," attending to feelings, exaggerating, catastrophizing, and two-chair work.

As a different consulting style, Nevis (1980) suggests a Gestalt therapy approach to assessment in which the organization gives up its data during a highly interdependent relationship with the consultant. Diagnosis in the traditional sense is immaterial to the organization. The Gestalt therapy approach is more open to observations, more contactful, and places more weight on the consultant attending to his or her own sensations and emotions. Assessment is seen as taking place continuously and not as one stage at the beginning of the change process. The consultant's style is highly involving and oriented to mobilize the organization's energy. Nevis' work and that of his colleagues at the Gestalt Institute of Cleveland open the door to new ways of consulting with enterprises and mobilizing their energy.

A fourth way of using Gestalt therapy is to make use of its concepts and technologies in the transformation process. This development is in its beginning stages. It could involve using such interventions as making explicit what is implicit; energizing by movement and exaggeration; expression of appreciation and resentment; differentiating between "should" and "is"; and variations on the two-chair technique. While it is yet in its infancy, the possibility of a transfer of techniques looks promising.

A fifth way of using Gestalt therapy for transformation is giving as many key individuals as possible a basic training in Gestalt therapy. This could have an energizing effect of major proportions, possibly creating the energetic source necessary for a transformation project.

There are various reports of using Gestalt therapy with firms, but no cases so far on its use in organizational transformation. Empirical data will be needed to substantiate the hopes that have arisen.

EVALUATION

Empirical Support

Most of the approaches described in this chapter are based on the experience of implementing them in practice. They used technologies that have been tried out. McWhinney supports his approach with a number of documented cases. Hawley's piece is based on a change project he implemented. The fusion team was used successfully in an army group. Some of the other approaches have varying degrees of support from trials in practice. Sometimes, however, the implementation is only in the stage of a series of workshops that have resulted in a transformational change in a management group, without documentation of this affecting the organization.

Purposing, Formulating the Core Process, and Aligning Around a Common Vision

These three approaches deal with changing the organization's mission and purpose. However, purposing (as described in Chapter 3) differs from the other two approaches in some basic ways. Reformulating and aligning are group activities and processes, while purposing is basically a top executive activity and responsibility. In purposing, a new vision is created by the top executive and then communicated to employees. In the other two approaches, the new vision emerges out of group activity.

In reformulating and aligning, the creation or discovery of a new vision, the alignment and attunement are a continuous, group process, while in purposing, the task of the leader is to transmit his vision to employees, and help them accept it and align around it. Moreover, aligning and, mainly, reformulating involve deep insight, a high level of openness, and intense emotional experience, while purposing involves mainly intuition and rational process.

Involving organization members (in small organizations) and a management team (in large organizations) in the process of discovering a new vision or purpose, alignment, and attunement appears to be a promising approach to creating high spirit, enthusiasm, and motivation for organizational transformation.

The Complementarity of Approaches

Five approaches to rechanneling energy and revitalizing an organization have been described. The first approach, the flow state, stresses a particular style of management as an essential ingredient in ensuring the unblocking of organizational energy. The second approach suggests a variety of structural methods that encourage the free flow of energy. The third approach, the alchemic way, creates energy by raising awareness and reformulating the core process. The fourth approach, close to the third, revitalizes by aligning members around a common vision. Gestalt therapy may unblock energy flow.

These five may be not differing but complementary approaches. it may be feasible in revitalizing an organization to approach it with a combination of all five: changing management style, freeing structure, raising awareness and reformulating the core processes, aligning members around a common vision, and unblocking energy.

Is Energizing a Necessary Phase in Transformation?

Energizing appears to be an approach to organizational transformation. What is not clear, however, is whether every transformation process necessitates an energizing phase. Is energizing needed only in particular cases? Is a high level of channeled energy an essential aspect or a necessary stage in the transformational process? If this is so, then possibly some organizations may have sufficient energy for transformation while others may not. Perhaps only the latter may be in need of revitalization. Alternatively, all organizations in transformation may need an energizing phase, in which case energizing would be an essential part of every transformative process. These issues need further study and clarification.

The Difficulty in Practice

Except for the structural approaches, most of the methods described in this chapter demand a high level of openness to intense emotional experience on the part of management. Probably not very many hardheaded administrators of business concerns would be willing to submit to the kind of intensive, deep, personal processes used by some of these methods. It seems reasonable to expect much resistance. In a personal note on this matter, McWhinney writes (personal communication) that it is indeed difficult to get people to do this: "It takes a bit of magic, sometimes called charisma to move a group so deeply. So you start up building trust and it takes time and courage." McWhinney's words indicate the possibility that a manager or consultant of exceptional stature may be needed to facilitate such processes.

7

Raising and Changing Consciousness

This chapter describes approaches, models, and technologies that focus on raising, expanding, and changing consciousness. Consciousness evolution and transformation is a common theme in transformation writings (Allen & Kraft 1982; Hawley 1983; Johnston 1983). Some scientists argue that organizational transformation is basically a change in the members' consciousness (Harrison 1984). This type of strategy is embedded in theories on consciousness evolution (Jantsch 1976; McWaters 1982), new-age thinking (Ferguson 1980; Hubbard 1982), and, more specifically, in transpersonal psychology (Walsh & Vaughan 1980; Walsh & Shapiro 1983; Wilber 1983), Eastern wisdom and practice, and intuitive and creative thinking (Tilden 1983).

A simple definition of the term "consciousness raising and changing" is provided by Harrison (1984). Essentially it means

> ... becoming aware of the transformative process in which we are involved. As we become aware, we can begin to begin to participate voluntarily in our own evolution. ... We can influence the quality of life on earth through our thoughts and beliefs. Thought is seen as the **source** of reality. We create reality through thought. Thus we need not struggle with things as they are. Instead, we may change our mode of perception and thus the quality of our experience. At any moment, the possibility of transformation of our reality into new paradigms exists. (p. 98; emphasis added)

Harrison provides the two basic, interrelated processes involved in consciousness change. The first is awareness of the evolutionary process that takes place at different levels, of its nature, of its characteristics, and of its logic. The second is being aware of how our thoughts and beliefs create reality and can change reality. These two ideas are guiding interventions for consciousness change, some of which focus more on awareness of the evolutionary process, others more on changing reality by changing thought, and others on combining the two. In most cases, this type of strategy sets the stage for a relatively long and deep "going inside" process. Techniques such as meditation and other modes of relaxation are commonly used.

A CASE STUDY: THE TRANSFORMATION OF THE AMERICAN WILDLIFE SOCIETY

This is a short description of an intervention conducted (and described) by Brown (1983) in the American Wildlife Society (A.W.S.). The organization has six departments: fund raising, programs, public relations, its magazine, administration, and endangered species. There are 6 directors and a support staff of 18 at the national headquarters. In 1982, the organization was in a deep crisis. This was a period of recession. Membership had fallen off and funds dropped dramatically. There had been a great shrinkage in participation in the public programs. These facts had forced the firing of staff personnel, and the future of the organization was in doubt.

For six months, communications within A.W.S. had been tense and strained. The directors were so busy keeping their particular projects afloat that there had been almost no dialogue among them. There was not a sense of a larger purpose, nor did a program of revitalization exist. The organization was trapped in a vicious circle that was ever deteriorating. It was in this state that the organization asked for the help of Brown, an organizational consultant who developed an intervention based on psychosynthesis therapy (Assagioli 1971) called "creative explorations of inner space." The intervention consisted of two-day workshops for the six directors, and follow-up sessions.

The purpose of this type of intervention was to help participants expand their awareness of present situations, to generate a new sense of purpose and direction, and to empower or energize participants in applying their visions in daily life. The intervention was based on a sequence of very structured techniques, some of which are left-brain and others right-brain.

The workshop was based on the confrontation of four basic questions:

1. What are the present realities within my department with which I must be concerned?
2. What is the best and most realistic future for my department?
3. What blocks, fears, or defenses within me or within significant people in the organization may inhibit or prevent the realization of the new plan for my department?
4. What specific steps must I take now and in the near future to move toward the realization of my new goals for my department?

Each of these questions is addressed separately by a sequence of 11 structured steps or techniques that elicit participants' intuition, imagination, inspiration, insight, and thoughts. The workshops consisted, therefore, of four sessions, each session addressing one of the above questions and consisting of the same 11 steps. The steps and the whole intervention are described in the following sections.

First Session

Step 1: Preparation

The workshop started with an "icebreaking" exercise and continued with the power object. This exercise honors the uniqueness of each individual and at the same time helps to form a sense of cohesion. Each person was asked to bring into the group an object that held a special value for him/her. Then each described the value of his/her object. The objects were passed around the group so that each participant could see, feel, and appreciate the meaning of these unique items. Then the group selected one of these items to represent the group spirit, purpose, and power. This item was called "the group power object."

Step 2: Deep Relaxation

Participants were asked to close their eyes and begin to tune in to themselves. They were instructed to focus their awareness on the experience of breathing, to let this natural rhythm carry them into deep relaxation. The consultant spent 20 minutes helping them let go on deeper and deeper levels, and get into a primal "I am right here, right now" state of awareness.

Step 3: Reflective Meditation

The consultant had the directors write on the tops of their papers the focusing question, "What are the present realities within my department with which I must be concerned?" He gave them 25 minutes to do a thorough review of their most important issues and concerns, and to write down in outline form the contents of their reflections.

Step 4: Receptive Meditation

The participants were asked to sit in a quiet and receptive way with eyes closed, and allow deeper thoughts and feelings to come into their field of awareness. Some of the more subtle issues and dynamics were identified through this and, as they were, the people were asked to open their eyes and write them down. They would pulse from receptive meditation to writing and back to the receptive meditation.

Step 5: Visualization

Participants were again asked to close their eyes and breathe deeply. Then they were asked to allow a mental image to come into their field of awareness that would express in a visual way all the cognitive information of which they had become aware. They were advised to deal with the very first image that came to mind, to focus on this image with full attention, noticing its size, shape, color, and the context in which it appeared. They were asked to pay particular attention to how they felt or emotionally resonated with the inner image.

Step 6: Symbolic Drawing

Participants were asked to make a drawing of their images.

Step 7: Cognitive Analysis

The directors were asked to analyze their drawings in writing and in detail for about 15 minutes. "What is the image? Describe it fully in words. What does it stand for? How does it pull your thoughts and feelings together in a synoptic way? What does it mean to you? What does it reveal to you about your department that you might not have appreciated earlier?"

Step 8: Symbolic Dialogue

Participants were asked to close their eyes, take a few deep breaths, and bring the image back into their field of awareness. Only when they could visualize the image very clearly were they to ask this question directly to the image: "What do you have to teach me at this moment in my life?" They were instructed to listen with their intuitive minds to the answers that would come into awareness, and then write the answers underneath their drawings. After four or five minutes, they were invited to ask the image this question once more, or any other clarifying questions that came to mind, and to write down the responses.

Step 9: Symbolic Identification

Participants were asked to stand up, their eyes closed, and allow the image to return to their field of awareness. Visualizing the image clearly, these men and women were asked to let themselves go in imagination, to become one with the image, move into it, let it move into them physically. They were asked to allow their bodies to move, gesture, assume whatever posture would best express the living reality of their images, and to allow whatever sounds, noises, or spontaneous music that might want to happen. When the participants completed this step, the consultant had them sit down and write about their experiences in great detail.

Step 10: Grounding

Participants were asked to reflect for a period of time on the implications of all that they had experienced in this creative exploration of inner space, and then write down their reflections. Next the consultant invoked the use of the power object to let the people talk about what they had experienced. One by one, they began to tell their stories, share their insights, reveal their drawings and the meanings of their drawings, talk about the messages they had heard from them. Each person spoke as much about himself or herself as he or she did about departmental realities.

Step 11: Closure

The consultant suggested to the directors of the A.W.S. that they consider displaying their drawings in the room so that they could see them many times during the rest of the workshop. This would help them keep their intuition open and available, insights would continue to emerge, and they would have important data about which to speak with one another.

Second Through Fourth Sessions

In the second session participants passed through the same 11 steps but addressed the second question (What is the best and most realistic future for my organization?). In the third session they had to address the third question by going through the 11 steps. The fourth session was devoted to addressing the fourth question by going through the 11 steps one more time. The results of the intervention are described by Brown in very general terms:

> ... the group realized that A.W.S. would not only survive, but also grow.... New directions had been envisioned. The fear, negativity, and poor communications ... had been transformed. The directors came together frightened and fatigued, under pressure and feeling alone. They left rested, personally empowered and collectively inspired, open to their own intuition and inner guidance, and united in a dynamic sense of fellowship. The transformation of their organization would become a little more possible by virtue of their willingness to take a deeply human and personal inner journey, to connect them with their own Higher Selves, to access the vast reservoir of human potential within them, and then to strategize the grounded and specific changes which needed to occur. (p. 20)

TRANSPERSONAL PSYCHOLOGY AND ORGANIZATIONAL TRANSFORMATION

The practice of organizational transformation is strongly affected by transpersonal psychology and Eastern practices (Johnston 1983; Berger 1984). This section summarizes the main ideas of transpersonal psychology and their application to organizational transformation.

Transpersonal psychology is an offshoot of humanistic psychology; it aims at expanding the field of psychological inquiry to include areas of human experience and behavior associated with extreme health and well-being. Such inquiry includes altered states of consciousness, peak experiences, self-transcendence, meditation, yoga, and other methods of expanding awareness. As such, it draws upon both Western science and Eastern wisdom in an attempt to integrate knowledge concerned with utilizing consciousness for the fulfillment of human potential.

A clear, short description of transpersonal psychology is provided by Walsh and Vaugahn (1980):

> Transpersonal psychology is concerned with the study of optimum psychological health and well-being. It recognizes the potential for experiencing a broad range of states of consciousness, in some of which identity may extend beyond the usual limits of the ego and personality. (p. 9)

The major themes of transpersonal psychology are related to concepts such as consciousness, conditioning, attachment, the nature of personality, and disidentification.

Consciousness

Transpersonal psychology holds that consciousness is a central dimension that provides the basis and context for all experience. It views our usual consciousness as a defensively contracted state. This usual state is filled to a remarkable and unrecognized extent with a continuous flow of largely uncontrollable thoughts and fantasies that exert an extraordinarily powerful, though unappreciated, influence on perception, cognition, and behavior. Skillful self-observation inevitably reveals that our usual experience is perceptually distorted by the continuous, automatic, and unconscious blending of input from reality and fantasy in accordance with our needs and defenses.

Optimum consciousness is viewed as being considerably greater, and potentially available at any time, should the defensive contraction be relaxed. The fundamental perspective on growth is therefore one of letting go of this defensive contraction and removing obstacles to the recognition of the expanded, ever present potential through quieting the mind and reducing perceptual distortion (Vaughan 1979).

The transpersonal perspective holds that a large spectrum of altered states of consciousness exists, that some states are potentially useful and functionally specific, and that some of these are true "higher" states. "Higher" means that they possess all the properties and potentials of lower states, plus some additional ones (Assagioli 1971; Wilber 1981). On the other hand, the traditional Western view holds that only a limited range of states exists (such as waking, dreaming, intoxication, delirium). Each state of consciousness reveals its own picture of reality; therefore, it follows that reality as we know it is only relatively real. The reality we perceive reflects our own state of consciousness, and we can never explore reality without, at the same time, exploring ourselves, both because we are and because we create the reality we explore.

The highest levels of consciousness are assumed to be related to human spirit and spirituality. Spirituality is defined by some transpersonal psychologists as "the courage to look within one's self and trust. What is seen and what is trusted appears to be a deep sense of belonging, of wholeness, of connectedness, and of openness to the infinite" (Johnston 1983, p. 1).

Conditioning

Transpersonal psychology holds that people are vastly more ensnared and entrapped in their conditioning than they realize, but that freedom from this conditioning is possible. The aim of transpersonal psychology is essentially the extraction of awareness from this conditioned tyranny of the mind. One form of conditioning that Eastern disciplines have examined in detail is attachment. Attachment is closely associated with desire and signifies that nonfulfillment of the desire will result in pain. It therefore plays a central role in the causation of suffering, and letting go of it is central to its cessation.

Attachment is not limited to external objects or persons, but encompasses patterns of behavior, self-image, belief systems, and the prevailing status quo as well. Among the strongest attachments are those of suffering and unworthiness. Insofar as we believe that our identities are derived from our roles, our problems, our relationships, or the content of consciousness, attachment is reinforced by fear for personal survival. We believe that we are our attachments.

Personality

Traditional psychology holds that a person is his or her personality, and that health involves a modification of personality. From a transpersonal perspective, however, personality is accorded relatively less importance. Rather, it is seen as only one aspect of being with which the individual may, but does not have to, identify. Health is seen as primarily involving a shift from exclusive identification with personality rather than the modification of it.

Identification and Disidentification

Transpersonal psychology and Eastern disciplines maintain that identification with internal phenomena and processes is more significant than external identification. Here "identification" is defined as the process by which something is experienced as self. It sets in train a self-fulfilling process in which experience and psychological processes validate the reality of that with which a person was identified. With identification the person is unaware of the fact that perception stems from a thought, from a context. The context cannot be seen; rather, it is that from which everything else is seen and interpreted.

Assagioli (1971) writes that we are dominated by everything with which our selves become identified. We can dominate and control everything from which we disidentify. Thoughts and beliefs constitute the operators that construct, mediate, guide, and maintain the identification construction of consciousness and act as limiting models of whom we believe ourselves to be. As such, they must be opened to review in order to allow growth. The mind is usually filled with thoughts with which we are unwittingly identified; hence, our usual state of consciousness is one in which we are, quite literally, hypnotized.

As in any hypnotic state, there need not be any recognition of the trance and its attendant constriction of awareness, nor memory of the sense of identity prior to hypnosis. While in a trance, we think we are the thoughts with which we are identified. To put it differently, those thoughts from which we have not yet disidentified create our state of consciousness, identity, and reality. The task of awakening can thus be viewed as a progressive disidentification from mental content in general and from thoughts in particular. This is clearly evident in practices such as insight meditation, where the student is trained to observe and identify all mental content. Awakening is a process of "dehypnosis," of reaching "pure awareness." Finally, awareness no longer identifies exclusively with anything, the me-not me dichotomy is transcended, and the person experiences himself or herself as being both nothing and everything. Freed of consciousness distortion and limiting identifications and contexts, awareness is now capable of clear, accurate perception.

Organizational transformation as a practice focuses on the very first stages of the process of change. These stages (see Chapter 6) include "awakening," increasing the members' awareness of changes in the environment and in the organization, awareness of where the organization is located in the second-order change cycle, awareness of the effects of the current paradigm, and awareness of dysfunctional behavior. It therefore is useful to use transpersonal psychology methods and ideas to facilitate these stages.

A few consultants have applied transpersonal psychology concepts and definitions (at the individual level) to describe organizational phenomena. Some have defined organizational transformation as basically a change in the members' consciousness (Hawley 1983; Harrison 1984), others have studied the phenomenon of "organizational consciousness" (Berger 1984), and some have described the purpose of organizational transformation as moving the organization and its members into the highest level of health and well-being. Johnston (1983), for example, uses the definition of Walsh and Vaughn (1980) for transpersonal psychology to describe the purpose of organizational transformation:

> To facilitate the expansion of individuals' and organizations' consciousness to include the highest, deepest, and broadest range of optimally healthy states and realization of human potential, some of which may extend the usual limits of beliefs, values, ego, and personality. (p. 9)

Another approach is to recognize the existence and importance of the spirit and aspects of spirituality in the organization's life. Transformed individuals and organizations are described as spirited entities (Connelly 1984; McKnight 1984; Johnston 1984; Ritscher 1983). The concepts of "identification" and "disidentification" are also widely used (for example, McWhinney 1980), and some use Eastern techniques in their transformation efforts (for example, Brown 1983).

CONSCIOUSNESS HIERARCHY AND TRANSFORMATION

Whereas the last section dealt with some major themes in transpersonal psychology, this section examines the issue of altered states of consciousness, consciousness hierarchy, and evolution, with regard to their direct applicability to organizational transformation. Some scholars believe that the evolution and transformation of social systems consist of the evolution and transformation of human consciousness (Jantsch 1976). Various techniques for expanding and changing consciousness have been used as a vehicle for transforming organizations (for example, Johnston 1983).

"Living systems" theory (J. Miller 1978), "evolution and consciousness" theory (Jantsch 1976), and "growth" theory (Land 1973) all hold that nature consists of hierarchical wholes. There exists an energetic, dynamic, and creative evolutionary process in which more and more complex inclusive wholes are produced. Some transpersonal psychologists hold that the same process can be found in the psyche, the same hierarchical arrangement of wholes within wholes, reaching from the simplest and most rudimentary to the most complex and inclusive (Pelletier & Garfield 1976; Wilber 1981).

The idea that the psyche consists of hierarchical wholes and that a whole at any level is merely a part of the whole of the next level is commonly accepted in developmental psychology and humanistic psychology. The cognitive studies of Piaget, the works of Loevinger (1976) on ego development, of Maslow (1971) on the hierarchy of needs, and of Kohlberg (1969) on moral development all subscribe, in whole or in part, to the concept of stratified stages of increasing complexity, integration, and unity.

Transpersonal psychology, however, went further and looked for the highest stages of unity, which are beyond those described by developmental psychology. The main focus of those interested in altered states of consciousness, and in consciousness evolution and hierarchy, is typically empirical and scientific. How many altered states exist? What are the conditions that bring them about? What phenomenological experiences do they engender in the experiencing subject, and how do these differ from the contents of ordinary, waking consciousness? The effort to find answers to these and other closely related questions is what characterizes this rapidly growing field.

An altered state of consciousness is best defined by Tart (1972). In this state the individual

> clearly feels a *qualitative* shift in his pattern of mental functioning, that is, he feels not just a quantitative shift (more or less alert, more or less visual imagery, sharper or duller, *etc.*) but also that some quality or qualities of his mental process are **different.** (p. 176; emphasis added)

No attempt will be made to review all the states of consciousness except to bring forth some exemplifying studies. Krippner (1972) has identified 20 different states of consciousness. Thought to be semiautonomous, these states include dreaming states, sleeping states, lethargic states, and hysterical states. Pelletier and Garfield (1976) studied three states of consciousness: psychotic states, psychedelic states, and meditative states. Meditative states are the highest and involve a "profound state of passivity accompanied by an apparently paradoxical state of complete awareness" (p. 115).

An important contribution to the studies of consciousness taxonomy, hierarchy, and evolution was made by the studies of Wilber (1981, 1983). He distinguished three main developmental states of consciousness.

The lower realms involve simple biological functions and processes — that is, somatic processes, instincts, simple sensations and perceptions, and emotional-sexual impulses. Wilber included within this stage all the stages of Western psychology, with the exception of transpersonal psychology.

The next level is the intermediate realm, denied by Western psychologists — called "beyond ego." Here the consciousness starts to become transpersonal. The point is that consciousness, by further differentiating itself from the mind and the body, is able in some ways to transcend the normal capacities of the gross body-mind, and therefore to operate upon the world and the organism in ways that appear, to the ordinary mind, to be quite fantastic and farfetched. This state of consciousness can be called an over-mind or supramind. "It embodies a transcendence of all mental forms, and discloses, at its summit, the intuition of that which . . . all men and women would call God" (Wilber 1983, p. 347).

The highest level of consciousness is called the ultimate realm. This is difficult to explain in everyday language. It is the emptiness of everything that allows the identification to take place — the emptiness that is in us coming together with an emptiness that is the deity. By visualizing that identification, we actually become the deity. "The subject is identified with the object of faith," writes Wilber (1983, p. 347).

One more model of consciousness hierarchy is that of Assagioli (1971). He developed a theory and method of therapy he called "psychosynthesis," based on ideas very similar to those of transpersonal psychology. Assagioli blended the traditional wisdom of Eastern and Western psychology and philosophy to provide a view that recognizes authentic individualities as the cornerstone of the evolution of a better society. He distinguished four levels of unconsciousness:

1. Lower unconscious. This is the domain of consciousness in which reside the roots of all our present patterns, past experiences, fears, basic needs, drives, and desires. This level must be acknowledged and dealt with in order to release the stress and tension that block creativity and self-expression.
2. Middle unconscious. In this level exists all the information to which we must have access in order to survive in the everyday world. The middle unconscious is that domain in which we mull over important information outside our immediate awareness.
3. Higher unconscious. In this domain reside all the undiscovered and undeveloped talents, abilities, capacities, and functions of human nature. All that we can become, that we have not realized or actualized, exists in this dimension, waiting to be discovered, explored, and developed.
4. Collective unconscious. This is the external context that shapes our perceptions and thoughts; it is the culture and history of other people who influence our world without our being aware of it.

Assagioli distinguishes between the "I" and the "higher self." The I is the actor in the world that chooses, fears, resists, or desires to grow. The higher self is the inner principle to which the I turns for guidance. It is the inspiration, intuition, and insight. The higher self is thought not to be embedded in the physical plane, but exists "above" or outside it, transcending matter, time, and space.

While Wilber's and Assagioli's models refer to the individual level, other models refer to the system level. Markley (1976), for example, defines "human consciousness" as social beliefs, assumptions, and fundamental premises held about human beings' origin, nature, abilities, characteristics, relationships with others, and place in the universe (p. 214). He describes developmental stages of human consciousness according to the guiding images embedded in the systems' culture. Studying the history of different social systems, Markley concludes that consciousness evolution tends to be nonincremental in character; it proceeds through periods of crisis, resulting in a relatively distinct consciousness characteristic, ever higher in terms of complexity and integrity.

An important contribution to the understanding of the process of consciousness evolution was made in the studies of Wilber (1981, 1983). He suggests that the process of psychological development proceeds in a most articulate fashion. At each stage, a higher-order structure — more complex and therefore more unified — emerges through a differentiation of the preceding, lower-order level. This higher-order structure is introduced to consciousness, and eventually the self identifies with that emergent structure. As evolution proceeds, however, each level in turn is differentiated from the self sense. The self disidentifies with a lower-level structure, detaches itself from exclusive identification with that structure in order to identify with the next-higher-order emergent structure.

The point is that because the self is differentiated from the lower structure, it transcends that structure and thus can operate on that lower structure by using the tools of the newly emergent structure. Thus, as the body-ego was differentiated from the material environment, it operated on the environment by using the tools of the body-self (muscles). As the ego-mind was differentiated from the body, it operated on the body and the world with its tools (concepts). And as the subtle self was differentiated from the ego-mind, it operated on mind, body, and world using its structures (psi).

Thus, at each point of psychological growth we find that the following occur:

1. A higher-order structure emerges in consciousness.
2. The self identifies its being with that structure.
3. The next-higher-order structure emerges.
4. The self disidentifies with the lower structure.
5. The self shifts its essential identity to a higher structure.
6. Consciousness thereby transcends the lower structure and becomes capable of operating on that lower structure from the higher-order level.
7. All preceding levels can then be integrated into consciousness. As

evolution continues, more complex, more organized, and more unified structures emerge until there is only unity.

Wilber's model is very much in congruence with theories on the evolution of open systems, such as Kuhn's theory on scientific revolutions, Jantsch's theory of "self-organizing systems," and Prigogine's theory of "order through fluctuations." However, while these theories emphasize accumulation of anomalies, fluctuations, critical points, crisis, and a sudden shift to a higher order, Wilber's emphasis is on the importance of identification with the emerging new cognitive structure and disidentification with the old ones. These two processes are crucial for people to be able to manipulate and transform lower structures into higher ones.

To summarize, transpersonal psychological concepts that are relevant for second-order planned change may be summarized in the following generalizations:

1. Consciousness is a central dimension that provides the basis and context for all experience. Consciousness expansion is a powerful change agent.
2. Organizational members are under the "bondage" of, and are managed by, beliefs, values, attitudes, roles, behaviors, or possessions with which they identify, to which they are attached or addicted.
3. Members can transcend and manage any belief, value, role, or behavior with which they disidentify.
4. Individuals and organizations are capable of growth and transformation far beyond traditionally recognized levels of health and normality.
5. The process of disidentification with involuntary conditioned content and processes has important implications for people in organizations, in that their whole perspective on self-identity changes. As a result, they find greater vitality, creativity, strength, and satisfaction. Problems that previously seemed insurmountable may now be viewed as soluble or irrelevant.
6. In the ultimate states of consciousness, members will experience spirituality (in nonreligious terms).

APPROACHES FOR RAISING AND CHANGING CONSCIOUSNESS

In this section some intervention models, approaches, and technologies, based on transpersonal psychology and Eastern wisdom, concepts, and methods, will be described and analyzed. Also, creative thinking methods will be briefly described because of the similarity between consciousness expansion and creative thinking. Hence, this section deals with two change techniques: consciousness raising and creative thinking.

Methods for Raising and Changing Consciousness

Culbert's Five Stages Model

One of the first to develop an intervention model of consciousness raising was Culbert (1976). The model has two components: the personal and the system. The personal component involves developing an understanding of who we are naturally — that is, without our adaptations to the system — and to recognize which parts of the system fail to suit our needs. The system component involves our seeing what the system stands for, what its world view is, and how it actually works — as contrasted with how we have been conditioned to see it. The model is shown in Figure 7.1

The model has five stages. The output of each stage provides the input for the next. The model describes skills that need to be learned by the participants in each stage and group or organizational support that may enhance the learning. The main thrust of this model is that second-order change involves awareness of the underlying assumptions that shape the system's goals and the individual's image of the system. Challenging existing premises enables participants to envision new alternatives.

Stage 1: Recognizing what's "off." Consciousness raising starts with feelings that something is off in the interaction of members with the system. Participants can discover what brings about the discrepancy in their relationship with the system by dealing with mutual expectations

Figure 7.1. Consciousness-Raising Model for Social and Organizational Change

Stage 1: Recognizing What's "Off"	Skills for self-accepting, non-evaluative analysis	Identification of Discrepancies
		a. between what the system expects of us and what seems natural or consistent with our self-interests
Feelings of Incoherence		b. between doing what comes naturally and what seems acceptable to the system
	Support that bolsters feelings of self-adequacy and encourages self-valuing of experience	
Stage 2: Understanding Ourselves and the System	Skills for "divergent problem-solving"	Increased Awareness
		a. of self: our nature and ideals
Discrepancies		b. of the system: what it is and how it works
	Support that helps us resist convergent problem-solving and cope with the tensions which result	
Stage 3:: Understanding Our Relationship with the System	Skills for explicating assumptions and determining how they were acquired	Increased Awareness of Our Relationship with the System
		a. assumptions which underlie our goals and how we go about achieving them
Increased Awareness of Self and System	Support that challenges existing premises, beliefs, and idiosyncratic assumptions	b. assumptions which comprise our image of the system
		c. assumptions which explain how we and the system influence one another
Stage 4: Formulating Alternatives	Skills for seeing where existing assumptions are inconsistent with our nature, interests, and ideals	Envisioning Alternatives
Increased Awareness of Self and System		a. which change the system
Increased Awareness of Our Relationship with the System	Support that helps us reflect on personal priorities and consider a range of alternative actions	b. which change our relationship to the system

Figure 7.1. Continued

Stage 5: Affecting the Lives of Others		Changes and Improvements in the System
	Skills for thinking about change in a "statespersonlike" way	
		a. making alternative responses to the system
Envisioned Alternatives		b. devising alternative systems and putting them into action
	Support that monitors change projects and helps us maintain focus when encountering resistance	c. helping others to envision their own alternatives

Source: Culbert 1976.

(members vs. system expectations) and discrepancies in values and norms.

Stage 2: Understanding ourselves and the system. Recognizing discrepancies in expectations, values, and norms offers members the understanding of symptoms and problems as they are usually defined. In order to engage in a fundamental change, there is a need to delay any corrective action and use the discrepancies that members had noted to deepen their understanding of their own world view, reality, or context and the system's world view or underlying assumptions. The technique used here is called "divergent problem solving." It is a process of viewing the discrepancies as symptoms, not problems.

Stage 3: Understanding our relationship with the system. In this stage, participants examine their assumptions about their own goals and the means for achieving them, about the system's purpose and values, and about the ways members and system influence each other.

Stage 4: Formulating alternatives. This stage involves reexamining how participants focus on inconsistencies in assumptions. This process stimulates thoughts about what would constitute a better situation.

Stage 5: Affecting the lives of others. In this stage, other groups in the system are involved in the process. All parties will look for ways to change the overall functioning of the system, changes that bring each party closer to a more fulfilling existence of the system.

The Paedogenic Model

McWhinney (1980) suggests an intervention mode termed the "paedogenic mode." This intervention mode is aimed explicitly at transforming members' realities by setting a process of discovery. McWhinney has applied this mode in facilitating second-order change in a large catering firm and in a subsystem of an aircraft manufacturer (McWhinney 1980, p. 286). In contrast with other designing modes, the paedogenic mode does not start from a basis of existing constraints or goals. It transforms by creating a new reality that contains solutions "to be discovered." It implies a return to a nonmature form of the system, when it was more flexible, less habituated, less invested in present reality, and unencrusted.

Paedogenesis begins with breaking; it is revolutionary. It suits a turbulent environment, a decaying society of disequilibrium and breakdown of norms and values. Paedogenic intervention begins with stepping back from available technology and current situations, to more fundamental levels of central processes in the design activity. It moves inward in search of deeper awareness of meaning and of the environment in which one exists. The paedogenic intervention mode takes the form of a cycle: a disequilibrating event, a retreat for a better start, a founding or a reassertion of identity, a return that produces the new direction.

Disequilibrium. The disequilibrating event is a visible, often dramatic turning point in an ongoing process. It may be the final step in an evolution of forces that have weakened the system's integration. It may be the loss of a source of raw material. As Prigogine (1984) suggests, the system is pushed beyond the limits of its flexibility. The system experiences a deep crisis — for example, a competitor is markedly more successful, or there is a revelation of rising expectation.

The retreat. The intervention starts by encouraging participants to step back, to evaluate the situation, to loosen existing constraints, and to notice faults. This is the phase of "releasing" traditional modes, basic assumptions, values, and attitudes, and enabling members to find new directions and new choices. The retreat may begin with a general question such as "Why am I doing what I am?" or "What business are we really in?" or it can begin with less articulation and deal with anger, fear, guilt, or "here and now" feelings.

McWhinney suggests three different techniques of retreat: letting go of history, of social identity, or the cohesiveness of the current mode of operation. The first is called rejuvenilization, which is an explicit retreat to an immature form, less channeled in its responses to the environment. The individual retreats to a state where he or she is more flexible in reference to ecological challenges. The child trapped in the mature adult is released, and thus the conditions for creation of a new direction are set up.

The second technique, called relaxation, is characterized by "loosening" rather than "letting go." It "unfreezes" the forces that hold the system in its present configuration. Relaxation proceeds by reducing tension, communication, time pressures, and physical proximity. It consists of techniques such as focusing, meditation, relaxation, and visioning. Going to a retreat to avoid intrusions is part of this loosening.

The third technique, called dissolution, is the extreme of relaxation; it is the dissolution of the central organizing force of the system. It leaves the components operative — for example, the companies of the dissolved conglomerate are still functioning. The process begins with the "sloughing" of the systemwide constraints. It continues with a redirection of issues at the level of the whole (conglomerate business) to rebuild a system at the original level. Dissolution (such as divorce) provides the occasion for the deepest reexamination of meaning, for it confronts us with questions of identity and purpose.

Founding. The founding is an event that creates a base to which to return from the deep experience of retreat. It is the creation of new integration, new ideas, new institutions. It is a process that results in uncovering, revelation, an "Aha!" It is the creation of energy. The founding stage consists of creativity techniques, visualization and future imagining, and results in the emergence of a new idea, metaphor, or purpose for the system.

Return. The purpose of this stage is to articulate the new idea and to translate it into procedures, structures, and technology. Once a new context is discovered, it is time to design the system within the new context.

McWhinney also proposes a "lotal" design. He describes it at the individual level. One selects an image and focuses on it in meditation until another image develops. When this happens, one quietly observes it, examines it, and releases it. Returning to the focal image, one lets another new image develop, and so on, until a sense of completion is achieved. McWhinney does not detail how he uses this design on the organizational level.

Maps of Consciousness

Johnston (1983, 1984) developed intervention techniques based on both Eastern and Western methods of consciousness expansion. Among them are different types of meditation, psychosynthesis, methods of visualizing, dream work, biofeedback, and maps of consciousness based on Jungian psychology. The techniques are used in management workshops and as an integral part of transformation interventions.

The intervention suggested by Johnston is similar to that suggested by McWhinney. It begins with a process of clarifying the underlying assumptions and hypotheses that shape the organization's beliefs, values, procedures, and policies. It then proceeds to clarify strategic policy-type objectives with the top management. These strategic objectives represent actual transformation from a transpersonal/spiritual perspective. Among them are the following:

- To foster an organizational climate that is conducive to centering, balance, optimal health, strength, creativity, competence, productivity, and prosperity
- To assist the client in focusing on the inner work leading to self-realization, transcendence, and self-management rather than on the solution of particular ego problems
- To assist the client in integrating physical, emotional, mental, spiritual, social, technological, and economic dimensions
- To develop a value system that transcends the limitations of involuntary conditioning and encourages taking responsibility for designing organizational life in harmony with nature
- To help members develop methods for voluntary control of internal states and the expansion of psycho-spiritual-organic consciousness.

Johnston's intervention approach is complex and multidimensional. It can be summarized by its developmental stages, and proceeds through the following steps:

1. Clarification of assumptions and hypotheses

2. Clarification of strategic and operational objectives
3. Discovery of involuntarily conditioned attachments within the organization
4. Disidentification with those attachments
5. Transcending the attachments
6. Ownership of the former attachments, now perceived as options
7. Management of voluntary conditioning
8. Progress review.

Using Eastern Methods

The use of Eastern methods for consciousness expansion and organizational change seems to have expanded rapidly. The basic methods used are different types of meditation. The literature surveyed points to the possibility that although there are surface differences among various meditation practices, all meditations fall into one of two major categories. The first is concentration meditation. Such meditation emphasizes techniques of focusing the mind on a single objective, such as a sound (mantra) or a visual image. These techniques often lead to deep relaxation and good feelings. Transactional meditation is an example of this approach. The second category is awareness or insight meditation. It focuses attention on present inner and outer experience, fostering a capacity for increased self-awareness.

Frew (1974) used transactional meditation to increase creativity and productivity in work groups, and reported positive results; Shapiro (1978) reported attitudinal and behavioral changes as a result of a "zen" experience workshop; and Kindler (1979a) reported positive effects of different meditation relaxation techniques on group problem-solving effectiveness.

In addition to the basic practices of concentration and awareness training, guided meditations are used by some practitioners to promote disidentification and transformation. These practices, such as psychosynthesis, make extensive use of guided imagery in which participants are encouraged to focus attention on images and specific sentences. This intervention approach was exemplified in the case study provided in this chapter.

Intuitive and Creative Thinking

Encouraging creativity and creative thinking is an important part of facilitating transformation. Creative thinking interventions proceed through developmental stages very similar to those of consciousness raising. These stages are preparation, incubation, illumination, and verification (J. L. Adams 1974). After conventional approaches are tested and found to be inappropriate for dealing with the current situation, the next step involves deliberately setting aside the assumptions that are conventionally made about reality, and engaging in techniques that open up one's self to more primal and direct perceptions of reality. Such perceptions are less strongly filtered by convention, and often result from deliberate use of altered states of consciousness.

Some focus their interventions on developing members' intuition and creative thinking. Agor (1984), for example, developed an inventory for assessing intuitive and creative thinking. This inventory was used as a tool for developing creativity in organizational settings. The inventory is part of an intervention aimed at transforming organizations.

Tilden (1983) developed a model that connects spontaneity, intuition, and creativity. Tilden's main premise is that these three elements are interrelated, and that they are a matter of "trusting one's own inner wisdom," even in the face of social distraction or opposition. Those moments of insight, inspiration, and breakthrough are connected with the ability to disengage and relax.

Tilden describes a six-month training program for top executives that includes meditation, focusing on stress reduction, and creative techniques. To date, some 120 managers have completed this program. The results showed significant changes in stress reduction, and in perceptions and attitudes away from the intellectual, analytical, and quantitative toward "softening culture" — that is, more toward spirituality, connectedness, and care for others. It should be noted that both Agor and Tilden do not substitute left-brain thinking for right-brain thinking; rather, their efforts are to establish a more integrated ability.

Talbot and Rickards (1984) describe in detail their course for developing creativity in problem solving for managers. The course consists of five days:

Day 1. Problem finding: exercises in defining and redefining problems
Day 2. Idea finding: exercises in idea generating

Day 3. Idea development: exercises in developing ideas into feasible solutions

Day 4. Implementation: exercises in anticipating and dealing with blocks to acceptance of a new idea

Day 5. Integration: tackling problems, using all the above techniques.

Mangham (1984) points to the importance of matching creative individuals with creative organizations. He suggests some management actions for facilitating member and organization creativity:

1. Values and rewards: praise and reward creativity
2. Compensation: creativity and not only productivity should be measured and rewarded
3. Channels for advancement: there should be channels for advancement and status within the area of creativity
4. Freedom: giving members freedom in choice of problem and method of pursuit
5. Communication: free and open channels of communication, both vertical and horizontal
6. Project leaders: assign project leaders who have sufficient risk-taking and creative problem-solving experience.
7. Selection: select personnel (for a project team) who have diverse ideas and skills, with a marked skill in their particular domain; with ability to tolerate ambiguity, to be flexible and undogmatic.

To summarize, consciousness raising and creative thinking interventions proceed through similar stages, as shown in Table 7.1.

Table 7.1
Models of Raising Consciousness

Consciousness Evolution (Wilber 1983)	Consciousness Raising (Culbert 1976)	Paedogenic Design (McWhinney 1980)	Creative Thinking (Adams 1974)
1. Disequilibrium event or	process		
2. Identification	awareness	retreat	preparation
3. Disidentification	envisioning	dissolution	incubation
4. Transcendence	change	founding	illumination
5.		return	verification

Source: Prepared by the authors.

The developmental stages are very homologous. The change, transcendence, founding, or illumination comes after a relatively long process of discovery.

EVALUATION

The technologies used in the case example were deep relaxation, meditation, balancing the two sides of the brain, visualization, guided imagery, breath and movement exercises, focusing on specific objects and questions, symbolic artwork, and contact with nature. They encouraged participants to expand their consciousness of the present situation. They helped participants to explore the limits of their human potential and to develop their deeper human resources. They helped to elicit new choices and new directions. These technologies drew upon Eastern and Western therapy methods.

The intervention process is very similar to the creative thinking process. It takes the same stages:

- Preparation (relaxation)
- Incubation (meditation)
- Illumination (visualization)
- Verification (symbolic identification and grounding).

The intervention is not only a "step-by-step" process but also very structured, planned, and well-designed. It proceeded through seven steps.

1. Crisis. A crisis had developed at the A.W.S. A threat to the survival of the organization triggered action. The directors became aware that drastic changes were needed and accepted the need for change.
2. Separation. The directors chose to become fully conscious of the situation by taking a two-day retreat and focusing on it.
3. Awareness of present situation. The focus was on "what" and "how" questions; that is, on present processes, on what was going on and how each process contributed to the deterioration of the organization.
4. Envisioning the future. The next step was to gain a new sense of purpose and direction, a "growth step."
5. Grounding (return). When the directors had acquired a new sense of purpose and direction, they had to anticipate the difficulties they

would encounter in trying to implement the change program.

6. Planning. Having identified the likely problems that would arise, it was time to make some concrete plans.

7. Implementation. Brown does not elaborate on this stage, but assumes that once the directors returned to the A.W.S. with energy, enthusiasm, and change programs, they would be able to implement change successfully.

Environmental and Organizational Characteristics

Like many of the case studies presented in this work, the change effort was triggered by a threat to the survival of the organization. Drastic changes in the organization's environment (recession and rapid decrease in members and funds) led to crisis. Top management tried to cope with the crisis by doing "more of the same," incremental changes or what Lindblom (1959) calls "muddling through." The result was a deepening of the crisis and a threat to the survival of the organization (firing of staff personnel). Only after it was obvious that the old way of doing things would not work, were managers ready to try a new direction.

Intervention Outcomes

Like most of the interventions described here, this intervention focused on the very first stages of the change process. There is no empirical data about the final results of this intervention. Therefore, the main result of this intervention appears to be the discovery of new directions, and a new purpose for the organization.

Examination of consciousness change interventions and technologies points to the conclusion that they are of value in helping members to expand their consciousness beyond the limits of existing beliefs, values, and presuppositions. They may help members discover new possibilities based on a new and different logical framework. As such, changing consciousness interventions can be seen as a partial step in the process of second-order planned change.

A comparison of reframing intervention with consciousness change intervention is helpful in the understanding of the main characteristics of each approach. The two approaches are aimed at reaching similar goals:

changing members' perceptions of reality and creating new choices, new directions, new ideas based on a different logical framework or higher levels of consciousness. They are both short, intensive, and structured interventions. However, there are major differences in the models, approaches, and technologies they utilize.

In reframing, the consultant usually introduces his or her own logical framework, using sophisticated technologies that are carefully designed. The intervention is very experiential, here and now, and behavior-orientated. The sudden insight, illumination, or shift in perception results from experiencing current behavior brought to an extreme or absurdity. The change is introduced from outside by the consultant.

In consciousness changing, the consultant sets the stage for a relatively long and deep process of going inside. The emphasis is on the participants' searching for and discovering new realities. The sudden insight, illumination, or shift in consciousness comes after a deep process of focusing, relaxation, and detachment. The intervention is experimental and learning-orientated. Participants learn different principles and techniques, and learn to disidentify and "not to think." These types of interventions are more open-ended; they are less concerned with finding solutions to specific problems. The change is introduced from within.

Organizations needing transformation may be in completely different states and conditions. They are not alike. It therefore seems feasible to assume that the different approaches described in this book are not all equally suitable for any particular organization. Further trial in practice and study are needed to clarify which particular approach suits which particular set of organizational conditions. However, it seems reasonable to propose that the paedogenic intervention of McWhinney might be a suitable approach to helping a declining organization (Merry & Brown 1986) that is in a deep crisis. McWhinney describes conditions suitable for his approach as broad disequilibrium and decay of the fundamental fabric of society. This is very descriptive of the state of a declining organization. The practical problem might be how to encourage such an organization to open itself to the deep processes and experiences of the paedogenic design.

PART II

TRANSFORMATION STRATEGIES

8

The "Transformation" and the "Transition" Strategies

This chapter describes two basic strategies to facilitate second-order change in organizations. A review of the practice of second-order planned change points to the possibility of making a theoretical and practical distinction between two different strategies. The first is better known and more utilized; it is a goal-oriented strategy in which the change efforts are focused on managing the transition from a present state into a new state that is already known. The second is less known and less developed, and is the main subject of this book; it is a process-oriented strategy in which the main efforts for change are focused on consciousness raising and processes like understanding present and alternative realities, choice making, and searching for a new vision and purpose. This approach is focused on transformation processes. The goal-oriented strategy is termed "transition," and the processes-oriented strategy is termed "transformation."

These two strategies are not mutually exclusive. In "real life" change efforts, they might be used as mixed strategies or one after the other, depending on the organization situation, the manager, or the consultant. But because of their different methods and approaches, transformation strategies are more useful for facilitating the first phases of the change process, while transition strategy is more useful for facilitating the later phases of the process (such as planning, implementing, and "tuning up").

In this chapter an effort will be made to define and to analyze transformation and transition strategies. An examination of their characteristics, advantages, and disadvantages, and the circumstances

165

under which each strategy seems to be more helpful will be made. Examples of using these strategies will be provided through a case study that will be analyzed. The chapter will close with an effort to integrate the issues into a more comprehensive model.

THE ORGANIZATIONAL TRANSFORMATION STRATEGY

Introduction

Organizational transformation is based on, and embedded in, macro theories, especially those of Kuhn (1970), Prigogine (1984), and the evolution and consciousness perspective. It is also rooted in the phenomenology and learning views on change. According to this strategy, the main task of the manager or consultant is to help the organization's members to be aware of the existence of the processes of evolution in their organization and of its stages, its characteristics, and its impact, so that they will be able to consciously and deliberately participate, effectuate, and manage the process.

Transformation consultants, like organizational development consultants in its first years, find it difficult to define and explain specifically what organizational transformation is. There are some obvious reasons for this. First, organizational transformation is a new field; its theory and practice are not yet well developed, organized, and integrated. Second, organizational transformation taps the "soft side," the unconscious, the "flow states" of the organization, which are hard to describe in words. Third, organizational transformation points to a new direction in the study of organizational change that entails using new terms and new metaphors for describing neglected aspects of change. Fourth, organizational transformation is not a structured, goal-oriented, analytical strategy. It does not have specific, defined models or stages. And fifth, organizational transformation is not a solid field. It includes many different approaches to intervene and to facilitate change, as has been shown in Part I. These interventions focused, for example, on the organizational myths, energy, spirit and spirituality, paradigms, reframing, and networking.

Descriptions and Definitions

There are various definitions and descriptions for explaining what transformation is. Boskin and Phillips (1983) describe transformation by its key components. They say that transformation is a process aimed at helping members to explore and address key aspects of processes, such as awareness of purpose and vision, and the role of belief systems. Transformation is defined as allowing the emerging of a new state of being.

Hawley (1983), together with a group of organizational transformation consultants from Los Angeles, describes transformation as follows:

> O.T. recognizes the dynamics of paradigm shift, the building up of pressure to replace old theories, and the sudden shift from the old to the new. O.T. is discovering the natural base structures in our organization world while recognizing those structures are always evolving. O.T. helps make conscious what lies largely at the unconscious level in organizations. (pp. 7–8)

The verbs used in the above description best express the basic organizational transformation intentions: recognizing, building up pressures, discovering, and making conscious what lies at the unconscious level.

A short and precise description is provided by Johnston (1983), who mentions both individual and organizational levels. According to Johnston, the purpose of organizational transformation is:

> To facilitate the expansion of individuals' and organizations' consciousness to include the highest, deepest, and broadest range of optimally healthy states and realization of human potential, some of which may extend the usual limits of beliefs, values, ego, and personality. (p. 1)

"Expanding consciousness" and "extending the limits of beliefs and values" are the basic expressions in this definition.

Perhaps one of the most clear, precise descriptions of the organizational transformation is provided by McWhinney (1982). He adds to the above descriptions the notion that transformation denotes helping organization members discover the existence of alternative realities and develop their ability to choose a reality that fits their needs:

> It is a process of continuing redefinition of the environment and of identification of direction. It is also a process of creating reality. . . . Its direction is to take what is and transform it through clarification and redefinition. . . . Choice making, not problem solving, is the major focus. (pp. 77–78)

The expressions used in this description are "identification," "clarification," "redefinition," helping to "make choices," and facilitating the process of "creating new reality."

To summarize, the above descriptions provide a general idea about what transformation is and what is the basic role of the manager or consultant in the change process. All the descriptions deal with the very first stages of the process of organizational second-order change. The main focus is on awareness processes, making the unconscious become conscious, discovering new alternative realities, and choice making. The verbs used to describe transformation are "allowing," "recognizing," "building up pressures," "discovering," "energizing," "midwifing," "expanding consciousness," "redefining," "reframing," "clarifying," "choice making," and "extending the limits of beliefs." Following Owen (1983c), we suggest that organizational transformation as a practice takes place in the open space between what was and what will become.

Organizational Transformation Characteristics

Harrison Owen, one of the main spokesmen of organizational transformation, wrote an article on its intellectual roots (1983b). In this article, Owen distinguishes between organizational transformation as a phenomenon and as a practice. He then makes the connection between the two. As a phenomenon, organizational transformation is

> . . . the creation of new organization life forms in response to a changing world environment. Transformation is therefore not something that you do to an organization but rather something which **happens quite naturally** as the organization seeks to cope with an emerging and strange world. (Owen 1983b, p. 7; emphasis added)

The practice of organizational transformation is to enable members to consciously participate in, manage, and effectuate the process that is, according to Owen, always toward growth and a better way of being. Therefore, Owen describes the role of the organizational transformation consultant and manager as "midwife," and the verb he uses is "midwifing." Owen defines organizational transformation as a practice as follows: "The essence of O.T. is **energy** and **spirit**. O.T. is the natural process whereby human energy and spirit exercise and fulfill the search for a better way to be . . . a new life form" (p. 7; emphasis added).

The words "spirit," "spirituality," and "energy" are key elements in almost all descriptions of organizational transformation. Hawley (1983) describes organizational transformation as follows: ". . . a basic change in the organization energy. O.T. is a spirit and energy change. . . . O.T. is infusing organizations with new energy, heart, and spirit for their encounters with the massive changes assailing our world" (p. 7).

Organizational energy is defined as "human potential for action or the accomplishment of work" (Adams 1984b, p. 277), and organizational spirituality is defined as "individuals and organizations having transcendent purpose which enables them to be part of a bigger cause beyond their immediate needs" (McKnight 1984).

Another set of elements characterizing transformation is the organization purpose, mission, and vision. Hawley (1983), for example, writes that "Organizational Transformation is oriented toward meaning, purpose, and vision" (p. 8). Kiefer and Stroh (1984) also claim that the primary emphasis of the organizational transformation strategy is on the organization's purpose and vision, and the alignment of members with these elements. A vision created out of the organization's and individuals' needs tends to "pull" the organization toward its fulfillment.

The last set of elements characterizing organizational transformation is its dealing with the belief system and the symbolic expressions of the organization. Hawley (1983) puts it simply by saying, "O.T. recognizes the symbolic as an important reminder of a deeper reality in organizations" (p. 7). Owen (1983c) points to the importance of the organizational myths reflecting the collective or consensual beliefs of a group or organization. Some use the term "paradigm" to describe a prevailing organizational world view or collective belief system (Sheldon 1980).

To summarize, the main components of the transformation are neither forms nor structures; rather, they are abstract, fluid, and dynamic elements that are hard to define and deal with. These elements are the organization unconsciousness, energy, spirit, spirituality, mission, purpose, vision, belief systems, world view, myths, symbols, paradigm, and state of being.

It is important to note what organizational transformation is not. It does not deal with forms, structures, and solutions. Nor is it a problem-solving process. It does not deal with how to plan and implement a specific change program, nor does it utilize analytical, step-by-step methods. Organizational transformation is not something that consultants "do" to organizations. It is a more "right brain" process that taps organizational processes largely ignored in the literature on change. Organizational transformation helps organization members to recognize and accept the need for second-order changes, to cope with the process until they are willing to take responsibility for the process. Hence, organizational transformation deals with the very first stages of the process of second-order change.

Organizational Transformation and the
Cycle of Second-Order Change

The main purpose of organizational transformation is to help organization members to accept the need for changes in their world view, to let go of the old, and to discover new choices. Therefore, organizational transformation seems to be useful for facilitating the first stages of second-order planned change. What are these stages, and what are the operations in each stage?

Ackerman (1983) argues that the first three stages of a radical change process are the following:

1. Understand and accept the need and opportunity. The task at this stage is to help members be aware of changes in the environment and their impact on the world view of the organization. The task is to focus the organization's intention, to create energy for the change.
2. Assess the situation. Whereas the first stage focuses on what is happening in the organization and in the consciousness of its members, this stage focuses on the relations between the organzation and its environment. Searching for opportunities and sensing the environment's learning possibilities are the processes in this stage.
3. Design the desired future. In this stage the purpose is to collectively envision the desired state, to create an attractive, meaningful, relevant vision, and to build a commitment to this vision.

A very similar process is suggested by Buckley and Perkins (1984). They termed their first three stages "unconscious," "awakening," and "reordering."

1. Unconscious stage. Second-order change begins gradually, with an unconscious period. The first clues that something basic is wrong appear: unconnected bits of random information, sporadic symptoms, and tentative new ideas. There is growing internal dissatisfaction or drastic environmental changes. The system is in decline. First-order change is attempted with no positive results.
2. Awakening stage. In this stage dominant coalitions or a subunit suddenly becomes aware of the need for change and of possibilities. This might be the result of a crisis, a failure in the system, or an articulated new vision. It can also be triggered by a new chief executive officer with new ideas and perspectives.
3. Reordering stage. This stage involves the decision to challenge the current world view. The organization, now aware of its situation, can decide whether to take the traditional route of minor incremental changes or to embark on a major one. In this stage the task of the manager or consultant is to help members pass through internal changes in thoughts, perceptions, and beliefs. This internal alteration causes emotional insecurity as individuals "let go" of the old and adopt new attitudes, perceptions, and behaviors. This stage is usually termed "reframing."

The last example is the model suggested by Tichy and Ulrich (1984). They suggest the following stages.

1. Trigger event. Environmental pressures or internal needs trigger the process.
2. Feedling a need for change. Dissatisfaction with the status quo.
3. Creation of a vision. Transforming leadership provides the organization with visions of a desired future state.
4. Mobilization of commitment. A critical mass accepts the new vision and mission, and instigates it.
5. Institutionalization. The ideas and vision are transmitted into practice.

These three models exemplify the "fit" between the natural process of transformation and transformation practice. Organizational transformation appears to be useful in helping organizations cope with the first stages of second-order change. There is almost no mention in this approach of planning and implementing a complex, multidimensional change.

Organizational transformation does not, however, deal only with the first stages of the process of second-order change. It also deals with the aspects of departure from the past, or what Tannenbaum (1980) defines as the process of "letting go, holding on, moving on." Transformation includes endings; there is a sense of loss and dying, denial, fear, anger, and resistance. The past cannot be buried without effort. Yet the past should provide new directions and opportunities, not old memories (Biggart 1977).

Two exemplifying models are presented. The first is suggested by Tichy and Ulrich (1984). The model includes four processes arranged in a sequence according to their depth: (1) disengagement from physical settings; (2) unidentification with past roles and people; (3) disenchantment, which entails recognizing that the positive feelings toward past situations cannot be replicated; (4) disorientation, which entails experiencing the loss of familiar trappings and the acceptance of the transition. Albert (1984) suggests a model that consists of a set of four processes: (1) summary, in which all important aspects of the past are evoked and summarized; (2) justification, in which the grounds for termination are stated and defined; (3) continuity, in which a link is discovered or invented between past and future; (4) closure, in which the value of that which will be lost is celebrated in order to create the possibility of closure.

To summarize, organizational transformation deals mainly with the first stages of the process of second-order change. It helps the organization's members recognize and accept the need for a radical shift in their beliefs and perceptions, and encourages them to explore new possibilities. It also helps members cope with deep feelings of loss and with the need for letting go of the old, holding on to what is still important, and moving toward the new. In this book we have concentrated on describing the transformation strategy and many of its approaches, models, and techniques. We have done so purposely because it is a developing field, less recognized and less used by managers and practitioners than the transition strategy. In the next section we describe the transition strategy and some of its models and approaches; thus the reader will have a more comprehensive perception of the complexity of managing second-order change and of the differences betwen the two strategies.

ORGANIZATIONAL TRANSFORMATION AS DESCRIBED IN THE CASE EXAMPLES

McWhinney's intervention in the city college, which was described in Chapter 6, and the other case examples of transformation enable us to analyze some of the basic elements and characteristics of organizational transformation as it emerges from the above case examples:

1. Consciousness and free choice. Transformation is a process of consciousness raising that facilitates the ability to respond with choice, to select which messages and in what way they are to be responded to. It is learning to be aware of choices and to act more freely, not from an immediate stimuli–response option. It is a process of extracting information from the unconscious in order to be free to make choices. The use of images and metaphors goes beyond both the rational and the emotional. These kinds of exercises and techniques tap the domains of instinct, imagination, intuition, creativity, emotion, and spirit. Through these domains, participants learn to open the doors of perception, to deepen their awareness to what motivates them, to recognize their values, beliefs, attitudes, and complex interdependency.

2. Centering and clearing. The process started with clearing away that which blocks the perception of the individuals. It begins with focusing on the level of the individual, releasing him or her from current forces, categories, stereotypes, shared beliefs, and assumptions. The basic assumption of organizational transformation is that without clear perception, participants can neither focus on their task nor see the directions available to them.

3. Self-integration. This is the process of becoming integrated with one's self, of dissolving extrinsic demands, expectations, and fashions. It is the acceptance of uniqueness into the form of a greater whole. The assumption here is that the process of transformation is possible only if the participants are integrated individuals who are aware of their uniqueness and of their power to create alternative realities and to choose the most appropriate one. This process operates both at the individual and the group levels. An integrated group that is aware of its uniqueness and power can create realities and choices.

4. The emergence of a vision of the desired future. The transformation process facilitates the emergence of vision as a meaningful driving image. This vision can be displayed as a metaphor, image, picture, phrase, or concept.

5. The use of noncognitive learning processes. Almost all the exercises and the techniques used noncognitive, nonanalytic methods. Processes of raising awareness and learning by experiencing continue until consensus emerges on basic issues.

6. Emphasis on the first phase of the change process. The transformation strategy focuses its efforts on creating or allowing a clear vision of a desired future to emerge. It does not focus on implementing this desired state. The implicit assumption of organizational transformation is that once organization members are aware of needs and of their power to create and choose directions, and once they have a vision of the desired future, they can implement this vision alone or with the help of experts in specific fields. The purpose of the transformation approach is therefore not only to facilitate the emergence of a common vision, but also to empower individuals and groups to implement it in real-life situations and to create the energy needed for this.

7. Some possible difficulties and pitfalls
   - Efforts to bring about change that invest too much time and energy in the diagnostic phase cause the system to remain exhausted and unable to gather enough energy for implementing the change. This argument might also be true for transformation strategy, unless a more balanced division of efforts along the whole change process is made.
   - Transformation strategy, as described here, uses learning methods and techniques that may evoke resistance and anxiety because they tap deep personal levels and utilize uncommon learning processes.
   - It ignores the fact that people have different learning styles, and that some people learn better through cognitive, analytic, and nonexperiential processes.
   - There may be a lack of continuity between what the "core team" agreed upon and what the "implementing team" may do with it. It is possible that what was agreed by the "core team" will not be accepted by the implementing team.
   - There is a possibility that too much emphasis will be on abstracts and not enough emphasis on concrete programs. The spirit and energy created by this strategy may be without base in the day-to-day reality.

8. Some possible advantages
   - Transformation seems to be useful for facilitating second-order change in organizations that are in a state of crisis or

chaos, unaware of the need for a radical shift in their ideology, culture, purpose, and procedures.

- Transformation seems to be useful for infusing deteriorating organizations with high spirit and enthusiasm.
- Transformation seems to be useful in helping organizations in crisis to be aware of internal and external processes affecting the organization, and to accept the need for a radical shift.
- Transformation seems to be useful for creating or discovering a new direction for the organization.
- Transformation seems to be useful for helping organizations' members let go of dysfunctional beliefs and processes, hold on to what is needed for the future, and move on toward a realization of a new, desired future.
- Transformation seems to be useful for the alignment of members with a new vision and for gathering members' commitment to engage in the process of change.

THE TRANSITION STRATEGY

Introduction

The transition strategy is embedded in perspectives on second-order change such as strategic choice, developmental stages, and organizational life cycle. It is also based on the traditional approach to planned change. From these perspectives, organizations eventually proceed through distinct stages, and the task of managers is to effectively manage the transition from one stable state to another. Transition seems to start where transformation ends. Whereas the main purpose of transformation is to help organizations to accept the need for change and to generate a new vision, the main purpose of transition is to turn these into reality.

Yet, although transition may be seen as complementary to transformation, it does not automatically follow that this is the case in reality. Some managers and consultants prefer to use either one of them, while others incorporate both in their work. Moreover, in many cases managers use methods derived from the two approaches and mix them, as will be shown later.

Unlike transformation, transition is a homogeneous, structured, step-by-step, organized approach. It was developed out of organizational development in the mid-1970s, mainly by Beckhard and Harris (1977), and was further developed and used by other consultants and managers (Ackerman 1982; Nadler 1982; Kimberly & Quinn 1984). The transition strategy is well known and utilized; therefore, our main efforts will be to make the distinction between the two strategies and the conditions under which it is more effective to use either one of them.

The Transition Strategy: Definition and Characteristics

In this book the definition provided by Ackerman (1983) is used not only because it is simple and precise, but also because it accurately represents the purpose of the strategy. Ackerman writes:

> In situations where clients have a clear future state in mind, like reorganization . . . the transition management process is used to achieve or **implement** that desired state. Its focus is over a set period of time, at the end of which the "future" becomes the "present" way of operating. (p. 3; emphasis added)

Practitioners, managers, and scholars who write about transitions use the verb "managing," not "facilitating" (organizational development), nor "midwifing," "allowing," or "energizing" (organizational transformation). Beckhard and Harris (1977) use the term "organizational transitions: managing complex change"; Kimberly and Quinn (1984) use the term "transition management"; and Tichy (1983) uses the term "managing strategic change." The verb hints at the basic characteristics of this strategy. It is a goal-oriented or task-oriented strategy. Its main purpose is to provide managers with models and techniques for coping with a transitional period and for managing, planning, and implementing a complex, multidimensional change.

The strategy takes into account human as well as formal structural needs of the system as the implementation proceeds. The change process is not unlike that of organizational development, but has a greater emphasis on the entire system, on elaborating the desired state, on the impact of the desired state on the present state, and on planning, implementing, and managing the change. The transition strategy is future-oriented. It does not focus on a thorough, all-embracing diagnosis and search for causes; the energy and attention are focused on practical issues related to implementing the desired state.

Transition is an analytical, rational, and pragmatic strategy. Its main focus is on analyzing and evaluating the impact of the future state on the present state, and deducing what action steps need to be taken. In order to cope wth multidimensional changes, to evaluate and to plan for implementing them, transition often utilizes computer programs and a manual.

The Stages of the Transition Strategy

Beckhard and Harris (1977) were among the first, in the field of planned change, to notice that wide-ranging, complex change effort involves three distinct stages. Figure 8.1 presents these stages of the process.

Beckhard and Harris developed a model, based on the above idea, that consists of a sequence of six distinguishable stages:

1. Assess the present condition, including the need for change
2. Define the new state or condition after the change
3. Define the transition state between the present and the future
4. Develop strategies and action plans for managing this transition
5. Evaluate the change effort
6. Stabilize the new condition and establish a balance between stability and flexibility.

Ackerman (1982) further developed the above model by adding the impact analysis stage, in which managers analyze and assess the impact of the desired state on present structures, procedures, technologies, and people. The model consists of the following stages:

1. Understanding and accepting the need for change and the opportunity for change
2. Assessing the situation; this phase includes assessing the scope of the field and building up a readiness and a willingness for the change

Figure 8.1. Transition Stages

Source: Beckhard and Harris 1977.

3. Designing the desired state; this phase includes building commitment and drama (the plot of the whole process), and collectively envisioning the desired state
4. Impact analysis; this phase includes a profound examination of the impact of the desired state on every dimension and level of the organization, and evaluation of the results
5. Organizing and planning for the change, designing the process of the change
6. Implementing the change
7. Formalizing the new state, celebrating the achievement
8. Evaluating the process, learning what has happened
9. Monitoring and fine-tuning.

The change effort, as facilitated by Ackerman (1982), is governed by two "management structures." The task of the first is to manage the "business of the business," while the task of the second is to manage and orchestrate the change process.

A further example of a transition strategy is provided by Tichy (1983). He also argues that second-order change typically starts with a new vision that represents a new world view. However, Tichy emphasizes the importance of what subsystems are needed to be changed in order for the desired future to be realized. He argues that in order to implement a desired state or a new mission, managers should assess its impact and implication on three basic subsystems: the cultural, the political, and the technical. From this point of view, the transition strategy aims to help managers change those three subsystems so as to be consistent with the desired future.

Tichy's model provides guidelines for transition management:

1. Review the present state and the desired state change in order to determine the technical, political, and cultural adjustments required
2. Analyze the changes in the technical, political, and cultural systems
3. Plan for unbundling and uncoupling the three systems in order to manage the transition in each
4. Plan for managing the transition in each system
5. Plan for recoupling the systems: How will the technical, political, and cultural systems mesh in the desired future?

Tichy's approach is important because it integrates different views on planned change. Organizational development has traditionally focused on culture changes (values, attitudes, relationships). Engineering has traditionally focused on technical and structural changes, and management has focused on changes in dominant coalitions, power structures, and management.

The last model of sequential phases of transition managing is suggested by Lundberg (1984). He distinguishes three transition stages: induction, management, and stabilization. In each stage three planned change processes need to be pursued: diagnosis, planning, and action. The model is shown in Figure 8.2.

To summarize, transition is a rational and analytical strategy aimed at helping managers to implement second-order change in their organizations. The strategy typically starts with dominant coalitions having a basic idea about the desired future. The approach includes analytical models and methods guiding specific phases, operations, and change targets to be achieved in order to implement the change successfully.

The transition strategy was developed by experienced consultants out of their own experiences in facilitating large-scale, complex changes in large organizations. From this perspective, second-order planned change appears to be a very complex process. It involves managing two contradictory processes at the same time (stability and change); it involves assessing, planning, and implementing a multitude of very different

Figure 8.2. The Cycle of Planned Transition Processes

TRANSITION STAGE	DIAGNOSIS	PLANNING	ACTION
INDUCTION	INDUCTION DIAGNOSIS	INDUCTION PLANNING	INDUCTION ACTION
MANAGMENT	MANAGEMENT DIAGNOSIS	MANAGEMENT PLANNING	MANAGEMENT ACTION
STABILIZATION	STABILIZATION DIAGNOSIS	STABILIZATION PLANNING	STABILIZATION ACTION

Source: Lundberg 1984.

changes (technological, structural, behavioral). It takes at least a few years to implement such a change, as the case studies indicate (for example, Kimberly & Quinn 1984).

For a better understanding of the characteristics of the transition approach, its advantages, disadvantages, and pitfalls, a case study will be presented and analyzed. The case chosen is one in which one of the authors was involved as a consultant. The case was selected because it enables us to examine not only the transition approach but also some of the basic questions that arise from the theory and practice of second-order change in organizations.

A CASE STUDY: THE TRANSITION FROM LOCAL TO REGIONAL HIGH SCHOOL IN THE UNITED KIBBUTZ MOVEMENT IN ISRAEL

This is a retrospective case analysis of a dramatic change that took place in the mid-1970s when about 100 kibbutzim changed their high school education system from a local, small, closed, intimate, and ideological system to a regional, large, open, organic, and academic system. About 100 local high schools were united into 15 regional high schools, which were newly built in the center of each region and belonged to kibbutzim in the area.

The old high school educational system in the United Kibbutz Movement was based on local schools. These schools had between 10 and 100 students, depending on the size of the kibbutz. The students were the children of the kibbutz only. Almost all the teachers were kibbutz members, and each school was a "family oriented organization" (Talmon 1972). The relationship between teachers and students was close and informal. The orientation of these schools was toward "socialistic humanistic education," not quantitative learning. Most of the time was devoted to the study of socialism, the history of the kibbutz, Jewish history, and agriculture.

The study groups were small, sometimes including students from two or even three grades. Each group had its own teacher of all the humanistic subjects who followed the group for at least two years. There were no learning tracks, no final exams, and no graduation certificate. The evaluating system was based on the efforts in class, on individual papers, and on midterm exams. The system as a whole strongly rejected the idea that students be evaluated by quantitative criteria, especially as the governmental graduation exams emphasized quantitative knowledge in math, English, and Bible, which were secondary subjects in the kibbutz high school. The consequence of this attitude was that kibbutz students could not apply for academic institutions unless they passed the graduation exams.

This system was private and financed mainly by the kibbutzim. Hence the buildings, the facilities, and the equipment were usually poor, old, and outdated. In the small kibbutzim there were no laboratories nor libraries. Another important aspect of the local system was to instill the students with a feeling for physical labor. They studied in the mornings, and worked in the afternoons. Whenever necessary, they were taken to help pick the crops. At least 21 learning days a year were spent on work.

Thus the children were raised in and by their communities, close to their core, involved in the good and the bad, protected from a hostile and changing environment, until they left for the army. Adversaries and cynics called them "the children of the cream"; supporters called them "the elite."

The new regional high school is different in almost every educational aspect. It is a modern building (or buildings) with modern facilities and equipment, modern laboratories and libraries. It includes about 500 students from the region, about 60 percent of whom are kibbutz students. There are many learning tracks, the groups are mixed, and students can choose tracks and subjects. The traditional teacher and class have disappeared. Teachers are experts in subject teaching and they do not have their own classes.

The government curriculum and the graduation exams are a legitimate, integrated part of the system. Most of the teachers are not kibbutz members. Competition, learning achievements, scores, and exams are integrated into the system. The traditional subjects have disappeared; math and English have become the most important subjects. The students study five days from 8 a.m. to 3 p.m. and work one day for six hours. Work needs do not interfere with studies.

Radical changes in the kibbutz, and in its environment and mometum opportunity (government support and financing), facilitated the change. Many changes took place in the kibbtuz during the 1960s and the early 1970s. The essential changes were economic success and a rise of the standard of living; industrialization; new technology in agriculture; the computer revolution; the rising demand of the young generation for academic education; the need for experts in various areas; the ongoing resistance of the universities to accepting kibbutz students without graduation certificates; and the change in the basic orientation of the kibbutz from a social change, ascetic movement to a productive, consuming, high-standard social community. More and more people felt that the old educational system was unsuitable for the needs of the modern kibbutz.

Radical changes also took place in the kibbutz environment: rapid urbanization in the surroundings; the expanding socioeconomic gap between the kibbutzim (which consist of European families) and their neighbors (mostly North African families); the establishment of kibbutz regional industry with nonkibbutz workers; ongoing pressure from the environment on the kibbutzim to "open their gates" and to be involved in economical, social, and cultural issues in the region; the rising power of the regional municipalities; and the government decision to transfer the responsibility for the schools, buildings, facilities, and equipment to the regional authorities.

The momentous opportunity to implement the expensive change was provided by the government. In the early 1970s the Ministry of Education decided on "integration" in public schools. School districts were changed so that at least 30 percent of their students would be from North African families. The government now encouraged the kibbutzim to change their systems and to accept nonkibbutz students by providing financial support through the regional municipalities.

The transition process included the following phases.

The Establishment of the Transition Committee

The process started when groups of parents initiated discussions on changing the system in all the kibbutzim in the region. The leader and instigator of these groups was the chief executive of the regional municipality, a kibbutz member who saw the opportunity to enhance cooperation in his region, as well as his authority and power, if the change took place. The discussion showed clearly that most of the parents were in favor of the change, while the old generation (now the minority) was against it. In order to avoid a conflict and a split, the kibbutzim decided to establish a committee that would investigate the educational, organizational, and financial implications of the change, and then reach a final decision.

The Development of the General Model and Its Implications

The committee consisted of representatives of the kibbutzim in the region and the various groups in each kibbutz. The leader of the team was an expert in education and administration, an instigator and a "doer" who supported the change, and wanted to be the founder and the first principal of the new school. He was supported by another powerful group member, the chief executive of the regional municipality, also a "doer" who saw in this project the summit of his achievements.

The group first worked on "team building," and on clarifying values and attitudes concerning education. Then it divided into subgroups to work on three basic issues. The first task was to develop an ideal model of an educational system based on humanistic orientation that suited the kibbutz needs. The second task was to investigate the financial aspects of the change and the construction of new buildings, purchasing of land for the school, and so on. The third task was to work on the construction and architectural aspects of the schools. This phase took about six months, at the end of which the group provided all the kibbutzim with the new model of the educational system and the financial implications of the change, as well as general ideas about the location of the buildings. The general assemblies in all the kibbutzim approved the change by a large majority.

Impact Analysis and Preparation for the Change

In order not to miss the momentous opportunity for government financial support, and in order to shorten the transition period, the group decided to work in two teams and to open the new school within two years. The first team, headed by the chief executive of the regional municipality, worked on raising financial support, purchasing the land for the site, and constructing the building and the facilities. The other team, headed by the group leader, worked on developing and translating the ideal model into an operational and practical program. It worked on the curriculum, the learning tracks, the evaluation system, the organizational and managerial system, rules, regulations, classes, and hours.

The next step was conducting an impact analysis in which the implications of the new system on the present system were analyzed and evaluated. This analysis was made by examining the impact of the change on different groups and dimensions. Groups were students, teachers, parents, the kibbutz; the dimensions included work, busing, and communications. The implications were analyzed and evaluated, and decisions were made about how to solve these various problems.

The analysis showed, for example, that teachers from distant kibbutzim rise early in the morning (6 a.m.), return home at 4 p.m., and work a five-day week. This would mean a sharp worsening in their work conditions. Teachers had already started to oppose the change. As a result, the committee decided that these teachers would work a four-day week, and transportation would be provided for them.

Transition Period

New teachers were hired. Teachers and the staff passed through workshops and training programs in which the educational policy, the values, and the procedures were studied and discussed. An effort was made to bring the students from all the different schools to the same level of study. The buildings, the facilities, and the equipment were all in progress. The maintenance staff and the working staff were organized, and passed through the training programs.

Implementing the Change

In September 1977, everything was ready for the transition. The school was named, and the head of the transition group was elected the first principal. Although not everything was completed (the library and the sports hall had not been built because of financial problems), the school was opened on time. A ceremony and celebrations were held in every kibbutz to symbolize the new change.

Tuning Up

It took at least one year to solve unforeseen problems and to tune up the system. Some changes were made to bring the idea to reality. For example, in the first year, students could choose all their classes. In the second year, some classes became required (such as literature and

English). It took three and a half years from the first formal decisions until the change was implemented.

EVALUATION

The above case study enables us to examine the basic elements and characteristics of the transition strategy. It also enables us to further understand the differences between the transformation and the transition strategies. Transition strategy, as it emerges from the above case study, is characterized by the following elements:

1. Dealing with an existing image of the desired future. In this case study the idea of regional, open high schools already existed in the mind of a network of people before the process began. There was no need to pass through deep awareness processes for generating directions or choices. It points to the possibility that awareness of environmental changes and/or of the emergence of new needs is an incremental process. Some individuals are more aware of or sensitive to these changes than others. Warning signals from the environment may be detected first by sensitive individuals or at the organizational margins. This phenomenon is dependent on many elements, such as dogmatism (May 1972) or neurosis (Perls 1981) at the individual level, or disturbances of the feedback processes (J. Miller 1977), or inability to examine the basic assumptions underlying the system operations (Argyris 1978). Adams' (1983) study on networks showed that in every system, one can find people who are more willing than others to accept change and to support it. These people are less committed to existing operations and values, and more committed to development and change.

2. No diagnostic phase. The above case study is characterized by not having any analytic diagnosis of the problems of the existing system. There are assessment processes related mainly to the establishing of the new system. Thus, there is an assessment of the needs that the new system should fulfill. There is an assessment of the situation and of forces that might hinder or enhance the change. There is an impact analysis. All these processes are goal-oriented and are directed toward facilitating the implementation of the existing idea.

3. Political campaign. Transition strategy also entails managing a political campaign. Success depends on political awareness, power

struggle, and conflict management. It entails the ability to persuade external agencies to provide financial as well as political support. Schattschneider (1975) claims that reform movements succeed because their leaders know how to make the conflict dominant over other existing conflicts, and "dominance is related to intensity and visibility" (p. 72). In this case study, as well as in others representing the transition strategy, the final decision to transform the system was preceded by political campaigning that was managed democratically. The ability to establish support for the change includes using collaborative and participative processes and conflict management.

4. Goal orientation. The purpose of the transition strategy is to implement existing ideas. In order to achieve this goal, one has to set schedules, objectives, and task teams, and to be task-oriented. The above case study shows that transition strategy is typically managed under time pressure because of cost reduction, or utilizing the momentum opportunity, or reducing the problems created because of the transition period.

5. Rational and analytical orientation. Unlike the transformation strategy, transition strategy, as displayed by the above case study, is more a "left brain" process. It includes rational and analytical processes such as impact analysis and assessment needs. The only place for a more "right brain" process was in the training program for the personnel. In the above case study, much freedom was left for the teachers to explore, discover, imagine, and generate ideas about new ways of teaching, class arrangements, and evaluation systems. As in the case of the new alternative school (Gold & Miles 1981), this process was facilitated partly by external consultants who used "right brain" processes for generating new ideas.

6. Possible difficulties and pitfalls.
   - A study conducted by Nadler (1982) on the transition period at A.T.T. showed that once the solution has emerged and is agreed upon, it is very hard to change it during the transition period, even when circumstances have changed.
   - A study conducted by Ackerman on transforming a large oil company using transition strategy showed that during the transition period, there is a rapid deterioration of the old system because most energy efforts, resources, and attention are given to the establishment of the new system (Ackerman 1982).

- Too long a period of transition and not clarifying with the employees what their positions will be in the new system may create resistance and anxiety, and may hinder the change.
- The above case study was characterized by emphasis on form and structure, not on processes and maintenance. Too much goal orientation generated implicit resistance to the change, which became explicit when the new system started to operate.

Some Theoretical Aspects Derived from the Case Study

The retrospective analysis of the above case study enables us to examine some of the crucial issues relating to second-order planned change:

- Was the change inevitable? (the question of voluntarism vs. determinism)
- Was this transition a second-order change?
- What made the change possible and successful?

Was the Change Inevitable?

In order to address the question, one has to examine what happened to all the high schools in the kibbutz movement, and the differences among them before the change and after it. At least three facts emerge immediately. The first is that there were only marginal differences among the local high schools before the change. The second is that although the majority of the schools were transformed into regional ones, at least four communities decided not to participate in this process, and to transform their systems by renewal. The third is that among the regional high schools there are some basic differences.

Four communities decided to keep their local systems but to transform them into more modern ones. These communities opened their high schools to nonkibbutz students who came from other areas and were "adopted" by families in the kibbutz. This act both enlarged the student population and opened the school to its remote environment. Mainly, it enabled the communities to get government financing for building a modern local high school.

Differences exist not only between those systems that passed through the transition and became regional systems and those that remained local, but also among the regional systems. There are basically three types of regional systems. The first is the "regional boarding school." These high schools were built as if they were "mini kibbutzim." Each school has a farm and is managed by the students, who study, work, and live there. The second type is the "regional kibbutz school," which includes kibbutz children only. There are no graduation exams, and the system is relatively closed. The third type is the "open mixed school," which was described in this case study.

The conclusions are that although the second-order change was inevitable for the survival of the system in a radically changed environment (the close environment, the kibbutz; and the remote one, the region and the state), the direction of the change was in the hands of those who managed it. This proposition confirms voluntaristic-based theories.

Was This Transition a Second-Order Planned Change?

The regional high school is different from the local high school not only in quantitative measures (size, number of teachers, students, learning tracks) but also in qualitative measures. It is based on a different value orientation and is guided by different implicit premises. It is beyond the purpose of this study to elaborate on the values and underlying suppositions that guide each of these systems. However, the basic differences are summarized in Table 8.1.

The above case study shows that a second-order change in a system can be seen also as a first-order change from the metasystem perspective. Systems theory (for example, J. Miller 1978) provides the notion that

Table 8.1.
Comparison of Local and Regional High Schools

Local	Regional
Closed system	Open system
Homogeneous	Heterogeneous
Learning to work	Learning to study
Ideological system	Professionalism
Integrated into the kibbutz	Apart from the kibbutz

Source: Prepared by the authors.

every system has subsystems and is also a subsystem of a higher-level system. Thus a local high school is a system that has subsystems (classes, groups) but is also a subsystem of the kibbutz or the high school system in the United Kibbutz Movement.

Therefore, from the perspective of the local high school system and that of the kibbutz high school system as well, the change was a second-order change. But from the perspective of the individual kibbutz and the kibbutz as a movement, this change (in one subsystem) was a first-order change. The change affected some dimension in the kibbutz life; however, the kibbutz as a social system did not change drastically.

What Made the Change Possible and Successful?

- Drastic changes in the immediate environment of the school (the kibbutz) and in the remote environment (the region, the state) made the old school system irrelevant
- Awareness of these changes and the failure of incremental, minor adjustments to provide satisfactory adaptation and solutions
- The emergence of clear ideas about the direction of the needed change, and the evergrowing network of people who were willing to support and struggle for the change
- Strong leadership with both a vision and a mission, task and people orientation, and strong political awareness
- Participative processes that enabled all the involved groups to take part in the transition and that enhanced their commitment to the project
- Momentary opportunity
- The ability to cope with anxiety, to go through processes of "letting go," "holding on," and, most important, "moving on"
- The ability to implement the change in a relatively short time.

What Holds the Change from Restitution?

The new educational system has persisted for about seven years, and the change has now been accepted as an inseparable part of kibbutz life. There are indeed some statements about "those good old days," but these seem to mourn the past rather than envisage the future. Glorifying of the past by those who made it seems to be an inseparable part of every change. The following facts are related to the persistence of the change: The new system is not a vision of a leader only, nor does it satisfy parents' needs only. It is embedded in changes, values, and needs of higher-level systems. It is consistent with the values and purposes of the kibbutz and of the kibbutz environment (the region), and with the values and purposes of the Ministry of Education. Hence the system is supported financially and politically by both the region and the Ministry of Education.

In regions where the school consisted of kibbutz children only, it was supported and maintained by the kibbutzim that owned the school and by the kibbutz movement. There are indeed pressures from the region and the Ministry of Education to open the system. However, these kibbutzim addressed this problem by encouraging their students and their members to be involved in other social activities in the region. As long as these kibbutzim have the resources and support of the movement, and not too much pressure from the region and the government, the change will probably continue.

SUMMARY

In this chapter we have distinguished between two types of second-order change strategies: transition and transformation. When organizational leaders decide to change what exists and to implement something new, they engage in transition processes. A transition is the process of achieving a known new state over a set period of time. Transformation is the emergence of a new state of being out of the "remains" of the old state. In contrast with transition, the new state is unknown until it takes shape. Table 8.2 summarizes the main differences between the two strategies.

Figure 8.3 suggests that the two strategies are basically complementary. Whereas the transformation strategy focuses on making what lies largely at the unconscious level become conscious, on helping people accept the need for a change, on allowing new visions or world views to emerge, and on facilitating the process of "letting go," the transition strategy focuses on applying the new world view or vision to day-to-day operations. Joining the stages or main actions of the two strategies will give the model in Figure 8.3.

The model suggests that the basic strategy used for facilitating second-order change is dependent on the location of the organization in the cycle of change. As we move toward the later stages of this process, it is more useful to use the transition strategy and vice versa.

Table 8.2.
Basic Differences Between Transformation and Transition

Transformation	Transition
• helping members to accept the need for second-order change	• helping the organization to plan and implement the change
• helping the organization to discover and accept a new vision, a new world view, and to align members with this vision	• helping the organization to elaborate the new vision, to implement it, to legitimize and institutionalize it
• focusing on the first stages of second-order change	• focusing on the later stages of second-order change
• open; going with the client's needs, nonstructured, nonanalytical process	• rational, analytical, step-by-step, and collaborative process
• focusing on changes in individuals' consciousness	• focusing on changes in the interactions in the organization
• dealing with flow states and abstracts	• dealing with the organization subsystems and concretes
• changing perceptions, beliefs, and consciousness	• changing forms, procedures, roles, and structures
• a process that might include moments of insight and a sudden shift in perceptions and behaviors	• an incremental process that might include political campaign and conflicts
• facilitating and allowing	• managing and applying
• spirit and spirituality	• practicality, pragmatism
• energizing and empowering individuals, creating critical mass	• utilizing the organization's energy and resources for implementing the change
• allowing death and rebirth	• shaping the new form

Source: Prepared by the authors.

The model suggests that transformation is more helpful than transition in organizations in ongoing crises, that are stuck, or that are in a long chaotic period; that have tried first-order changes several times without solving their problems; that are paralyzed by conflicts embedded in different points of view. The transformation strategy seems also to be useful in situations where organization members are unaware of or deny the need for second-order change.

The model also suggests that in order for second-order change to take place and to be institutionalized, transformation has to be followed by transition, with or without professional guidance. Awareness and acceptance of the need for second-order change, and even having a new vision, are necessary but not sufficient. The model suggests that transformation may also be used partially in the later stages of the change

process when crises occur or realignment with the new vision and
ideology is needed.

Figure 8.3. The Cycle of Second-Order Planned Change

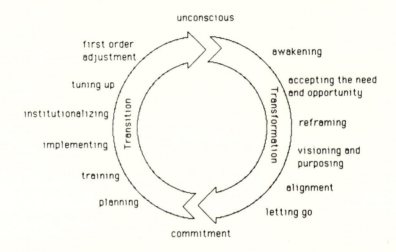

Source: Prepared by the authors.

9

The "New" and "Renew" Strategies

This chapter deals with two different strategies to implement transformation. Facilitating and implementing transformation involve coping with strong resistance to change. A review of case studies showed that there are basically four strategies in implementing transformation and dealing with the resistance to change:

1. Initiation of a new freestanding organization, totally different from others of this kind (Gold & Miles 1981)
2. "Sponsorship," whereby an existing organization develops a new organization or subunit, totally different from the sponsor (Shortell et al. 1984)
3. Merger or consolidation (Sheldon 1979)
4. Renewing already existing systems (Warren 1984).

In this chapter an effort will be made to examine and compare the two extreme strategies. The strategies that implement the change by initiating a new freestanding organization (no. 1) or by developing a new "sponsored" organization or subunit (no. 2) are termed "new." The strategy to implement the change by revitalizing existing organizations (no. 4) is termed "renew."

The idea that human systems transform in two different ways was raised by Sahlins (1960), who studied the evolution of cultures. He argued that "evolution moves simultaneously in two different directions. On one side, it creates diversity through adaptive modification: new forms differentiate from old. On the other side, evolution generates progress: higher forms arise from, and surpass, lower" (p. 12).

The question of how people can consciously participate in these two evolutionary processes and shape them is the subject of this chapter. The literature on planned change completely ignores the issue. No theoretical distinction is made between the two processes, and almost no conceptualization exists. The idea proposed here is that the transformation approach seems to be useful for renewing existing systems because of its focus on raising consciousness and awareness of the need for change. On the other hand, in creating a new organization that is based on new ideologies, new cultures, new procedures, and new purpose, the transition approach seems to be more appropriate because here the main problem is to implement new, already existing ideas.

Hence, the purpose of this chapter is to make a distinction between two strategies to implement second-order change and to examine their advantages and disadvantages. For a better understanding of the two strategies, two case studies will be described and analyzed.

THE "NEW" STRATEGY

Organizations can be transformed by creating a new system in a new place with new personnel, or by renewing the old system in the same place with the same personnel. The literature review showed that almost all the case studies and the examples of second-order planned change represent the "new" alternative. When second-order change was conducted by taking the "renewal" alternative, it usually entailed the positioning of a new top manager or top managerial team.

In business organizations, DuPont, like many other firms, created separate pilot plants to develop new technology and new products (nylon, rayon, Corfam). In total institutions, the creation of a radical new prison that really rehabilitates was possible by starting out with a new plant, guards carefully chosen to be rehabilitators, and a new, dedicated staff. Even the prisoners were new (McCleery 1957). In medical systems, the creation of a new, revolutionary health care system based on prevention and holistic medicine was made possible by establishing a new system in a new area with new personnel (Shortell et al. 1984; Tichy 1977). In education systems, the creation of an open alternative school (although it was a failure) was conducted by establishing a new school with new personnel (Gold & Miles 1981; Dwyer et al. 1983).

The perception that the "new" alternative in second-order planned change is much more utilized than the "renew" alternative also gains support from empirical studies in specific domains. There is a great deal of evidence that in school systems, for example, almost the only means of achieving second-order change is by creating an alternative school system, or by using unutilized buildings for innovative educational purposes (G. V. Bass 1978; Broad 1977; Flaxman & Homestead 1978). Studies on change in social institutions and programs, such as government services, mental health systems, and criminal justice systems, pointed in the same direction (Heller & Monahan 1977).

Studies on overcoming resistance to radical and widespread changes have shown that the most successful strategy is the creation of a new organizational unit, such as a separate college or a pilot plant (Mintzberg 1979). Hage (1980) claims that the human resistance to change, and the difficulties of changing existing procedures, processes, and structures, are so great that "the best approach would be to create a new unit in which new personnel are recruited and trained, and which has its own source of resources and enough time to work on the implementation" (p. 244).

Hage's claim is based on long-term field studies. Chandler (1977) comes to the same conclusion in his study on new products. He points out that the first production of a car, plane, radio, television set, or computer represents major departures from regular production processes, involving not only new output and production technology but also a wide variety of other changes, including marketing, logistics, input, and management. All of these occur in new organizations and tend to have been the simplest solution to the problem of overcoming resistance.

It should be noted that second-order planned change implemented by creating a new system is different from creating a new system. It is a much more complicated process. New organizations are being created daily, but they are not completely different from the other organizations of their kind. They are probably different in one or a few dimensions (such as new product or new technology), but as a whole they are not different. Second-order planned change implemented by creating a new system entails creating a completely different system, a system that represents a different world view, different culture, different purpose, and different procedures.

In order to better understand the "new" strategy, its advantages, and its difficulties, a case study will be presented. It is a case study representing a failure. It enables one to see how complicated and difficult it is to accomplish second-order change even when taking the "new" strategy. The case studied is an attempt to create a new open school based on new ideas and principles.

A Case Example: Whose School Is It, Anyway?
Alternative Public Schools

Attempts at change from within existing school systems were abandoned by a substantial bloc of educational reformers in the early 1970s. Instead, much effort was devoted to creating alternative systems based on a new education philosophy. Whereas in public schools the emphasis is on basic skill acquisition and future vocational success, alternative systems emphasize helping actualize each student as a human being and allowing the student to take responsibility for his/her individual learning priorities. Alternative schools attend to the process of learning rather than to its content, and to students' feelings as well as their thoughts. They emphasize greater freedom and choice for students and teachers.

An in-depth description and analysis of the creation of a public alternative school is provided by Gold and Miles (1981). It is a study of the creation of a new and completely different elementary public school in a district that already had 15 public schools. The initiation of the idea came from one of the members of the district board who had recently completed his degree in education and was well acquainted with organizational development and humanistic education ideas.

The first vision of the school was developed by this person together with other board members who supported the idea of building a new, open elementary school. The vision was expressed as follows:

> The major focus is on educational change and the change process . . . to create an institution that responds to the changing needs of society and the needs of individual kids. . . . In this school we want a redefinition of education, a redefinition of the institution, a redefinition of the parents' involvement in the school, and a redefinition of education as opposed to instruction. . . . Education is a set of learning experiences designed to help each youngster learn how to do, how to create a better society. (Gold & Miles 1981, p. 49)

The first vision included more specific ideas on the structure, the buildings, and the curriculum:

... an organizational structure, not a vertical one ... but a horizontal one, kids with groups of adults. The function of the adults here would be to help the kids become involved. Groups would be autonomous ... curriculum is the interaction of people in the process of studying something. We need a high degree of trust, competency, planning skills, imagination, and creativity: a complementary relationship between school, home, and community. We will organize in teams, each responsible for a group of kids. It would be a multi-age group; the focus would be on the developmental aspects of the kids, their motor development, sensory and emotional development, etc. (Gold & Miles 1981, p. 50)

The small team of "true believers" succeeded in gaining the approval of the district board and the city council. A site was located and funds were provided for the project. The next step was the nomination of a school principal who was willing to make the dream come true. After a long process of selection, the appropriate person was found. He recruited teachers who were enthusiastic to work in a new, different system. The teachers, together with the small team, developed the school curriculum, structure, and goals. They passed through training programs, workshops, and organizational development training.

The project began with greater enthusiasm, strong devotion, and high energy. The personnel felt that they were part of a new experience providing new hope for public education. The problems arose when the parents in the neighborhood in which the school was to be built demanded to participate in the decision-making process of the planning. Behind this demand was their resistance to the change. As the project developed and the buildings were erected, the resistance of the parents grew. During the first year of operation, the parents threatened to stop sending their children to the school. After a bitter conflict, the school district and the school personnel were forced to change the school, which became a regular elementary school.

Advantages of the "New" Strategy

Developing a completely new organization has some decisive values as an approach to organizational second-order change:

1. In a new organization, the constraints of the established system can be bypassed, and the vested interests of various parties set aside for a moment.

2. Personnel favorable to the new system can be recruited, so that resistance is absent and the energy of well-trained true believers is brought to bear.
3. Protection of the new system from the environment means that all energies can be fully focused on the task; experimentation and "fine-tuning" are possible, so the vision can be actualized in something like its "pure" or optimal form, free of expedient alterations.
4. There are personal benefits for those who participate in the creation of a new system: the excitement of creation, the freedom to innovate, and the autonomy involved in creating something for which one is responsible.
5. Most reformers believe, with some justification (Gold & Miles 1981), that a new system is an obtrusive and clear demonstration of a new set of ideas, and hence it can do far more to diffuse these ideas because potential adopters can see it working.
6. The creation of an alternative institution, especially a public service or a social institution, provides citizens with choice.
7. The development of alternative institutions creates heterogeneity and helps to meet the needs of specialized groups.

The only disadvantage of creating a new system is that it cannot solve the problems of an existing system that faces the choice of disintegration or transformation.

Failure Analysis

The failure to maintain the change brought to mind the notion that while it is probably easier to implement second-order change by creating a new and different system than by changing an existing system, it is, however, very difficult, in both alternatives, to maintain the change and avoid going back to the old ways of doing things. Studies on the persistence of first-order changes in organizations show that failure to maintain the change is related to intraorganizational variables, such as lack of sufficient commitment of management to the change, the reward system, and socialization (Goodman & James 1982).

Second-order change entails not only intraorganizational changes but also changes in the relationships between the system and its higher-level systems, and between the system and its environment. Second-order change includes changes in input and output forms and structures, changes in strategy and policy, and changes in ideology, all of which are linked to how the system relates to its environment and higher-level systems. Therefore, maintaining second-order change is a much more complex phenomenon than maintaining first-order change. It is related not only to complex interorganizational processes, but also to processes in which the organization has no influence on the nature and direction.

Dwyer, Smith, and Prunty (1983) conducted a follow-up study of an innovative elementary school established in 1964. In 1979, the school, very similar to the one mentioned above, was a regular elementary school. The buildings were reconstructed; open spaces were changed to regular rooms. Teachers and principals were changed. Curriculum, grading, teaching processes, and policy were reversed. Analyzing the reversal process, the researchers came to the conclusion that it could be explained only by looking at the "nested systems" and their effect on the school. The multiple categories of antecedents for the reversal at the school fell along geographical (population changes), political (changes in policy, in redefinition of school areas), cultural (values and attitudes of the community toward education), and organizational (changes in superintendents) lines at the national, state, county, community, district, and school levels. Only the support of these environmental factors would have made the change possible.

Analyzing other cases (failures) of creating new systems based on new points of view, cultures, procedures, and purposes (Tichy 1977; Walton 1975) showed very similar conclusions. Change did not persist long because of changes in personnel (management and professionals) and because of lack of support from users and metasystem levels. The above studies indicated that second-order change in systems tightly coupled with, and highly dependent on, metasystems (in terms of finances, personnel, rewards, policies) can persist if the metasystems support the change. However, because of changes in metasystems (in management, in policies), it is possible that this support may change in time.

It is, therefore, proposed that for a second-order change to persist over time, commitment of managers and personnel is crucial, but not sufficient; there must also be indifference or support from the metasystem, in order for the change at the system level to persist. However, because these situations rarely occur, the system can maintain the change by what Aldrich (1979) calls "finding a new niche" or by what others call "networking" (Adams 1983). It entails looking for, and finding, alternative metasystems, customers, and environments. It entails creating a network of new environmental metasystems.

THE "RENEW" STRATEGY

A survey of the literature shows that only a very few case studies featuring the "renew" strategy have been published. This fact may represent reality and be in accord with Hage's (1980) finding that the "new" strategy is preferred because of the system's resistance to large-scale change. However, studying deviant cases may deepen our understanding of the conditions under which second-order change may be implemented and maintained successfully.

The discussion on renewing existing systems is important because of three issues:

1. The practical issue. In many cases the people in the organization are willing to transform their organization, or at least to engage in this process, in order to survive. It may also be that there is no option but to change the organization from within. It is also possible that in many circumstances renewal is much less expensive and less time-consuming.
2. The ethical issue. The belief that organizations can be transformed only by creating a new unit entails a hopeless future for almost everyone who works and lives in old, declining systems. For some it means unemployment; for others it means living in deteriorating systems in crisis and uncertainty. For those who live in communities and in total institutions, this issue is crucial. Those who have the freedom and the power to choose where they want to work and live will find that there is no problem for them. But what about those who have no choice but to stay where they are?
3. The theoretical issue. Some life cycle theories suggest that social systems, like all living systems, are born, mature, and die. Evolution theory proposes the notion that the "natural selection law" applies to human systems. These are deterministic and somewhat pessimistic viewpoints. But there are other, more optimistic perspectives.

Argyris (1977), in his theory of "double loop learning," claims that human beings are capable of learning not only to correct deviations and to improve their organization's functioning, but also of learning how to learn. Jantsch (1980) claims that social systems have the capability for "self-organizing" and "self-transcendence." Prigogine (1984) argues that although second-order change is an inevitable phenomenon in social systems, its nature and direction are in human hands. The cases cited in this book show that Argyris' viewpoint is the more practical and optimistic one. Although it is very hard to renew social systems, it is nevertheless a matter of learning. For further understanding of the renewal process, its characteristics, and some of the conditions necessary for its success, another case example will be presented and analyzed.

A Case Example: The Transformation of the County Jail*

This is a short description of change effort facilitated by internal and external consultants (Gluckstern & Packard 1977). In July 1973, the Berkshire County Jail, the county sheriff, and the University of Massachusetts School of Education became partners in an effort to transform a traditional, repressive, authoritarian, closed jail into an open, self-organized, rehabilitative, and educational system. The reasons for this change were many: growing hostility of the community and its readiness to provide the jail with resources for change; the fact that most of the prisoners went back to crime after their release; and changed views about prisoners' rehabilitation.

The change was possible only after the nomination of a new warden and mainly because the university received a grant for studying and implementing education and rehabilitation programs. The change process lasted for about three years, during which the buildings, the facilities, the organizational structure, and the decision-making process changed completely. Prisoners had to take responsibility for their lives and to participate in educational, vocational, and rehabilitational programs. Prisoners went from being treated like irresponsible, mistrusted kids to being treated as human beings. There were changes in roles, values, and attitudes of prisoners and personnel.

The first step started with the development of an ideal model by the university. It was then shared and discussed with the county sheriff and the jail management team. The ideas were elaborated into action programs. Then the university nominated an external consultant and the jail appointed internal consultants who worked with a task team headed

---

*The case was taken from Gluckstern and Packard (1977).

by the chief warden, in order to facilitate and implement the change. The main goals of the change or the action steps were the following:

1. To create an environment within the jail that supported the change, and facilitated learning and change of the inmates and personnel
2. To develop educational, vocational, and rehabilitation programs together with the inmates and the personnel; to use this process for socialization and attitude changes
3. To transform the jail into a self-governing institution; to change the decision-making processes, procedures, and structures
4. To create new roles for correctional officers as teachers, advisers, and psychologists, and to provide training programs for them
5. To change the reward and punishment system, and the regulations and procedures for taking leave from the jail
6. To change the structure and to add modern facilities, such as sports facilities and production workshops
7. To open the jail so that community resources available from individuals and institutions could be utilized.

The First Year

This year was devoted to overcoming the resistance to the change, to releasing fear and distrust coming both from the personnel and from the inmates. The consultants were faced with cynical attitudes about "liberal do-gooders." To overcome these feelings, they interviewed all the inmates and personnel, emphasizing that the project addressed the needs of the individuals in the institution. Step by step, they established workshops, discussion groups, and task groups, some of which included personnel and inmates together. The basic strategy was to develop the change in an emergent way and not to impose the model on the jail. From the group meetings emerged needs and ideas about meeting those needs. The meetings were held in a democratic, collaborative style, thereby providing training in managing the jail in a new way.

During this year some of the personnel left, but most of them decided to stay and to cooperate with the consultants. Toward the end of the year, suggestions for change were translated into programs for change, and some obvious changes were made so that everyone could realize that these changes were possible and were for the benefit of all. At the end of the year, some important decisions were made. The community decided to provide the jail with an occupational training program held in the jail and to raise money for vocational classes; a drug rehabilitation program was opened; an educational policy-planning committee was elected that included inmates; and the university's suggestion to open an adult education program and degree study program through an open university was accepted.

The Second Year

During this year a governing board was established that included inmates, administrators, correction officers, the project team, and the consultants. The board first worked to implement the above changes, and then was willing to work on changing the whole institution. It first decided to develop a new mission and purpose for the jail, and then to elaborate upon it and translate it to everyday life. A new vision emerged: that of open, educational, rehabilitational, self-governing institutions. Task teams were formed to work on changing the buildings, the facilities, the structure, and the decision-making process.

The consultants, with the help of the university, worked on redefining the roles of inmates, correction officers, and administrators. New roles were created and training programs for the personnel were opened by the university. Toward the end of the year, some of the changes were in the process of implementation and some were already implemented. New facilities were built; the buildings were in a process of change; the vocational, educational, and rehabilitational programs were operating. At the end of this year, the personnel and the inmates were ready for changes in the structure and the decision-making processes, and the new roles.

The Third Year

In this year the transformation of the jail was completed and the efforts were devoted to two main issues. The first was the institutionalization of the change, making explicit what was implicit or uncertain, and stabilizing the procedures and the regulations. The second was securing funds and financial aid from local and federal agencies, because the funding for the change and the research given to the university was already exhausted.

One more concern was the ability of the institution to maintain the change after the consultants and the university team left. This problem was solved by placing the internal consultant in charge of the new training programs, and by continuing the training programs for the personnel through the university. At the end of 1976, the project was successfully completed.

Evaluation

The above case study enables us to analyze the conditions that favored the change effort.

Environmental Characteristics

- Both the community near the jail and the Sheriff's Department supported the change and helped to implement it.
- The initiative for the change, the funding, and the professional skills were provided by the university.
- The university provided not only funding and professionals, but also training programs and ideal models.
- A momentous opportunity was provided by the university's adopting the project, and this was fully utilized for transforming the institution.
- Ideological and value changes in the perception of jails and their functions had developed in the county.

Change Agent Characteristics

- The internal and the external consultant collaborated.
- The internal consultant provided access to the system, acquainting the "outsiders" with the politics, the regulations, and the formal and informal structures of the jail. He served as a mediator, enabling both sides to understand each other better.
- The external consultant provided the skills and the knowledge about change principles and processes.
- The two consultants were able to work together, using each other's skills and advantages.

Intervention Characteristics

- Long-time preparations by the intervention team. It took about six months for the university to study the problems in the jail and to work on a general model for an alternative system.

- A long period of time was devoted to building up trust and breaking resistance. This period took a year of hard effort.
- Starting with the needs of the clients. Although the consultants had an ideal model in their heads, they did not impose it or try to work on it. Only when the system was ready for the change and trusted the consultants was the model provided. This happened in the second year of the intervention.
- Emerging approach. The strategy used by the consultants was to enable changes to emerge and to proceed with emerging needs for further changes.
- Task orientation combined with learning new skills. Most of the work was done in small task groups. All these task groups were managed in collaborative, democratic style. This approach was probably more appropriate for prisoners. A workshop for direct attitude change or sensitivity training was not provided.
- Professionalism, collaboration, and ability to empower and energize tired and skeptical individuals.
- Multidimensional effort. The change effort did not focus only on attitude or relationship changes, but on every organizational dimension. Each dimension was equally important.

Organizational Characteristics

- Relatively small institution. The jail housed 80 male inmates, most of whom were transferred from other jails to serve the last two to three years of their sentences.
- Top wardens who not only supported the change but also took an active part in it.
- A total institution in which both inmates and personnel can be transferred if they resist the change.
- A total institution with well-defined procedures, regulations, roles, and norms that can be easily located and worked upon. It is relatively easy to be aware of "what is" and "what is not."
- The whole organization could pass through changes over a long period of time without profound harm because there is no competition with other institutions.
- Time and money were available without serious restrictions.
- Prisons are relatively simple and homogeneous organizations. There is no production system, no selling, and not many subsystems.

Outcomes

- The outcome of the intervention was change in the four basic dimensions of second-order change. Changes occurred in the world view of the system, in processes and structures, in culture, and in the purpose of the system.
- No follow-up study was conducted, and thus no data are available about the persistence of the change.

In summary, skeptics might find many conditions, not commonly encountered in other situations, that favored the change. From this perspective the above case study emphasizes how difficult it is to renew existing systems. Optimists might be encouraged by the fact that collaboration and professionalism, thorough preparation, and multidimensional intervention might result in positive outcomes. Recent studies on successful change efforts have shown that thorough preparation, going with the clients' needs, helping the clients to be aware of the need for a change and accepting it (readiness), and multi-dimensional interventions are positively related to success in terms of implementing the change (Clark & Burke 1984).

SUMMARY

The "new" and "renew" strategies to deal with second-order change are actually two poles of the same continuum. Figure 9.1 shows this continuum.

The literature survey of case studies pointed out that in each case a "new" element was present. The most common element was a new top manager, usually an outsider, not committed to old ideas and existing

Figure 9.1. The "Renew" and "New" Strategies as Poles of the Same Continuum

RENEWAL				NEW
SAME SYSTEM SAME SITE	NEW MANAGER ONLY	NEW MANAGER NEW TOP TEAM ONLY	NEW MANAGER NEW TOP TEAM NEW PERSONNEL	NEW MANAGEMENT NEW PERSONNEL A NEW SITE

Source: Provided by the authors.

dominant coalitions, who was willing to invest his energy in reorganization, and already had some basic ideas about the desired future. The case study analysis pointed out that the more the intervention included "new" elements, the less difficult it was to change the system. Hence, as one moves along the above continuum toward the right-hand side the less resistance to change occurs.

The reversal of the change of the innovative schools shows that second-order planned change can be reversed, even after the change has been implemented, institutionalized, and accepted, if important interests in the environment oppose it. Further, it shows that irreversibility is not a differentiating feature of second-order change. In order for one to understand the conditions under which second-order planned change is irreversible, one has to examine specific internal and external processes and the interactions between them.

The case analysis suggested the following proposition: The more an organization is dependent on outside systems that oppose its changes, the less the chance that the change will persist over time.

For a second-order change to persist under the above conditions, the organization will have to find alternative support systems and redefine its relevant environment. Using the terms provided by Ferguson (1980) and Aldrich (1979), the organization will have to find a new "niche" and to "network." And, last, the outcome of second-order change needs to be measured mainly by its persistence over time, not just by its implementation.

10

The "Top-Down" and "Bottom-Up" Strategies

Approaches to transformation can be classified into two basic categories: those which attempt to bring change through the upper echelons of the organization and those which attempt to bring change through the lower echelons of the organization. Most of the approaches described in this book have been top-down and collaborative. The focus has been on the roles and behavior of managers and management consultants in initiating, facilitating, and managing the change. Training programs, models, and approaches that may help managers to become transformation leaders have been described and emphasized. Participative and collaborative methods have been important for the success of the change effort.

Some of the approaches we have described represent the bottom-up strategy. Networking (Adams 1983), paradigm reframing (Nicoll 1980), and consciousness raising (Culbert 1976) are basically bottom-up approaches. Bottom-up strategy involves problems and difficulties many managers and practitioners tend to avoid. The main turf of this strategy is power, politics, and conflict management; this strategy deals not only with organizations but also with communities and social movements. The purpose of this chapter is to concentrate on the bottom-up strategy, to clarify its context and its basic principles. It will both deepen our understanding of the complexity of transforming existing systems and provide us with a view not many managers and practitioners are acquainted with.

Case examples of bottom-up transformation can be found mainly in the literature on community development and change, and on social movements (Lewis & Lewis 1977; Heller & Monahan 1977; Lees & Mayo 1984). Not many examples of this strategy are available in the literature on management and organizations. One may construe from this fact two possible explanations: either this phenomenon is very rare in work places or, if it exists, it is seen by scientists as belonging to the political and revolutionary domain. We believe there is a ring of truth in both perspectives. We believe that organizational change, particularly transformation, involves dealing with the political system, and aspects such as powerlessness that many consultants and managers tend to avoid. Further, the case examples presented hitherto have tended to coincide with the evolution-progress-growth perspective and not so much with the political perspective on organizational change.

TRANSFORMATION, POLITICS, AND POWER

Transformation, and particularly transformation through bottom-up strategy, entails political action and transforming the power structure in the organization. Bottom-up strategy is embedded in the conflict and political perspectives on change and stability in organizations. From the political perspective, organizations are coalitions of various interests. Employees, shareholders, managers, customers, suppliers, and government departments all impinge upon the organization; within it, personnel people, engineers, accountants, marketing persons, and production workers also have interests. Each group may have a distinct and different set of preferences for organizational action, and each group employs different criteria for evaluating organizational outcomes. What is good for marketing is not necessarily so characterized by production; what suits the employees may not coincide with the preference of managers.

Different groups have different values and cultures. Second-order change is about renegotiating dominant beliefs, values, and attitudes in the organization in order to introduce new beliefs, new systems, new order. Under such circumstances, visions and values are not apt to be shared, the likely result being a clash of wills. Successful change involves one person or group influencing the organization according to their values and vision. Change involves win-lose rather than win-win situations (Mangham 1979).

Power is an important concept for understanding life in organizations. In organizations, dominant coalitions maintain their power through decision-making processes, controlling conflicts, and preventing certain issues from being discussed. Yet one of the most important resources of power through which dominant coalitions maintain their position is their control over ideologies and socialization processes. Consensus or even homeostasis in organizations can be misleading. Dominant coalitions exercise their power to prevent members from having grievances by shaping their perceptions, cognition, and preferences in such a way that they accept their role in the existing order of things, either because they see or imagine no alternatives to it or because they see it as natural and unchangeable. The absence of grievances in an organization may represent a false or manipulated consensus (Kakabadse & Parker 1984).

Deluca (1984) suggests that organizational politics — or, more accurately, the sociopolitical context — is a major component in any large-scale change effort. The term "sociopolitical context" refers to the power, political activities, and informal social network among actors in an organizational setting. Furthermore, in second-order change efforts, the sociopolitical context should be viewed as the primary component or the ultimate target of the intervention; it is both context and object of the change effort. The purpose is not to present new processes of technologies but to alter the values and ideology of the organization in a desired direction. Real change is about changing dominant ideology and power structure.

Harrison (1972) argues that in many organizations the dominant culture (in terms of norms, values, and beliefs) is what he calls the "power culture." Power culture is characterized by centralization of power and decision making. An organization with a power culture attempts to dominate its environment and vanquish all opposition. It is unwilling to be subject to external law or power. Within the organization, those who are powerful strive to maintain absolute control over subordinates. Power cultures are proud and strong, able to move fast and react to threat or danger; they support "power-oriented," politically minded, "risk-taking" individuals; they are competitive, jealous of territory, and self-serving.

In a power culture, some people are powerful and some are powerless; relationships nearly always have a vertical (one-up, one-down) character; even colleague relationships are often arenas for competitive striving and gamesmanship. The power to define reality and relationships lies in the hands of a very small number of people at the center, and the ability of other members of the organization to raise and define issues is drastically curtailed. In power culture organizations, any move to explore the reality of the organization and any suggestion of a renegotiation are seen by the dominant coalition as a threat. There is some evidence that in this type of organization, top-down strategy for change does not work, and a bottom-up strategy should be attempted (Reason 1984).

There is much evidence that successful transformation leaders and consultants operate not only on the model of openness, frankness, and consensus, but also on the political model (McClean 1982). There is also much evidence that unsuccessful transformation is related to failure in changing the power structure in the organization (Kakabadse 1984; Nord 1976).

SOCIAL ACTION: EXAMPLE OF BOTTOM-UP STRATEGY

An example of bottom-up strategy aimed at radical change in social systems is the social action strategy. Social action became prominent in the community organization field in the 1960s and the early 1970s. This strategy is used today by community workers and local leaders for transforming social services and communities. In the field of community development and change, there is a distinction between two strategies: community development, which is a bottom-up strategy aimed at first-order changes, and community action, which is a bottom-up strategy aimed at second-order change. Community action strategy assumes that real change requires a redistribution of power within the system so that influences and resources are shared more equally (Baldock 1980).

A clear definition of community action is provided by Rothman (1974):

> Community Action presupposes a disadvantaged segment of the population that needs to be organized, perhaps in alliance with others, to make adequate demands on the larger community for increased resources or treatment more in accordance with social justice of democracy. Its practitioners aim at basic changes in major institutions or community practices. They seek redistribution of power, resources, or decision making in the community or changes in basic policies of formal organizations. (p. 5)

The change expert who becomes involved with community action groups is actively aligning himself or herself with one side of a struggle or controversy. Instead of maintaining objectivity, he or she is joining forces with the powerless segments in the organization, in the hope that both power and resources can be shared more equally. He or she is making a commitment in the direction of social change.

In many organizations the basic issue lies in the conflict between a small group of privileged and a large group of the underprivileged. The primary goal of the privileged is not so much to run an efficient organization as to maintain their position in power. In this context, top management will resist any attempt to change the system. Freire (1970) suggests that it is the task of the underprivileged to change the system, since only power that springs from weakness is strong enough to do this.

In other words, the top-down strategy cannot alter the basic dynamics of the situation. It can be changed only through the development of a critical consciousness and action by those farther down in the organization; they "will not gain their liberation by chance but through the praxis of their quest for it, through the recognition of the necessity to fight for it" (Freire 1970, p. 29).

This line of thought suggests that successful intervention could be brought about through the underprivileged, by helping them to understand the nature of their situation, by organizing and building support groups, and by developing networks and finding the strength to challenge those in power. This would enable them to attempt to establish a dialogue with the privileged and to begin to negotiate a new reality. Freire has suggested that this might be done through a "pedagogy of the oppressed," through which they might "emerge" from their submersion and acquire the ability to intervene in reality as it is unveiled.

A major aspect of community action is organizing people into community-based coalitions through which they can act to help themselves. These coalitions or networks are formed around specific issues. Examples of special interest groups of this type include women's political action groups and minority groups. In these instances the groups' members are relatively powerless and must confront policies made by others. Their purpose often revolves around their need to exert a greater degree of control over their own lives and to protect their rights and dignity.

Another aspect of community action involves allowing leadership to emerge from within the group. While outsiders may participate in organizing and in sharing concrete skills, in the long run, real leadership must emerge from within the group itself. Only then can there be a guarantee that the issues being attacked are those that have the most meaning to the membership. Only then can a real, ongoing power base be developed with the assurance of some degree of permanence.

Community action gives people a sense of their own power and potential. This is usually done through maximum participation of the group members in the decision-making process. Experience seems to show that bottom-up strategies work most effectively when people begin their work with actions concerning concrete issues that are amenable to change. When the group experiences success in dealing with the environment — when a necessary change has actually been accomplished — the group is on its way as a powerful force for change.

The concepts of networking and coalition are particularly important. It must be remembered that, with regard to many issues, differing interest groups may have stakes in their resolution. It is possible that many organizations can come together to lend their strength to a particular change process and then work separately on other projects. The use of networking and coalitions can also help to resolve the problem of members' involvement and strength. Small organizations provide members with the opportunity to be actively involved, to identify, and to feel that they are important. Networking of small organizations provides the power and strength for the action. The combination of active involvement and success experiences can be brought about when a number of small groups band together for a common cause.

BOTTOM-UP TRANSFORMATION LEADERSHIP

Unlike the transformation leader described in this book, the bottom-up transformation leader does not hold any formal management position. He or she works his or her way up, not down. We found that transformation leaders who work uphill have the same characteristics as those who work downhill. They also have a vision, they know how to communicate their vision to followers, and how to align their people with this vision. Their vision emerges from the needs of the powerless and from their own needs. They know how to translate vision into actual programs. They are strong leaders with immense energy and motivation. They are determined, unyielding, persistent, and persevering.

They have the capability to make the impossible, possible; the unattainable, attainable. They infuse their followers with high spirits and energy. More than other transformation leaders, they are political leaders. The bottom-up leaders are not naive. They rise from the system, criticize it, and align themselves with those who are trying to transform it. Their actions are well organized and well planned. Their protest is politically designed. They are experts at using mass communication and modern technology in the service of their protest. Lobbying, networking, and establishing a coalition are important elements in their actions. They are aware of opportunities and threats, and know how to deal with them successfully.

Yet, we find that bottom-up transformation leaders differ from the transformation managers mainly by having rebellious characteristics. What are these characteristics? They are the capacity to sense injustice and take a stand against it — the capacity and the courage to fight against what is sensed as unfair. May (1972) makes a distinction between the rebel and the revolutionary that is helpful. The revolutionary seeks the total destruction of the system, replacing it with another system that is no better. The revolutionary substitutes one injustice for another. Revolution may do more harm than good. The rebel is motivated from within; he or she is restless, opposes authority and restraints. The rebel seeks above all an internal change in tradition, values, beliefs, and attitudes without destroying the whole system. Whereas the revolutionary tends to collect power, the rebel does not seek power as an end but tends to share it.

The rebel fights not only for the relief of others but also for his or her personal integrity. For him or her these are but two sides of the same coin. The slave who kills his master is an example of the revolutionary. He can then only take his master's place and be killed in turn by later revolutionaries. The rebel is the one who realizes the master is as much imprisoned as he is, by the institution of slavery; he rebels against the system that permits slaves and masters. His rebellion, if successful, saves the master from the indignity of owning slaves. May argues that there is humanity in rebels but not in revolutionaries. Organizations need rebels to shake the fixed mores and rigid order; and this shaking, though painful, is necessary if the organization is to be saved from boredom, apathy, and rigidity.

The rebel is continually struggling to make the society into community:

> In our particular day, the rebel fights the mechanizing bureaucratic trends not because these in themselves are evil, but because they are the paramount modern channels for the dehumanizing of man, the stultifying loss of integrity, and the indignity of man. (May 1972, p. 227)

The rebel is always restless; when one frontier is conquered, he or she soon becomes ill-at-ease and pushes on to a new frontier.

CHANGE EXPERT CONTRIBUTIONS

Experts who participate in bottom-up strategy are entering a new area, political action. Yet their skills and knowledge in management, human relations, conflict management, and problem solving, and their awareness of human needs and social processes, can be of much help. Some of the unique attributes that change experts can bring to the tasks of bottom-up change are the following:

1. They have a unique awareness of common problems faced by organization members and the ability to distinguish between development and real change. In their work with organizations, practitioners become aware of recurring themes, of large numbers of people facing the same difficulties and the same obstacles. They become aware of the organization structure, culture, procedure, and ideology. They become aware of failing attempted solutions; of first- and second-order problem resolutions. When experts become aware of the need for a second-order change, they can encourage action for change by making the organization as a whole aware of problems and their consequences for the organization and its members; or they can join the organization members or some of them in an attempt to help them to act for change on their own behalf.

2. They can encourage the development of new leadership and provide leadership training. When the expert has intimate contacts with the powerless segment of the organization, he or she can try to encourage and support the growth of active self-help organizing that can make demands and negotiate a new order. For that purpose, the encouragement of self-management and local leadership is important and possible.

3. They can put their skills at the disposal of the powerless segments of the organization. Experts can make a significant contribution by sharing their skills with the people who are attempting to organize for change. Team building, effective communication, conflict management, and political action are a few examples.

4. They can help to coordinate the efforts of groups attempting to maintain action for change. Experts can familiarize themselves with all of the groups and organizations that are attempting to bring about fundamental changes. They can help to create networks and coalitions, and help coordinate the action for change.

5. They can recognize their responsibility to the powerless. There are many qualities that change experts can bring to a movement for social change. Not many experts want to become directly involved in bottom-up

strategy. Such involvement implies, for one thing, a recognition that when the needs of the powerless come into conflict with the desires of the powerful, one side should be supported against the other. The decision to leave objectivity behind and to take sides in a struggle is a personal one that brings with it many risks.

PART III

RESEARCH AND THEORIES

11

Organizational Change

Hitherto we have described strategies, approaches, models, and technologies for managing and facilitating organizational transformation. The focus has been on planned and managed change. However, strategies and approaches are based on studies and embedded in theoretical perspectives that provide explanations of why and how organizations develop and transform, the variables and the processes involved, and the relationships between specific variables. Most of the studies on organizational change do not distinguish between first- and second-order change; however, many of them deal with major changes and not just with minor improvements. Hence they set the stage for further investigation of this phenomenon.

In this chapter we will concentrate on studies that explain why organizations develop and change, or that describe the driving forces for change. These studies are focused more on the content of the change than on the process of organizational transformation (such a classification was made by Goodman and James 1982). Theories on the process of transformation will be the topic of Chapter 12.

In describing each perspective, we will try to answer the following questions:

1. Does it distinguish between different types of change?
2. What is the cause or the source of the change?
3. What is the implicit assumption about determinism? Is change beyond the capacity of people to manage and shape?
4. Is it ahistoric or historic in its perspective?

MANAGEMENT PERSPECTIVE

This perspective takes a proactive stance regarding second-order change. It emphasizes the role of management behavior in initiating and managing first- and second-order changes, in order to gain advantages over their competitors and to achieve a better adaptation to the changing environment. The source of change is within the organization, and change is triggered by management behavior, decision-making processes, choice making, and strategic planning.

Lindblom (1959) was among the first to note that the decision-making process can be used as a tool for two different types of change. He outlines two modes of decision making. The first one is the branch method, which is an approach to first-order change. It is a decision-making process that is built out of the current situation. A step-by-step method, it provides limited changes and improves immediate situations. The second method is called the root method. An approach to second-order change, it is a decision-making process that always starts with new assumptions and from a new perspective. The root method is not based on past experience or on present operations and processes; it is a method that changes the whole context of the problem and opens new directions for the organization.

The main focus of Vickers (1965) is on the policy-making process as an approach to second-order change. He describes two methods of policy making. The first, called the executive method, is a method for first-order change. It gives effect to policies by maintaining the course of affairs in line with current governing relations, norms, processes, and standards. The second, called policy making, is an approach to facilitating second-order change. It forms new governing relations and new systems of rules, norms, and values.

Davis (1982) provides one more managerial method of second-order change involving strategic decisions and planning. He distinguishes between strategies that change content, and thus improve current situations, and strategies that change context, and thus create new directions and options for the organization. Davis utilizes the terms "normal change" and "paradigm change," which he took from Kuhn's theory on scientific revolutions. Hence, according to Davis' conception, strategic decisions and strategic planning can change not only content but also context, and thus change the organization paradigm.

In the early 1970s, the notion of organizational change as an adaptation process came to be a common theme in the professional literature, and the management proactive perspective was developed further by the studies of Child (1972). He argues that the strategic choices made by decision makers are essential to understanding how organizations adapt to their environments. Specifically, Child suggests that the dominant coalition has autonomy over many variables that enable organizations to change radically and to adapt proactively, rather than merely to accommodate to uncontrollable changes.

As examples, Child shows that organizations can choose the environment or market in which they operate; they can manipulate and control their environment; they can choose technologies that grant them subsequent control; they can employ control systems to deal with their large size; and they can analyze and evaluate their environments in ways that enable them to adapt creatively to contingencies. We also prefer a less deterministic view of organizational change and contend that top management always retains a certain amount of discretion to choose courses of action that serve to align the organization's resources with its environmental opportunities, and to serve the values and preferences of management. This view is dialectical rather than free-will-oriented; it is the degrees of strategic freedom and the reciprocal causality that are important, rather than an absolute choice between determinism and free will, between causes and effects.

To summarize, the above studies exemplify the perspective that emphasizes the importance of management behavior in the process of second-order change. The major source of the change exists within the organization, specifically in the decision-making system. From this perspective, first- and second-order changes can be deliberately planned and managed. Management perspective represents a micro level of theorizing. It focuses on specific internal variables in specific organizations.

INNOVATION AND CREATIVITY PERSPECTIVE

The human capability for creative thinking, creative behavior, and innovation is a major source of organizational change. This perspective is the most compatible with the strategic choice, or management, perspective. The source of the change is in the system and in the unique capabilities of people to be innovative and creative.

The concept that the process of second-order change involves creative thinking is expressed implicitly in many studies on creative thinking and creative problem solving (J. L. Adams 1974; Markley 1976; Watzlawick et al. 1974). The many studies in this field emphasize two important aspects of second-order change. The first is that in order to pass through or reach second-order change, one has to deliberately set aside the assumptions that are conventionally made about reality, and engage in techniques, activities, and processes that open up one's self to different or new perceptions of reality (de Bono 1971).

The second aspect is that the process of creativity involves higher states of consciousness and, in many cases, the use of intuition, imagination, and visioning (J. L. Adams 1974). From this perspective, the organization's rules and basic assumptions are an inseparable part of the organization's problems. Watzlawick et al. (1974), for example, argue that second-order change is ". . . an invention outside the logical process . . . a central act of imagination" (p. 23).

Kirton (1980) has developed a theory of change and innovation. He argues that individuals have characteristically different styles of creativity, problem solving, and decision making. Adapters tend to operate cognitively within the confines of the appropriate, conceptually accepted paradigm within which a problem is generally initially perceived. Innovators, by contrast, are more liable to intuitively treat the enveloping paradigm as part of the problem. Presumably, the proportion of innovators will affect whether and how quickly organizations can change their paradigm.

Some scholars write on specific stages of innovation (Daft 1978); others study the effects of individual, organizational, and contextual variables on innovations and change. Kimberly and Evanesco's (1981) and Moch's (1976) studies show that organizational variables such as size, specialization, functional differentiation, and decentralization affect an organization's innovation and, hence, its capacity to radically change itself.

Hage (1980) makes a distinction between output innovations, which are the new products and services that a specific organization produces within a year relative to its size, and process innovations, which are new throughput technologies, processes, and procedures. He defines second-order change as radical innovation in input-output and technology. He reviews the recent studies on this issue and summarizes the findings in propositions such as "Centralized organizations can introduce highly radical innovations if the dominant coalition has positive attitudes towards change and indeed pursues a pro-change policy" (p. 93) and "The more committed the dominant coalition is to the introduction of change and the greater the concentration of specialists, the more likely there is to be a radical innovation" (p. 194).

To summarize, creativity and innovation are important driving forces in the second-order change process. They are characteristics of human behavior in organizational settings. The main focus of these studies is on intraorganizational processes, and their effect on the environment and society. Like the previous perspective, this one takes a more voluntaristic standpoint, seeing change as dependent mainly on the behavior of the organization's leadership and members.

POLITICAL PERSPECTIVE

This perspective suggests that organizations are in part political entities (Tuchman 1977) and that they have many similarities to government (Denhardt 1971). The main focus of this perspective is on dynamic political processes in the organization, and their effects on change and stability. The political perspective challenges the humanistic perspective with a view that sees incompatible aims and rewards in organizational life, and points to decisions and conflicts as the important area for investigating the effects of these incompatibilities (Huff 1980).

Organizations are characterized by a delicate balance of power; by tension; by conflicts between interest groups, ideologies, and values; and by struggles for power, dominance, and rewards (Pondy 1967). Conflict is an inherent attribute of human interaction. Change is the result of political campaigns and the triumph of a coalition of one interest group and its values, ideology, and interest over others (Schein 1977). Organizational change entails rearrangement of existing relationships. Group survival dictates abandoning individual views and accommodating uncomfortable and even opposing views (Huff 1980), and the process of organizational second-order change includes a political campaign and the establishment of support groups, networking, and propaganda (Adams 1983).

Zald and Berger (1978) studied how interest groups and social movements in organizations can constitute an important source of second-order change. They describe organizational coups, bureaucratic insurgency, and mass movements as three types of social movements that enable organizations to adapt through major changes in top management, in goals, or in linkages to external elements.

Harrison and Pitt (1984) distinguish between adjustments and change, arguing that change involves both structure and power. Kakabadse (1984) distinguishes between maintenance change and visionary change, in which the existing ideology, values, roles, and power structure change. He argues that change does not come about by presenting rational truth or through sharing, caring, and participative models:

> Change is about renegotiating certain dominant values and attitudes in the organization in order to introduce new systems. Under such circumstances visions and values are not likely to be shared, with the likely result being a clash of wills. Successful change involves one person or group influencing the organization according to their values. Under such circumstances, change is a painful experience for those involved. (p. 182)

A more radical perspective on power and change is presented in studies by Freire (1970), Alinsky (1972), Nord (1976), and Reason (1984). Organizations are viewed as oppressive political systems in which dominant coalitions resist any change that might diminish their power and privileges. Change is a revolutionary process in which the oppressed develop awareness of the situation, and empower themselves with the ability to intervene in reality and change it so that power and privileges are shared more equally.

To summarize, the model of man and the model of organization suggested by the above studies emphasize dimensions and aspects neglected in the literature on planned change. The dark side of man is emphasized. Organizations are perceived as political entities in which dominant coalitions manipulate their power in order to preserve the status quo and maintain their privileges. Change involves power and usually comes from the bottom up.

NATURAL SELECTION PERSPECTIVE

This perspective on organizational change does not concede much importance to strategic choices and human creativity; indeed, it provides alternatives to models of managerial choice and planned change. The natural selection perspective has certain basic premises about change. First, change and development are functions of environmental changes. Second, the persistence of change has meaning only when viewed in terms of a population of organizations being differentially selected by the environment — after the selection has occurred, we can say that the organization has adapted. Third, managerial choice, planning, and changing are viewed as unnecessary or misleading explanations for the process of adaptation.

This perspective provides a post hoc explanation for organizational change and adaptation. Campbell (1969) proposes a three-step evolutionary model that Aldrich and Pfeffer (1976) elaborate. First, variations in structure occur. From an evolutionary perspective, the source of these variations (random, borrowed, or created by decision makers) is irrelevant. People may adapt to an environment, but all they have done collectively is provide a pool of variations in the population of organizations. In the second step, selection, the environment differentially selects one or more of these variations. Other organizations fail, which removes their variations from the pool. In the third step, retention, variations that were selected are retained. This model ascribes little importance to people's ability to adapt.

Aldrich (1979) elaborates the natural selection perspective by using the variations-selection-retention model. His book integrates a huge array of literature in such a way that he presents the natural selection model as a powerful and researchable alternative to models that draw primarily on managerial choice. Besides exploring the implication of this perspective on change, he directly challenges Child's (1972) arguments on strategic choice. Specifically, Aldrich argues that there are severe constraints on managers' choices of new environments and on their abilities to influence their environments. He argues that managers' perceptions of reality are so homogeneous as to make truly novel strategic choices improbable. These and other limits on managerial choice suggest that we must look elsewhere for explanations of the differential adaption and survival of organizations.

A number of other researchers have empirically tested and extended the natural selection model, or have employed it in their modeling. Notable among them are Nielsen and Hannan (1977), Brittain and Freeman (1980), Caroll (1982), Padgett (1981), and Rundall and McClain (1982). Hannan and Freeman (1977), for example, studied populations of organizations and argued that unstable environments select those organizations which have developed a generalist structure — that is, have not optimally adapted to any single environmental configuration but are optimal over the entire set of configurations (p. 946).

The strongest advocacy stand is taken by McKelvey (1982), who argues that systematics, which is the science of classification, is a prerequisite to understanding organizational development and change.

That is, we cannot develop an understanding of how organizations adapt until we can discriminate among different kinds of organizations, trace the linkages of these organizational differences, and develop procedures to identify and categorize organizational forms into classes. The tasks of systematics are taxonomy, evolution, and classification. Of these, evolution bears most heavily on our understanding of adaptation and change.

McKelvey's exposition of the evolutionary perspective is axiomatic and propositional. We can convey how he views organizational change by paraphrasing a few of his succinct axioms and propositions. Environments of organizations change. Organizations respond to environmental forces. Thus, organizations respond or adapt to changing environments. This adaptation to changing environments accounts for the evolution of organizations — the differences are incremental, sometimes revolutionary — changes in structures, processes, and competencies over successive generations. The specific course of organizational evolution and change is ultimately determined by characteristics of environments. In essence, adaptation to a changing environment explains organizational differences and, thus, change and evolution. To understand change, one has to study the differences of the environment.

To summarize, three works exemplify different natural selection approaches to development and change. Hannan and Freeman (1977) predict the occurrence and change of structures based on changes in environmental niches. Aldrich (1979) elaborates the three-stage natural selection model. Change derives from variations in organizational forms, one source of which is managerial choices that are selected and retained. McKelvey (1982) presents an axiomatic model of evolution that explains change in terms of organizations adapting to changing environments.

All the above works downplay or eschew the importance of managerial choice, and all of them view the source of change as an inconsequential artifact of evolution. They take a broad macro perspective by aggregating organizations into groups and populations.

ORGANIZATION AND ENVIRONMENT INTERACTION PERSPECTIVE

This level of analysis focuses on how organizations interface with environments, specifically, on how managers, in their interactions with their environments, make choices about their interactions. These choices, not the environment itself, are the most important explanation for change. From this perspective, second-order change is a choice made by dominant coalitions for a better interaction with the organizational environment.

Pfeffer and Salancik (1978) argue that there are two basic ways in which organizations develop and change: "The organization can adapt and change to fit environmental requirements, or the organization can attempt to alter the environment so that it fits the organization's capabilities" (p. 106). Organizations adapt their environments to them by such tactics as merging with other organizations, diversifying, co-opting important others through an interlocking directorate, and engaging in political activities to influence matters such as regulation.

Several studies have addressed the relation among strategies, organizational change, and the organizational environment. Hage (1980) investigates how a turbulent and hostile environment (low growth, inflation, regulation, and competition) would affect the change strategies used by top managers for organization survival. Using published data and field interviews, he finds that success in eight major domestic industries depended upon achieving either the lower cost or the greatest differentiation.

Lindsay and Rue (1980) and Khandwalla (1976) find that complex, uncertain environments elicit comprehensive and elaborate planning strategies. Davis (1982) investigates the relations between the organizational environment and two types of strategies: incremental strategy, which changes content, and revolutionary strategy, which changes context. Davis argues that top managers have the choice of applying either of the two strategies, depending on what they want to accomplish and on the type of the organization's environment.

Kurke (1981) examines how strategies change or persist over time. He uses a quasi-longitudinal laboratory design to test how uncertainty of the environment and frequency of the change in it affect the choice and perpetuation of decision-making strategies. Kurke finds that the frequency of change and uncertainty interact to produce a tradition of change among decision makers. This tradition of change enables decision makers to adapt their organizations quickly, by rapidly changing their strategies.

While the above studies focus on the relations among strategy, environment, and change, the following studies focus on the relations among structure, environment, and change. Social scientists accept the idea that the environment somehow affects structure: Burns and Stalker

(1961), Woodward (1965), and Lawrence and Lorsch (1976) convincingly demonstrate this relationship. Investigators have studied many different variables that may explain how and why the environment affects structure and structural change (DuBick 1978; Marks 1977; Segal 1974). Meyer (1979), for example, finds that bureaucratic structures do not change as rapidly as do shifts in the environment. As a result, the fit between organizations and environments is greatest at the time of formation and declines gradually thereafter, until reorganization or replacement of existing units becomes necessary. "Structure, which is initially an accommodation to the environment, eventually becomes an impediment to change and must be altered fundamentally" (p. 205).

Some explicitly combine strategy and structure, usually typologically, and study their relation to organizational change and adaptation. Most of the studies in this area were done by Miller (1982), Miller and Friesen (1980a, 1980b), and Miles and Snow (1978). Miller and Friesen propose a typology to categorize the various forms, or archetypes, that organizations use during periods of "revolutionary" changes and "momentum" changes. They argue that, in general, organizations are usually sluggish in adapting to environmental changes; there is tremendous momentum built into organizational structures that precludes rapid, revolutionary change.

However, the authors found that when organizations do change, there are revolutionary simultaneous reversals in many structural and strategic variables. Although organizations normally are resistant to change due to momentum, when they do change and adapt, they change in a revolutionary rather than an evolutionary fashion.

The archetypes they propose are the most typical configurations found during the revolutionary transitions. For instance, the archetype called "consolidation"

> ... is usually triggered by a perceived need to retrench and consolidate. For example, the firm may have diversified too quickly and into some unprofitable areas, or resources may have been taxed due to overexpansion. The decline in profit and the sense that the firm is out of control cause the realization that some sort of change is necessary. (Miller & Friesen 1980a, p. 282)

To summarize, the interactive perspective relates change and adaptation to both the environment and managerial choices. The studies on it represent a diverse set of theories, approaches, and methods. The level of analysis and theorizing is micro level; and the standpoint on human capacity to initiate, plan, and implement change is neither voluntaristic nor deterministic but interactive.

DEVELOPMENTAL STAGES PERSPECTIVE

From the developmental perspective, organizations, like all living systems, develop, grow, and change. In this perspective there are two groups. The first takes the life-cycle perspective. Organizations grow, mature, and decline. The second takes a more open-ended perspective, analyzing stages over a period of time.

Life Cycle

Much has been written about the organizational life cycle (Adizes 1979a; Haire 1959; Kimberly & Miles 1980; Lavoie & Culbert 1978; Lippitt 1969; Quinn & Cameron 1983). However, most of this literature is conceptual rather than empirical. Haire (1959) was among the first to argue that it is possible to talk of lawful processes involved in the growth of organizations, just as we can talk about laws of growth for living systems. Haire argues that the growth process in organizations is subject to natural laws, and that the discovery of these laws is the most reasonable approach to understanding the process of change in organizations.

The aforementioned studies suggest that the organizational life cycle consists of five stages: birth, growth, maturity, revival, and decline. This perspective suggests that each stage manifests integral complementaries among variables of environment, strategy, structure, and decision-making methods; that organizational growth and increasing environmental complexity cause each stage to exhibit certain significant differences from all other stages; and that organizations tend to move in a linear progression through the five stages, proceeding from birth to decline. This is implicitly a deterministic perspective. The nature of the change and its direction are predetermined. Lippitt (1969), however, suggested a more voluntaristic model with only three stages: birth, youth, and maturity. He argues that organizational decline can be avoided. It occurs only because management fails to notice the need for adjustment to changes in the environment. Adizes (1979a) has also developed a developmental model that allows for renewal.

Miller and Friesen (1983) empirically tested the life-cycle models. The results seemed to support the prevalence of complementarities among variables within each of the five stages and the predicted interstage differences. They did not, however, show that organizations proceed through the stages in the proposed sequence. It is important to note that life-cycle models postulate that the transition from one stage to the next is slow, smooth, and evolutionary. Incremental changes and developments, rather than jumps and discontinuities, are typical of the process.

The life-cycle perspective is a new micro version of the old "rise and fall" theories in history and sociology. Societies and cultures rise and fall, in a deterministic process inherent in the nature of all living systems. At the beginning of this century, Spengler wrote "Every culture passes through the age-phases of the individual man. Each has its childhood, youth, manhood, and . . . old age" (in Etzioni 1964, p. 23).

Developmental Stages

This approach is less conceptual and more empirically based. Unlike the life-cycle perspective, it shows that the transition from one stage to another is preceded by crisis, chaos, and muddling through.

Greiner (1972) provides an empirical model which postulates that growing organizations pass through five distinguishable phases of development, each of which is terminated by a crisis and revolution. Each phase is strongly affected by the previous phase. The future of the organization is much more a function of historical forces and decisions than it is of present environmental dynamics. Organizational structure, management practices, rewards systems, and control systems change dramatically in times of revolutionary crisis. Then comes the evolutionary stage, in which new practices, managerial perspectives, structures, processes, and employee behavior are institutionalized.

During the developmental process, the organization's processes and structures become more rigid and predictable, and more resistant to change even when they become outmoded. Top managers who are unaware of the growth phase of their particular organization, along with associated characteristics and problems, are likely to preside over an organization that is frozen in time. These managers may be unable to take advantage of opportunities, and the organization will be unable to adapt to predictable crises. These organizations, which cannot participate in and adapt to revolutionary crises, have good chances of failing.

Greiner's model is based on empirical data that he gathered during the 1960s while working as an organizational development practitioner. It is an attempt to portray the qualitative changes in an organization longitudinally. The main focus of the model is on internal processes and managerial practices. It does not stress the turbulent environment as a source of crises and change. It emphasizes continued linear growth and does not deal with phenomena of decay or decline. Greiner locates the management system as the main lever for evolutionary and revolutionary growth.

Researchers at Stanford University developed an empirical model based on Greiner's approach (Elgin 1977). It is a rather detailed model that deals with the extremes of growth and decline, and the limits to manageability of complex social systems. The model analyzes the process of evolutionary growth, which inevitably ends in crisis followed by either transformational change or termination.

These investigators describe four stages of evolutionary growth:

1. High growth. Growth in scale, complexity, and interdependence contributes to greater efficiency. Creativity is high and management is entrepreneurial. However, with increasing growth there arises a need for greater coordination and control; the structure becomes rigid. Security takes the place of creativity.

2. Greatest efficiency. System output is increasing but at a decreasing rate. Yet an impetus toward more growth prevails.

3. Diseconomics of scale. This stage is based on the economic law of diminishing returns: At some size, nothing is to be gained from greater size. However, the pressure of societal and organizational forces pushes the system into greater activity. The large increments in efficiency derived from centralization, decentralization, and technological innovation are approaching limits of saturation or exhaustion.

4. Crisis. The problems of the preceding stage are amplified to intolerable extremes. Internal forces and a turbulent, unpredictable environment contribute to precipitating the system into crisis. A tension between the need for radical change, and the organizational inertia and resistance to radical change threatens to break up the system.

5. Transformation or cessation of functioning. This stage is a function of three possible management strategies:
   a. Muddling through. This is an incremental approach often associated with Lindblom (1959). It is a cautious approach that does not question the soundness of underlying premises — what

was successful in the past should be equally successful in the present and near future. It is more of the same, a means of borrowing time, waiting for rescue from outside. The outcome is continued deterioration.

b. Chaos. Persistence in implementing dysfunctional policies can heighten the descent into chaos.

c. Authoritarian response. A typical response to inefficiency, threat, crisis, and chaos is an authoritarian management. Coordination and control structures are simplified and rationalized. Yet, in the longer term, the response will create a schism between the system and its environment.

One more empirical model explaining organizational developmental stages is provided by Miller and Friesen (1980a). In a retrospective case study conducted on business firms in the United States, these researchers tried to locate and identify patterns of organizational transitions. They found six patterns of transitions:

1. Revitalization. This transition describes the comprehensive and often dramatic movement away from traditions, rigidity, and conservatism, and toward adaptiveness, vigilance, and diversification. It is characterized by a new set of strategies and drastic change in the nature of the firm and its structure.

2. Consolidation. This pattern is characterized by replacement of an entrepreneurial manager with a more conservative professional manager, slowing down and consolidation of operations, control increases, and hiring of technocrats and experts. The emphasis is on stabilization and efficiency.

3. Stagnation. This is characterized by passive leadership, a "wait and see" attitude, diminishing control, and almost no innovation.

4. Centralization. This is characterized by a homogeneous management team that makes most of the key decisions by itself.

5. Maturation. This is the typical phase of old, large, complex systems. The decision-making process becomes increasingly decentralized.

6. Troubleshooting. This is the period of working hard to cope with ongoing difficulties. Decentralization is increased. Risk-taking innovation and proactiveness are reduced.

The researchers came to the conclusion that system changes tend to come in packages. Given a few changes of a certain type, a host of secondary alterations is likely to follow. Organizations are complexes of interrelated systems. One change provokes another. Striving for balance along one dimension may be harmful if it creates excesses or imbalances in others. The study proposes that organizational change is not only a determinable process of adjustments to environmental change but also, at the same time, a proactive human process. To put it in the researchers' words:

> While it is certainly true that some of the transitions portray environment as an incentive for changes in organization structure, strategy, and decision making style, it is equally true that past strategies, choices, and modes of behavior influence the nature of the [organization] environment. (Miller & Friesen 1980a, p. 289)

In sum, the developmental stage perspective provides empirical change models that can deepen the understanding of the dynamics of change and the stages through which organizations evolve. The models also provide knowledge about the nature of evolutionary periods and revolutionary actions as a source for changes both in the environment and in the organization. As organizations grow and evolve, they change; the problems of management change; and ultimately the organization's policies, procedures, and structures may have to change.

LEARNING PERSPECTIVE

This perspective is characterized mainly by the works of Argyris (1977) and Argyris and Schon (1978). The main focus is on how learning and reasoning processes affect first- and second-order change. Argyris and Schon suggest that there are important differences in the meaning created when people espouse their views versus acting them out. Individuals are often unaware of these differences. The source of meaning is in the theories of action people use, not those they espouse. These theories are reinforced by learning systems of society.

Organizational change is a learning process affected by the organizational and environmental conditions and by theories of action held by the organization's members. Organizations can create conditions that may significantly influence what individuals frame as the problem, design as a solution, and produce as action to solve the problem. However, individuals may also bring to the learning situation biases, beliefs, and theories that are relatively independent of the organization's requirements. These theories significantly influence how they solve problems and make choices.

Whenever an organizational error, deviation, or problem is detected and corrected, or solved without questioning or altering the underlying values or assumptions of the system, the learning is "single loop." The term is borrowed from cybernetics, where, for example, a thermostat is defined as a single loop learner. It is programmed to detect states of "too cold" or "too hot," and to correct the situation by turning the heat on or off. If the thermostat asked itself, for instance, why it was set at 68 degrees, or why it was programmed as it was, it would be a "double loop" learner. Hence double loop learning occurs when problems are solved or an organization creates a new state of adaptation by examining and altering the governing variables in which the problems or the misadaptation occurred.

The importance of this perspective is that it adds the learning aspects of initiating and managing second-order change, and it makes a distinction between first- and second-order change through learning processes. Individuals have the capacity to learn and deliberately change their organizations radically.

PHENOMENOLOGICAL PERSPECTIVE

Several conceptual articles have appeared that begin to explain, from a more phenomenological perspective, why structures appear, endure, and radically change. Most of the authors of these articles draw upon Berger and Luckman's (1967) work on the social construction of reality, and upon Weick's (1979) work on enactment. Like the explanation of enactment, phenomenological explanations of change rely on introspection, description, and interpretation to understand how social actors construct their life worlds and come to share them as if they were real.

From this perspective, environmental changes affect organizational change through the mediation of powerful members who perceive and enact them in various ways, and then translate them into decisions for restructuring. The focus of this perspective is more on organization members' "shared understandings" than on external factors. Second-order change is, first of all, change in the organization's world view, shared meanings, interpretive schemes, or what Weick calls schemata, which bring second-order change in structure and procedure.

An example of this approach is the work of Ranson, Hinings, and Greenwood (1980). They propose an integrative framework — a unified theoretical and methodological framework — that draws on three abstract conceptual categories. The first, provinces of meaning, embodies an interpretive scheme for organizational members that enables them to understand their worlds as meaningful and that provides values for implementing structures. The second, dependencies of power, enables different factions to resolve their alternative interpretive schemes and value preferences. The third category is contextual constraints that are inherent in characteristics of the organization and the environment. These frameworks imply that organizational change comes about by changing members' provinces of meaning, the dependencies of power, and the contextual constraints.

Pfeffer (1981) argues that organizations are systems of shared meanings and beliefs, in which a critical management activity involves the construction and maintenance of belief systems that assume continued compliance, commitment, and positive affect on the part of participants. Management creates and maintains these paradigms (belief systems) through language, symbolism, and ritual. In Pfeffer's symbolic world, second-order change would come about by managers applying different languages, rituals, symbols, and stories to change participants' shared meanings.

Daft and Weick (1984) present a model of organizations as interpretation systems. The two variables underlying the model are (1) management beliefs about the analyzability of the external environment and (2) organizational intrusiveness. These variables are the basis for four modes of interpretation: enacting, discovering, undirected viewing, and conditioned viewing. The model explains interpretation behaviors ranging from environmental enactment to passive observation.

Bartunek (1984) studied the relationship between second-order change in interpretive schemes and in structure. She shows that second-order change in interpretive schemes occurs through a dialectical process in which old and new interpretive schemes interact, resulting in synthesis. These changing interpretive schemes are both affected by and modify the organization's structure, but the relationship betwen schemes and structure is not direct. Rather, it is mediated by the actions that members take in response to changing understanding or structure, and the emotional reactions they have to these changes. An environmental impetus is probably necessary for change to begin, but the manner in which the environment affects the change depends on the organization's present interpretive schemes and structure.

To summarize, the phenomenological perspective provides a dynamic model that focuses on explaining how internal and external triggers for change are filtered through, and interpreted by, the organization members' shared meanings or interpretive schemes, and how changes in these interpretive schemes affect second-order change in structure, technology, and procedures.

INTEGRATED MODEL

The above perspectives on organizational change can be integrated into a more comprehensive and dynamic model that describes the driving forces for change and the relationships among them. Three types of driving forces for change were indicated:

1. Internal driving forces. These forces are strategic choices, human creativity and innovation, inner conflicts, emergence of new needs and new belief systems, and the inner urge or tendency of organizations to grow.

2. External driving forces. For their survival, organizations must adapt to their environments; there must be a fit between the organization and its environment. Changes in the market (new products, new technology), changes in population, changes in the economic situation, changes in policy, and cultural changes all push the organization to change in order to adapt to the new environment.

3. The interaction between internal and external driving forces. While internal and external forces can push the organization toward change, it is also possible that the interaction between the two forces will lead to change. This interaction creates choices that organization members might take. These choices are created by the human capacity to learn, to innovate, to be creative, to evaluate alternatives, and to make strategic choices. Further, there is a reciprocal relationship between internal and external forces. The creation of a new product or technology affects the organizational environment and vice versa.

Although internal, external, and interactive forces tend to push the organization to change in order to adapt or find a new fit, these forces are filtered through many organizational characteristics, processes, and structures. These elements may hinder or facilitate the change. Organizational characteristics are the more enduring, structural aspects of organizations, such as the type of organization (bureaucracy or total institution, for instance). Centralization and bureaucratization were found to be hindrances to innovations (Meyer 1974). Business organizations were found to be more vulnerable to changes in their environments than public organizations (Jackson & Morgan 1982).

Organizational change is a dynamic, systemic process that consists of elements affecting each other in multidirectional ways. The organization not only is changed by driving forces but also changes its external forces, internal forces, and the fit between external and internal forces.

Figure 11.1 shows the proposed relationships among the four dimensions. The model proposes that the implementation of organizational change is dependent upon the following factors:

1. The existence of internal driving forces for change and the relationship among these forces
2. The existence of external forces and the relationships among them
3. The existence of organizational characteristics that hinder or inhibit the change, and the relationships among them

Figure 11.1 Integrated Model

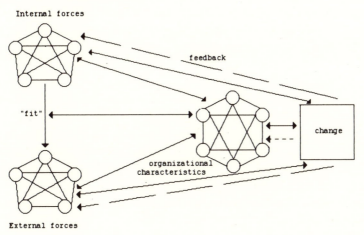

Source: Prepared by the authors.

4. The relationships among internal forces, external forces, and organizational characteristics, and the need to find a new "fit" among these forces
5. The existence of feedback loops affecting the change process by organizational sensing, monitoring, and learning.

An example of the complicated relationships among the four dimensions is the study of Hage (1980). He found that centralized organizations can introduce highly radical innovations if the dominant coalition has positive attitudes toward change and pursues a pro-change policy, and the organization is in crisis.

12

Transformation Theories

The purpose of this chapter is to describe theoretical perspectives explaining the process of second-order change in social systems. Unlike most of the previously mentioned studies, these studies and theories take a historical, evolutionary perspective explaining the differences between first- and second-order changes. They focus more on how living systems transform than on what is transformed and why. The theoretical perspectives described here also share the view that the evolution of social systems is shaped by both deterministic and nondeterministic processes that are mutually related. Hence, they share some basic assumptions about second-order change and therefore create a cluster of perspectives. This cluster of theories provides the context, the theoretical basis for the practice of organization transformation.

The theoretical perspectives presented in this chapter are the following:

1. Scientific revolution
2. Neo-Marxian
3. Order through fluctuations
4. Evolution and consciousness
5. Growth
6. Catastrophe
7. Futurist

In the final section, an effort will be made to integrate these perspectives into a comprehensive framework and to analyze some of the assumptions underlying them.

SCIENTIFIC REVOLUTION PERSPECTIVE

The common denominator of this perspective is the utilization of Kuhn's (1970) theory of scientific revolution for explaining the phenomena of first- and second-order change in organizations. Hence, following Kuhn's terminology, first-order change is called "normal change," and second-order change is called "paradigm change," or "transformation."

Kuhn describes and analyzes the dynamics of scientific development. He uses the term "knowledge paradigm" to denote

> the collection of ideas within the confines of which scientific inquiry takes place, the assumed definition of what are legitimate problems and methods, the accepted practice and point of view with which the student prepares for membership in the scientific community, the criteria for choosing problems to attack, the rules and standards of scientific practice. (1970, p. 11)

Kuhn portrays not only the formulation of the knowledge paradigm but also the dynamics with which such paradigms are created and replaced. He argues that science does not advance incrementally, with the discoveries of today being built on the theories and discoveries of yesterday. Rather, it advances by periods of evolution ("normal changes") and revolutions ("paradigmatic shifts").

Kuhn's main finding is that the scientific community, at any point in time, shares a common world view, a reality concept, a paradigm. He found that a dominant paradigm (for instance, the Newtonian paradigm) exists during each scientific period and provides the basic structure, the logical framework, within which all scientific thinking and experimenting is done. Thus, all experiments tend to support and entrench the dominant paradigm of the moment. The paradigm develops through scientific findings but remains basically unchanged. Kuhn calls it "normal change" or "normal science."

During this time the old paradigm is challenged. Contradictions within it are noted, and unexplained phenomena are pointed out. Contrary experimental evidence is gathered. Instances in which the theory does not predict are described. Some cling to and defend the old theory. They add new laws to explain the exceptions. They question the experimental expertise of their opponents. They accuse them of heresy.

Scientific revolutions occur in two complementary ways. The first is the accumulation of enough scientific observations contradicting the old paradigm and the existence of enough scientists who keep gathering data seeking new formulations to account for these observations. The second is through the vision of able individuals (like Darwin, Newton, or Einstein) who suggest an overarching new concept, a new world view so different, so stimulating, so "above the battle" that defending the existing ideas becomes less important than exploring the ideas suggested by the emergent paradigm.

The existence and dominance of a new paradigm are strongly related to the creation of new concepts, metaphors, and language. New paradigms always represent ideas that cannot be explained or articulated in the language of the old paradigm. Not only new language is needed, but also new scientific methods and tools. The revolutionary change occurs with a leap to a new level of perception. This perception usually comes from an overview that realigns thinking into a new and more enlightening framework. The old paradigm does not vanish; rather, it finds its niche within the new one.

Organization theoreticians argue that the way organizations are operating — their world view, culture, and belief system — actually represents a paradigm, an organizing paradigm (Markley 1976; Sheldon 1980). Further, they argue that organizations pass through periods of normal changes, in which they develop and change within the current paradigm, and periods of revolutionary changes, in which the organizational paradigm itself changes.

The overall pattern of change suggests that when crises are faced and normal modes of problem solving and management are first seen to be inadequate, calls often arise for going "back to basics." Failure here is usually followed by muddling through and massive tinkering with the system (Lindblom 1959). When this does not work, breakthroughs in basic approach are sought. Finding such breakthroughs inevitably entails the reexamination and restructuring of the fundamental assumptions, beliefs, and mental maps that underlie conventional wisdom. It leads to transformed perceptions of reality, to altered ways of organizing and behaving. It also stimulates a great deal of resistance as applications of the new paradigm are attempted (Nicoll 1980).

However, Kuhn's theory is also applicable for understanding the process of change in the science of organizations in both theory and practice. Organization paradigmatic change is intertwined with paradigmatic change in theory, inquiry, and practice. Kuhn's theory implies, therefore, that if one wants to help organizations change their paradigms, one needs to have a different theory, of higher logical level; one needs also to have a new paradigm for planned change, including new models and tools. Chase (1983) argues that many organizations of today are in need of paradigmatic change but the science of planned change offers theories and practices of normal change. Organizational transformation represents a new paradigm, a new theory and practice for facilitating revolutionary change.

Smith (1982) calls our attention to the fact that paradigmatic change includes the use of new terms, metaphors, concepts, and language. He demonstrates how language constructs actually represent world views. We think about and understand phenomena by using linguistic constructs such as metaphors and concepts. Revolutionary change entails a jump to a higher logical level that can be described and communicated only by using new language. The Einstein paradigm cannot be described, represented, and communicated by using metaphors and concepts taken from the Newtonian paradigm.

To summarize, a paradigm shift is triggered by organizational decline or crisis, and the accumulation of evidence that the old paradigm fails to provide new directions and satisfactory solutions, explanations, and legitimization to the present state. Further, it is triggered by the accumulation of evidence that there are, or might be, alternative ways of doing things, and alternative perspectives on present situations. And, last, a paradigm shift is facilitated by the activity of able individuals whose ideas, visions, innovations, or discoveries provide a new direction more satisfactory in terms of organization, adaptation, and members' needs. Paradigmatic shift is preceded by the emerging of new ideas based on new logic, and the emerging of new concepts and metaphors. Both the new ideas and the new concepts cannot be understood within the old paradigm.

NEO-MARXIAN PERSPECTIVE

The Hegelian-Marxian dialectical perspective implicitly inspired some of the new theories on, and approaches to, second-order change in organizations. Kuhn's theory of scientific revolutions and Prigogine's theory of order through fluctuations are two examples.

One of the first to apply Marxian theory and philosophy to social systems was Dahrendorf (1959), who explicitly rejects the deterministic aspect and the philosophical elements of Marx's class theory. He emphasizes conflict, evolution, revolution, and qualitative change as the main aspects of Marxian theory. According to Dahrendorf, every social system is characterized by

> ... the continuous change of not only its elements, but its very structural form. This change in turn bears witness to the presence of conflicts as an essential feature of every society. Conflicts are not random; they are a systematic product of the structure of society itself. According to this image, there is no order except in the regularity of change. (p. 28)

Hence, Dahrendorf argues that there are two different types of change: change of the organizational elements (first-order change) and change of the organizational "structural form" (second-order change). Conflicts and change, not equilibrium or steady state, are the important aspects of organization life.

Some scholars emphasize the dialectical aspects of Marxian theory as applied to organizations. Slater (1974), for example, argues that ". . . any pattern, value, ideal, norm, or behavioral tendency is always present in a [organizational] culture at any time along with its polar opposite" (p. 14). These elements turn into their opposites, "by being pushed to an extreme" (p. 167). Cumming (1977) expresses the same idea: "Firmly held values seems always to be accompanied by contrasting and even inimical latent values that are available for conversion into dominant ones" (p. 152).

There are scholars who emphasize that revolutionary change is a qualitative change, a change in the organization's ideology. The direction is toward equality and democratization. Grabow and Heskin (1973), for example, argue that organizational second-order change means actually changing the Western ideology of organizing. The purpose has to be the transformation of social systems into ". . . decentralized communal organizations" (p. 415). The same idea is expressed by Nord (1976): "Human development requires man to exercise control over his action, but achievement of that condition requires that control be shared by all" (p. 572).

Another important concept of Marxian philosophy is class-consciousness and consciousness raising. Through social interactions the "oppressed" learn about their situation and become more and more aware of the dominant ideology, the existing order, and their own powerlessness. From this perspective, people are willing to take an active role in radical change only after their consciousness is raised to a certain point, so that they can be aware of the existing injustice and of alternative possibilities for organizing.

The neo-Marxian perspective strongly influenced the political perspective on organizational change (see Chapter 11). It also led some scholars to suggest that practitioners should take a more active role in facilitating change in organizations. From this perspective, change is perceived as change in the ideology and in the order of the system. The change is toward sharing power and rewards, and toward democratization. The role of the consultant is not to help solve problems or to improve effectiveness. His or her role as change agent is to raise the consciousness of the lower levels of the system, to present a new possible order, based on a different ideology (Alinsky 1972; Freire 1970; Nord 1976; Grabow & Heskin 1973; Reason 1984).

Marxian philosophy is deterministic. However, the neo-Marxian perspective emphasizes nondeterministic aspects. Sztompka (1981) provides a nondeterministic interpretation of the Marxian theory as applied to social systems. He argues that evolutions and revolutions are natural processes of living systems; however, they are shaped by human thought and action. Moreover, Sztompka argues that through short periods of revolutionary change, social systems attain a higher and better order in terms of individual freedom, development and growth, social justice, and social security; however, this does not mean that there is only one way, or a specific ideal type, toward which all systems transform.

To summarize, the neo-Marxian perspective emphasizes the following propositions:

- That social systems pass through long periods of evolutionary change and short periods of revolutionary change
- That evolutionary periods are characterized by incremental changes and improvements in which the system as a whole (in terms of how the system operates, its values, its ideology, its world view, and its power structure) remains unchanged
- That social systems, social forms, and ideas contain their own destructive forces; every thesis creates an antithesis that leads to an inevitable clash, and to the creation of a new form and idea, qualitatively different from the former state

- That social systems are characterized by inner conflicts between interest groups holding different ideologies; these conflicts are the driving force of the revolutionary change
- That the dominant groups or coalitions develop a logical explanation, ideology, and culture to support their dominance, and to preserve the current order
- That revolutionary periods are short, occur rapidly and suddenly, and are preceded by inner tensions, conflicts, polarities, and crisis
- That through revolutionary periods the system transforms into a higher and better way of organizing in terms of social justice, social security, individual freedom, development, and growth
- That the interaction between human actions (voluntarism) and natural evolution processes (determinism) creates the tension, polarity, and crisis that lead to revolutionary change
- That the process of evolution involves consciousness expansion and increased awareness of people of that process; this awareness motivates people to take an active role in the evolution of their consciousness.

ORDER THROUGH FLUCTUATIONS PERSPECTIVE

This perspective is based mainly on the work of Prigogine (1984). The ideas have much in common with those of the evolution and consciousness perspective. However, Prigogine describes the whole process of system transformation, and his theory focuses on energy exchange processes, not on human consciousness. Some of this work earned Prigogine a Nobel Prize in chemistry in 1977. Nonequilibrium thermodynamics, and especially advances in fluctuation theory, provide improved tools for understanding the emergence and self-creation of new structures.

Prigogine's term for open systems is "dissipative structures." That is, the system's form or structure is maintained by a continuous dissipation (consumption) of energy. The energy moves through and simultaneously forms the dissipative structure. Hence, such a structure might well be described as a "flowing wholeness." It is highly organized but always in process. The more complex a dissipative structure is, the more components and connections it has, and the more energy it needs to maintain all those connections. Therefore, it is more vulnerable to internal fluctuations; it is said to be far from equilibrium. Because these connections can be sustained only by a flow of energy, the system is always in flux.

The more coherent or intricately connected the structure, the more unstable it is. The paradox is that increased coherence means increased instability. This very nature of open systems is the key to transformation to a new order, qualitatively different — a second-order change. The continuous movement of energy through the system results in fluctuations; if they are minor, the system dampens them and they do not alter its structural integrity. But if the fluctuations reach a critical point or size, they perturb the system. Positive feedback loops enhance the fluctuations, which increase the number of novel interactions within it. They shake it up. The elements of the old pattern come into contact with each other in new ways and make new connections. The parts reorganize into a new whole. The system escapes into a higher order.

Each transformation makes the next structure more complex or coherent, requiring a greater flow of energy for maintenance and exhibiting still less stability. Fluctuations increase through positive feedback loops until they exceed a critical point or threshold beyond which a new and more complex order will emerge. It is important to note that in open systems theory (cybernetics I), fluctuations have been viewed as equilibrium-disturbing. Hence, for a system to remain stable, the fluctuations must be minimized. In order through fluctuation theory (cybernetics II), however, fluctuations are viewed as a major vehicle for creating order, not destroying it. In fact, the theory of dissipative structures suggests that near-equilibrium order is destroyed, whereas far-from-equilibrium order is maintained.

Prigogine's theory has been applied to explain and understand organizational transformation. Smith (1984), for example, showed how management effort to restore order as quickly as possible — when something goes into chaos — may be dysfunctional. Managers believe that both long-term and short-term viability will be augmented by this action. However, it may well be that the most appropriate action for system viability is to encourage the chaos, and thus engage in the emergence of a new order.

Certain findings and theories in anthropology and sociology appear to fit well with the work of Prigogine. Back in the 1870s, the sociologist Herbert Spencer distinguished between growth and development in evolution. A system's growth is limited; beyond a critical point there can be no further growth without further organization. Spencer's ideas have been greatly extended by the anthropologist Robert Carneiro (1968, 1981). Carneiro notes that growth (first-order change) (a) consists of an increase in substance; (b) is usually manifested by a proliferation of structures already present; (c) is essentially quantitative; (d) can proceed, in the absence of new structures, only up to a point beyond which existing structures cannot support further growth, and growth declines or ceases. Carneiro calls this the "elastic limit." Development (second-order change), on the other hand, (a) consists of an increase in structure; (b) is characterized by the emergence of new structural forms; (c) is essentially qualitative; (d) is a response by the growing system to an increase in scale.

Carneiro describes the nature of development process or, as it is called in this work, second-order change, thus:

> But while growth [first-order change] tends to be continuous ... development is generally discontinuous and abrupt. It proceeds by a series of jumps, however small, from one level of organization to the next. ... Changes in natural phenomena proceed by the accumulation of relatively small quantitative increments, which every so often result in a sudden transformation and the emergence of something new and qualitatively different. (p. 179)

Carneiro's model is based on longitudinal and extensive study of the evolution of cultures worldwide. Both Carneiro and Prigogine point out that the development of the new qualitative order (second-order change) can be triggered either from within the system, deliberately, or from without, because of environmental changes or pressures.

Studies on changes in social systems over time seem also to fit with Prigogine's theory. Miller (1982) analyzed the evolution of business organizations and found that they proceed through relatively long periods of evolution and short periods of sudden, radical change in management processes, policies, and structures that Miller calls "revolution." In analyzing change in educational policies, Iannaccone (1977) differentiates between changes that are incremental and adjustive, and basic changes, cyclical in nature, that involve a complete shift in the educational leadership, policies, structure, and world view.

The above scholars argue that their approach to organizational evolution is not a deterministic one. Prigogine expresses his opinion on this issue thus:

> The evolution characteristics of complex systems ... present **real choices and real freedom**. In consequence, we have the responsibility of trying to

understand the dynamics of change in order both to formulate realistic objectives and to discover which actions and decisions should be taken in order to move closer to them. (Prigogine & Allen 1982, p. 38; emphasis added)

To summarize, Prigogine's perspective suggests that social systems will occasionally go into extreme fluctuation and perturbation, and appear to be falling apart. At a specific point the system either stops functioning or jumps to a higher, more complex order. According to Prigogine, the greater the turbulence and the more complex the system, the greater the jump to a higher order.

EVOLUTION AND CONSCIOUSNESS PERSPECTIVE

Classical social-evolution theory proposes that the evolution of social systems is a long, incremental, and relatively smooth process. The basic notion is that social systems inevitably tend to develop into ever more diversified, interdependent, complex systems. Tonnies' (1964) theory on the evolution of communities (gemeinschafts) to societies (gesellschafts) and Durkheim's (1947) theory on the evolution of mechanical solidarity to organic solidarity are two of many examples. Neo-evolution theories, such as the natural selection perspective, postulate that the natural laws of selection (variation, selection, retention) can be applied to social systems. The more micro evolution perspectives, such as the life-cycle and developmental-stages perspectives, focus on distinguishing between specific developmental stages typical of the evolution process. The basic premises of all the above perspectives are that evolution is a relatively smooth, incremental process and that it is deterministic.

Some new perspectives on the evolution of social systems propose that the evolution process is not a smooth and incremental process; rather, it is characterized by crises, chaos, catastrophes, and sudden shifts to a new order. However, like the above perspectives, these new perspectives implicitly propose that evolution is basically deterministic. People have only minor, if any, impact on both the nature and the direction of the process. Thom's (1975) catastrophe theory as applied to behavioral science (Casti 1979; Cobb et al. 1978) and Elgin's (1977) study on the inability to manage ever growing complexities at an ever-growing pace are two examples.

The evolution and consciousness or, as some scholars call it, self-organizing systems, perspective is actually a cluster of highly complicated ideas that draw upon new findings in biology, chemistry, quantum physics, thermodynamics, and brain research. It is an offshoot of general systems theory. Like the order through fluctuation perspective, it proposes that evolution is not a smooth process and that it involves periods of crisis and perturbations, and a sudden shift to a new order. However, unlike the former, this perspective emphasizes the voluntaristic aspects of evolution, how people can take, and are taking, an active role in the process. The evolution and consciousness perspective is an effort to integrate concepts from open systems, living systems, and evolutionary theories into a more dynamic, nondeterministic model.

One of the main spokesmen for this perspective is Jantsch, who studied the relationships between consciousness and system evolution. He claims that all living systems are autopoietic systems, that is, they all are capable of self-production, self-renewal, and self-organization. They do so through feedback mechanisms and consciousness capability. The self-renewing process consists of evolution and meta-evolution (or transformation) periods. Jantsch (1976) explains it thus:

> Evolution is open not only with respect to its products but also to the rules of the game it develops. The result of this openness is the self-transcendence of evolution in a "meta evolution," the evolution of evolutionary mechanisms and principles. (p. 8)

Hence, according to Jantsch, the evolution process consists of evolution and transformation periods; transformation periods are characterized by change in the "rules of the game," or what Smith (1982) calls "meta rules" (change in the rules of the rules). Another idea is that open systems are always in a state of fluctuation. Jantsch (1980) writes:

> Open systems are non-equilibrium systems, they are characterized by fluctuations within certain confines. During metastability periods the shift to a new structure is delayed during a finite period which is sufficient for the unfolding of life process. Metastability is delayed evolution. No complex system is ever truly stable. (p. 255)

The resistance of an autopoietic structure to its own transformation is an essential aspect of the comprehensive dynamics of transformation. Metastability involves resistance to transformation, which enables processes and structures to evolve, develop, and mature. Without metastability periods, "nothing much would come of evolution," writes Jantsch (1980). He explains:

> The higher the resistance against structural change the more powerful the fluctuations which ultimately break through — the richer and more varied also the unfolding of self-organization dynamics at the platform of a resilient structure. (p. 255)

The term "metastability" refers to a period of fluctuations within certain confines. Jantsch claims that systems are in a constant process of change; criticizing systems theory, he argues that "equilibrium is synonymous with social and cultural and also ultimately physical death" (Jantsch 1976, p. 1). His idea that resistance to second-order change has a positive function is supported by empirical studies such as that conducted by Miller (1982).

But perhaps the most important idea related to the current study is that which relates evolution to consciousness. Jantsch argues that all living systems are characterized by a certain autonomy vis-à-vis the environment that may be understood as a primitive form of consciousness corresponding to the level of existence of the system. Living systems' consciousness is related to their capability to be self-referential and self-descriptive. Self-referential is a configuration of a living system whereby it reenters its own boundaries so that it is both subject and object, both cause and effect of itself. A living system also defines itself by closing an informational boundary around itself. It describes itself and transforms itself through self-referential configurations.

The evolution of living systems to higher-level systems also involves the evolution of their consciousness to higher levels. The evolution of the human consciousness to ever higher levels makes possible more degrees of freedom, awareness of the evolution process, and an active role in the evolution and, thus, in shaping its results. Jantsch (1976) writes that consciousness evolution

> ... gives a chance to the individual and his creative imagination ... evolution is neither in its emerging and decaying structures, nor in the end result, predetermined. . . . **We are not the helpless subjects of evolution — we are evolution.** (p. 8; emphasis added)

The evolution and consciousness perspective emphasizes the role of people in evolution. Zeleny and Pierre (1976) put it explicitly:

Components of human systems are humans. As such they differ significantly from other components, mechanistic or biological, in their ability to anticipate the future, to formulate their objectives, to plan for their attainment, and to make decisions.... Social change results from free choice by independent decision makers; it is a teleological advance and need not be just the shaped outcome of external environmental pressures. (p. 164)

Three more important ideas of this perspective suggest that open systems not only are in constant nonequilibrium states but also that they are characterized by mutual causality, deviation amplifying, and positive feedback processes (Maruyama 1963). Maruyama was among the first to note that open systems have two different processes of feedback: negative feedback, which promotes self-regulation and equilibrium, and positive feedback, which amplifies deviations through mutual causal processes. The second process provides ever-growing inner conflicts until the system reaches a new "escape" state. This "escape" state is qualitatively different.

To summarize, the evolution and consciousness perspective suggests that human systems are in a constant state of fluctuation, disturbance, change, and development. The evolution process is not incremental and smooth. It involves perturbations that are amplified until they reach a threshold beyond which the system is qualitatively different. Evolution involves the evolution of human consciousness. This process enables people to take an active role in the process of change.

GROWTH PERSPECTIVE

The concept of growth, as usually used in organization theory, refers to quantitative change, a change that occurs over a time period in the organization's size, number of employees and managers, number and size of units, and/or volume of production and sales (Katz & Kahn 1978). It is argued that this type of change gives the organization better control over its environment, prevents radical changes, and enables incremental adjustments. Hence, "growth enhances the organization's survival value, by providing a cushion, or slack, against organization failure" (Pfeffer & Salancik 1978, p. 139). Further, it is argued that growth usually occurs without choice; nevertheless, organizations can deter or accelerate their growth by the choices they make.

The concept used mainly in the field of planned change to denote qualitative change is development. Whereas growth is an increase in size, development is a process in which organization members increase their potential and capacity to satisfy their own needs, and to attain the organizational goals and purposes. Development is more a matter of motivation, knowledge, understanding, wisdom, and quality of work life than of wealth and standard of living. Development is a learning process; it cannot be given to or imposed on one person by another. The most one can do is encourage and facilitate development. From this perspective, there may be growth without development and vice versa. Further, both types of change are incremental (Ackoff 1981).

The growth perspective presented in this section holds that there is a limit to the growth of organizations, beyond which they may die unless there is an increase in development (Carneiro 1981). Further, it holds that organizations tend to grow and evolve to higher and greater "wholes" in Darwinian terms. Once an organization's survival is assured, the basic drive for change is qualitative growth. An exemplifying study is that conducted by Land (1973).

Land studied the process of growth and change in living systems. His main argument is that in natural selection theory, the key issue is the drive for survival. But in modern social systems, the key motivator is not survival but growth:

> Physical, biological, psychological, and social systems are growth motivated; that is, their behavior acts in the direction of development of higher levels of and more widespread interrelationships. Thus, all systems tend to evolve more organized behavior, becoming integrated through the incorporation of diversity . . . this is a ubiquitous and irreversible process. (p. 197)

Land uses the term "transformation" to denote revolutionary change, which is always toward growth. His theory can be summarized as follows:

1. Transformation is a discontinuous and accelerating growth process represented by a series of "inventions" that elevate the level of organization through major reconstructions of information programs and growth systems. Therefore, in analyzing and assessing the shape of the future of our social systems, our evaluations of alternative courses must be made with the awareness of the possibility of

emergence of unique forms, not merely repetitions or extrapolations of the past and present.

2. As the evolved mechanism for evolution, man is therefore the sole responsible agent to and for his species and environment.
3. As an emerging species, we can continue to transform our environment through new growth processes and products, and select expressions of technology and society at ever increasing rates.
4. In our evolution, there is no finite or visualizable end to growth or to transformations to unique levels of growth on the part of each individual and of total society (pp. 193–94).

Hubbard (1982) suggests very similar ideas to those of Land. She views change as a continuum of dynamic interactions and not as a single event. Transformation is a natural part of evolution — the inner urge to grow. Hubbard points out that

> The balance of nature is continuous, progressive change with a recurrent pattern in the process: the creation of a new whole from out of the old through synthesis of separate parts. There is no point where the process remains static. The tendency in nature to form ever greater whole systems which are different from and greater than the sum of their parts is intrinsic — or we would not be here. (p. 5)

To summarize, growth perspective holds that the main purpose of all life — and particularly in the advanced industrial nations — is toward growth, toward higher and more complex levels of individuality and organization, higher-level needs and potentials. Evolution proceeds through the decline and death of the old, or what is termed here "destructuring," and the rebirth of higher-order structures.

CATASTROPHE PERSPECTIVE

Catastrophe theory, the discovery of French mathematician René Thom (1975), is an outgrowth of topology mathematics. The field of topology was of much interest, in the early 1970s, for family therapists who used its models to describe two types of problem resolutions: first-order change and second-order change (Watzlawick et al. 1974). Thom's approach is by itself rather hard to understand and to apply; his theory was modified and interpreted by Zeeman (1976) to form a concrete model that is applied to describing collective behavior and revolutionary change (Bigelow 1982; Casti 1979; Cobb et al. 1978; Guastello 1984; Olivia et al. 1981).

Unlike the other theories described in this chapter, catastrophe theory is based on mathematical models and constructs — and, hence, its application for explaining and predicting social phenomena is controversial. Furthermore, from this perspective, second-order change can be a sudden reversal, when an attitude or a system turns into the opposite. It is a more pragmatic approach to capture the dynamics of transformation, and scientists believe it is an invaluable means for conceptualizing radical, abrupt change in complex systems (DeGreen 1982; Smith 1984).

The central element of the theory is recognizing the discontinuous effects of continuous processes. Simply put, whenever a continuously changing force yields an abruptly changing effect, the phenomenon can be described as a catastrophe. A small change in stimuli or initial conditions can produce a major change in behavior or system state. A slight quantitative change in the continuous processes potentially describable by a differential equation can produce the sudden emergence of a qualitatively different kind of behavior. Any stable system can, on hitting an instability threshold, go through radical changes so that a new structure based on a new ordering principle emerges.

The theorem can be summarized as follows: For every situation representable by up to five independent, causal, or control variables and one or more dependent, effect, or behavioral variables, there is a set of potential functions such that

1. A line of three-to-many-dimensional surface called a manifold can be conceptualized.
2. Each singularity (threshold, breakoff point) is locally equivalent to one of a finite number of elementary catastrophes.
3. The situation is structurally stable at each point of the manifold with regard to small perturbations of the potential function.
4. Because of the qualitative equivalency of topological maps and graphs, a canonical form of the potential function can be substituted for the actual potential function, which may never be known.

With a large number of control and behavior variables, and therefore of dimensions, an infinite number of catastrophe types could be conceived. At least 25 have been identified. However, only 7 to 11 (with up to 4 or 5 control variables) have received much study, and of these only 3 have been applied to the behavioral sciences. These are the fold, the cusp, and the butterfly models. The fold model is two-dimensional because it involves one control variable and one behavior variable. The cusp and the butterfly are three-dimensional, involving three to four control variables and one behavioral variable.

In this book we describe only the simplest model, hoping that it will stimulate interested readers to learn more about this research and rather complicated methodology. Much literature is available (for example, Sheridan 1985).

Before examining the fold catastrophe, certain definitions must be qualified further:

- Control variables are causal factors or driving forces for change. They can be viewed as vectors, meaning lines with direction and magnitude. There are interrelationships among these forces. The exact values of the control variables need not be known. Indeed, they may be ordinal-level variables, representing a specific quality, that is, variables expressed only as greater than, less than, increasing, or decreasing.
- Attractors are the stable equilibrium positions.
- Repellers are the unstable or inaccessible regions.
- The inaccessible region represents the least likely behavior. It is usually displayed by a middle sheet over which behavior jumps.
- Catastrophes are the discontinuities or sudden jumps from one mode of behavior to another.
- Hysteresis is a lag in behavioral response due to inertia in the system. It is an irreversible jump from one behavior to another.
- The manifold is the graph, shaped like an *s*. It represents a set of equilibrium points.

The fold catastrophe is the simplest of the 11 elementary catastrophes. It involves a control variable and a behavior variable, and therefore can be drawn on a two-axis graph, as illustrated in Figure 12.1.

The graph has three main branches: a stable upper branch, a stable lower branch, and an intermediate unstable branch. As the control variable (for example, driving force for change) increases, behavior increases along some scale. We can visualize movement up and to the right on the lower branch of the manifold, until a critical point or threshold or fold point (T_1) is reached. At the fold point the graph folds

Figure 12.1.   Fold Catastrophe

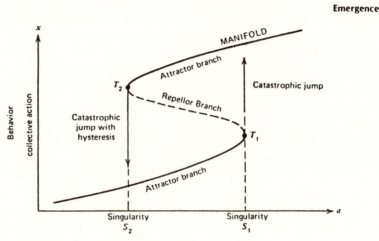

Source: Provided by the authors.

over continuously into the unstable repeller branch and behavior jumps catastrophically to the upper attractor branch. If the control variable is subsequently decreased, behavior does not immediately drop to the lower attractor branch. Rather, it can be thought of as moving downward and to the left along the top branch until another critical point (T_2) is reached, when it suddenly and catastrophically falls to the lower attractor branch. The lags or delays before the catastrophic jumps, coupled with path irreversibility, represents hysteresis.

People can suddenly change their attitudes from agreeing to dis-agreeing with respect to one and the same issue: a conservative monarchy unexpectedly changing to a fanatic, religious regime in Iran; a lighted metropolitan area turns abruptly into a dark one because two separate bolts of lightning hit two transmission towers, as was the case in New York in July 1977. The above examples show that in complex systems, certain unknown relationships exist within a complex web of variables. These variables, as well as the relationships among them, are usually in a process of slow, smooth change that is seldom noticed. When the change reaches a specific threshold and a stimulus is introduced into the system, an unexpected, sudden, and abrupt change that represents a new, qualitatively different (sometimes reversal) order, emerges.

Catastrophic change may occur without a similar abrupt, large change in the assumed causes. Instead, the presumed causes may change continuously, slowly, and smoothly. The theory implies that the more complex the system, the more the possibility for catastrophes to occur, unless sensing, monitoring mechanisms are present and resilient structure is applied. Catastrophe theory differs from all the other perspectives described in this chapter not only in its origins (topology mathematics) but also in its implications. It does not postulate that catastrophic change is always toward growth. It is also more pragmatic and deterministic. However, the theory provides models that help us to capture the dynamics of transformation; it is a means of explaining how discontinuities arise from continuously changing causal factors. These models help us to move away from a single-valued response surface. They are qualitative and not just quantitative. Finally, catastrophe theory models not only aid in the understanding of basic forces inside and outside the organization, but also help one to select appropriate variables to be brought under management control.

FUTURIST PERSPECTIVE

Futurists study and examine current discoveries, inventions, and developments at the cutting edges of various scientific and nonscientific areas. They try to locate trends, "to see the whole picture," and to forecast the future, all of which imply dealing with first- and second-order changes. The terms used by futurists to denote second-order change are usually "revolution," "paradigmatic shift," and "transformation."

Whereas the previous perspectives attempted to address the question of how second-order change occurs and what are the stages of the process, this perspective attempts to deal with the content of the process — that is, with what is changed. Many futurists use the previous perspectives as a contextual framework for understanding reality. However, their perspective is important for this study not only because it deals directly with the content of the transformation but also because of its basic premise that organizational transformation is part of a larger transformation process that includes individuals, organizations, cultures, and societies. A survey showed that there are many books and articles representing the above perspective. Therefore, in this section only a few exemplifying works that are directly related to transformation will be described and summarized.

Ferguson (1980) basically reports on discoveries, innovations, and trends related to personal, cultural, and social transformation. She argues that Western culture is in a deep crisis because of the difficulties present institutions have in coping with social problems and satisfying human needs:

> Our crisis showed us the ways in which our institutions have betrayed nature. We have equated the good life with material consumption, we have dehumanized work and made it needlessly competitive, we are uneasy about our capacities for learning and teaching. (p. 29)

Ferguson takes an optimistic viewpoint, asserting:

> Armed with a more sophisticated understanding of how change occurs, we know that the very forces that have brought us to planetary brinksmanship carry in them the seeds of renewal. The current disequilibrium — personal and social — foreshadows a new kind of society. Roles, relationships, institutions, and old ideas are being re-examined, reformulated, redesigned. (p. 29)

Further, she argues that for the first time in history, humankind has come upon the control panel of change, an understanding of how transformation occurs. We are living in the change of change, the time in which we can intentionally align ourselves with nature for rapid remaking of ourselves and our collapsing institutions. Ferguson describes some of the characteristics of the coming culture, the paradigm of the Aquarian Conspiracy, which

> ... sees humankind embedded in nature. It promotes the autonomous individual in a decentralized society. It sees us as stewards of all our resources, inner and outer. It says that we are **not** victims, not pawns, not limited by conditions or conditioning. Heirs to evolutionary riches, we are capable of imagination, invention, and experience we have only glimpsed. Human nature is neither good nor bad but open to continuous transformation and transcendence. (p. 29; emphasis added)

Ferguson not only describes the hoped-for future but also calls for creating a network of people willing to consciously facilitate the paradigmatic revolution.

According to Toffler (1981), change comes in waves that sweep across society, cutting through class, race, and special interest groups. The waves are chains of associated trends that reinforce one another, speeding up change and moving society in a new direction. The main components of this new direction are diversity and accelerated change. It is the convergence of many internal and external forces that build up the pressure for a revolutionary restructuring of economies. The result is a higher, far more complex level of development that is much more dependent on information.

The well-known physicist Capra (1982) offers a perceptual way of organizing or viewing the current experience of societal, organizational, or individual transformation. He suggests:

> The world is approaching a turning point. A massive shift in the perception of reality is underway, with thinkers in many disciplines beginning to move away from the traditional reductionist, mechanical world view to a holistic, ecological, systems paradigm. (p. 53)

Capra characterizes the traditional world view as the "mechanistic-Cartesian" paradigm that developed throughout the sixteenth and seventeenth centuries. This paradigm includes belief in the scientific method as the only valid approach to knowledge and the notion of the universe as a mechanical system composed of elementary material building blocks. The mechanistic view presents units as having closed boundaries. Change is seen as the replacement of a defective unit by a new unit, with the change having little impact on the larger system.

Capra claims that a new paradigm is now emerging, the holistic-ecological paradigm. We are in a profound shift in our thoughts, perceptions, and values, all of which form a new vision of reality. The new paradigm emphasizes the fundamental interrelatedness and interdependence of all phenomena, and the intrinsically dynamic nature of physical reality. According to Capra, the transformation that is taking place includes the following value trends:

- From competition to cooperation
- From unlimited expansion to optimal size
- From material growth to inner growth
- From central power to decentralization
- From hard technology to soft technology
- From specialization to synthesis and multidisciplinary approaches.

As the transformation takes place, the declining culture refuses to change, clinging ever more rigidly to its outdated ideas; nor will the dominant social institutions hand over their leading roles to the new cultural forces. But the old forms will decline and disintegrate while the new culture continues to rise. As the turning point approaches, Capra says, our greatest hope for the future is the realization that historic, evolutionary changes of this magnitude cannot be stopped by short-term political action.

Naisbitt (1982) analyzed trends and changes in major areas of the United States. Like Capra, he argues that we are entering a new era and that the United States is undergoing major cultural shifts. The main focus of this work is on describing ten megatrends or major socioeconomic shifts:

- From industrial society to information society
- From forced technology to high-tech, high-touch
- From national economy to world economy
- From short term to long term (profit and planning)
- From centralization to decentralization
- From institutional help to self-help
- From representative democracy to participatory democracy
- From hierarchies to networking
- From north to south (population shift)
- From either-or to multiple options.

A very similar study was conducted by Ayres (1984), who examined future trends in economy, industry, energy, and technology. He concludes that we are standing before a new industrial revolution characterized by petroleum substitutes, new materials, new information processing, new electronics and technology, that will radically change our way of organizing and socializing.

One more example of studies representing futurists' perspectives on transformation is Nicoll (1984b). Analyzing innovations and discoveries in brain research, quantum mechanics, and phenomenology, he suggests the following propositions:

1. Our world has changed and a revolution has occurred. This revolution has taken place in the beliefs, intentions, thoughts, and behaviors of people. A paradigm shift has occurred, and this process is at its midpoint.

2. The paradigm shift we are experiencing is different from any other the human race has experienced. It is the first one of which we are conscious while it is happening. We now truly understand that our presumptions — our paradigm — determine our experience.
3. The new paradigm will not replace the old one. Rather, it will build on the old, extend it, and include it.
4. The new paradigm is not bringing the millennium. It is not doing away with evil and pain. These things will remain, and will be dealt with long after the new world view is replaced.
5. The new paradigm is challenging our "common sense" views of the world, the logic of simple cause-and-effect relations.

The new paradigm is characterized by five major elements:

1. A metaperspective about ourselves that includes knowledge both of our own consciousness and of this paradigm shift
2. Limited arenas of knowledge where contingency perspectives and multiple realities are the rule
3. Hierarchies, heterarchies, and distributed functions
4. Multiple models of change and causality that emphasize interaction patterns, phenomenological intention, and love
5. And, by implication, conscious design of our new world.

Another common theme in futurists' writings that has affected the practice of transformation is the notion that revolutionary change is anticipated by an image of the desired future. Polack (1973) noted that when the dominant images of a culture are anticipatory, they "lead" social development and provide direction for social change. By their attractiveness and legitimacy they reinforce and influence decisions that will bring them to realization. As a culture moves toward the achievement of goals inherent in its dominant images, the congruence increases between the images and the development of the culture itself — the implications of the images are explored, progress is made, and needs are more fully satisfied.

Boulding (1978), Meadows (1982), Markley (1982), and Wilner (1975) have further developed and researched the issue. Markley added the notion that if the progress (development) of the human system outstrips its traditional images, its policies and behavior (which are based on the old images) become increasingly faulty — even counterproductive — precipitating a period of frustration, cultural disruption, or social crisis. The stage is then set for basic change in the underlying images that will then guide action in a totally new direction. Markley analyzed cultural transformation and concluded: "A substantial amount of evidence exists that successful responses to crisis tend to be **nonincremental** in character, and lead to restructured images and modes of system organization" (p. 215; emphasis added).

Wilner (1975) examined how healing imaginary visions emerge in periods of crisis and oppression, and how these images become powerful transformative tools for both individuals and collectives. She claims that these visions are produced out of a deep crisis of the social order; they are the product of individual imaginations that share in a collective experience of disorder, and are often radically transformative and regenerative, both for the individual psyches in which they occur and for the collectivities in which they find a communal resonance. Further, they often lead to radical realignments in sociopolitical structures that have become inadequate or oppressive. These writers also claim that Western culture and organizations are in a crisis that can be dealt with only by restructuring the underlying images of the desired future.

To summarize, the futurists' perspective, as presented here, takes an optimistic view of the future of mankind. The main propositions are that we are in the midst of a major shift in culture and habits. We not only can describe the main ingredients of the new emerging paradigm but also can consciously take part in this revolution. The different approaches describe different aspects of the new paradigm that are, to a large extent, complementary rather than contradictory.

INTEGRATION AND EVALUATION

The above cluster of theoretical perspectives can be integrated and summarized by the following propositions:

1. Organizations are in a constant state of movement and change. Periods of stability are only relative.
2. Evolution does not proceed in gradual steps, but with dramatic jumps. The evolutionary process of organization consists of long periods of development and change within a current paradigm, order, or state of being and short time periods of transformation resulting in the emergence of a new paradigm, new order, or new state of being.

3. This process is shaped by human creativity, thoughts, decisions, and actions that at the same time are shaped by this evolutionary process. Man is the changer and the changed at the same time.
4. Organizational decline is a cyclical phenomenon that leads back to rebirth and new life.
5. This death and rebirth tend toward growth, toward a higher and higher "Darwinian level," beyond mere survival and into levels of greater complexity and sophistication.
6. As higher levels are reached, there occurs an acceleration of change: the death and rebirth of organizations happen at an even faster rate.
7. Although the general tendency is toward greater complexity and sophistication, the process may include discontinuities, catastrophes, and reversals.
8. The evolution of living systems includes the evolution of the human consciousness. This process enables people to be aware of evolution and to take an active role in shaping its nature and its direction. Unlike other living systems, human systems are self-transcendent.
9. We are in the midst of a paradigm shift. The new paradigm can already be outlined, understood, and shaped by our thoughts and actions.

The above propositions quite naturally raise the problem of man's capability to manage increasing complexities at an ever growing pace. This problem has brought some scientists to a pessimistic view regarding the future of mankind (DeGreen 1982). However, some theoreticians argue that evolutionary processes include not only organizing modes but learning modes as well. Jantsch (1976), for example, further develops Bateson's (1972) learning theory and suggests a hierarchy of four learning modes: virtual, functional, conscious, and superconscious. Each learning/creativity mode is more sophisticated than that before it:

- Virtual learning: movement to change movement (response)
- Functional learning: response to change response (behavior)
- Conscious learning: behavior to change behavior (conscious action)
- Superconscious learning: consciousness to change consciousness (superconscious self-regulation of cultural and human processes).

Each mode includes lower-level modes. According to this model, there are mutual causality relationships between the evolution of learning modes and the evolution of organizing.

There are now new theories, derived from research on the brain and perception, very similar to the ideas and theories of Jantsch and Prigogine. These new theories were proposed simultaneously by two scientists unknown to each other, working in different disciplines in different countries. Pribram, a neurosurgeon from Stanford University, studied the brain structure and functioning. Bohm, an English physicist, studied the underlying structure of the universe and reality itself (in Cross 1982). The findings of these two scientists pointed to the possibility that both the brain and the universe exhibit several of Prigogine's requirements for an evolving, self-organized system:

1. The brain is complex — nature's most complex, highest-level organ.
2. The brain, an endlessly fluctuating medium, seems capable of "perturbing" itself into higher-order realms.
3. Only part of the potential of the brain has been used.
4. Every culture, including our own, has deliberately limited the brain function.
5. The brain is far more sophisticated than we ever realized. It is possible that it operates in dimensions beyond our conventional five senses.
6. The brain, in fact, meets all of Prigogine's requirements for triggering its own evolution. (Prigogine argued that the more complex a system, the greater its potential for transcendence.)

The idea that human beings are capable of shaping and managing ever growing complexities does not, however, automatically entail their doing it. There is already evidence that the pace of inventions and new technologies is higher than the pace of innovations in ways of utilizing and managing them (DeGreen 1982). Land (1973) puts it in a "must" proposition and argues that for man to shape and manage transformation processes

> ... will require a rapid and radical integration of the quality of human growth into the processes of planning, forecasting, and creating a future still and always unknown; but we can do so with the knowledge that by and through evolution processes, we can determine the quality of form, if not the content of things to come. (p. 195)

The implicit notion that periods of increasing perturbations are actually signals of upcoming transformation to higher-order and better ways of organizing, and therefore bad times are actually good times and the "more bad it is," "the better it is" (Cross 1982), needs to be reexamined. Two arguments are suggested for this reexamination. The first is the level of analysis. What seems to be positive from the macro perspective might be seen as negative from the immediate micro perspective. For specific organizations, industries, and communities, it sometimes means stopping functioning. For many individuals, it means unemployment and uncertainty.

The second argument is provided by Prigogine, who argues that perturbations can lead to either death or revitalization. Furthermore, history has shown that transformations may take very negative forms from the perspective of individual freedom and growth. It is important, therefore, to emphasize the point made by Jantsch and Land that for the evolution process to be positive, it needs the integration of human action and human responsibility.

The ideas of futurists that cosmic, social, organizational, and individual transformation is coming or taking place, and that the "Third Wave," or the "Aquarian Age" is happening now, are based on observations and analysis but are debatable. In this sense there is no difference between the futurists and religious and social groups who believe that the millennium is about to come. The ideas and the concepts used by some of the transformation practitioners are very positive, ignoring the dark side of human life and negative trends, such as increasing crime and hunger, and the arms race. This language might create an atmosphere detached from reality. Networking, caring, holism, cooperation, synergy, spirituality, transcendence, and win/win values are the common terms, not poverty, crime, power, or politics. Although some believe in affirmation, there is as yet insufficient evidence that using positive language causes the disappearance of evil.

To summarize, the above cluster of macro theoretical perspectives takes into account voluntaristic aspects of the evolution of social systems; therefore, they can provide the theoretical basis and framework for the emerging field of second-order planned change and, in particular, the approach called organization transformation. The value of these macro perspectives is that they identify a broad set of concepts that should be considered, and they provide the context in which second-order change takes place. There is also a problem with some of these theories. Critical variables sometimes are not identified, or remain abstract and undefined. Nevertheless, this cluster of theories as a whole adds depth and wide support to the approach of organizational transformation.

PART IV

SUMMARY

13
Models for Understanding
Second-Order Change

Progress in the domain of second-order change is constrained by a lack of adequate conceptual frameworks. Analytical reasoning that probes the dimensions and processes of such a crucial phenomenon has utility, for it begins to inform and guide practice, and to stimulate inquiry and, hence, enhance theory building. "Knowledge utilization" has become a rapidly developing field in organization science. This term indicates the efforts now underway to bridge the gap between empirically rigorous studies resulting in a focus on change in organizations, and applied studies and practices resulting in a focus on changing organizations (Glaser et al. 1983). This chapter suggests a number of conceptual models for understanding the phenomenon and the practice of second-order change.

Understanding second-order change can be assisted by addressing three questions. The first one is why organizations transform or what are the driving forces for this type of change. The second one is how organizations transform. This question includes organizational transformation as a phenomenon and as a practice. Explaining how organizations are transformed entails integrating theory and practice. The third question is what is changed in second-order change.

The early models of organizational life stages primarily examined the consequences of growing in scale and diversification (Katz & Kahn 1978). Other early models emphasized stages brought on by cycles of crisis (Greiner 1972). The models that followed examined the influence of cultural, economic, and technological factors. Other studies focus on stages of development models, as well as strategy, structure, decision making, and problem-solving style (Miller & Friesen 1980a).

Studies on the evolution and adaptation of living systems added new perspective to transformation. This cluster of studies suggests that what is experienced as an internal change may simply be an adjustment. An internal change may be a way for the system to remain the same. The concept of "order through fluctuation" and the theory of dissipative structures suggested that fluctuations are a major vehicle for maintaining order and for creating higher-level order. The concept of an "autopoietic system," which refers to a system capable of constantly re-creating the conditions necessary to sustain itself and capable of self-creation, deepens our understanding of self-organizing systems capable of self-transcendence (Jantsch 1980).

Studies in biology suggest that there are changes of a developmental nature; they operate according to the instructions encoded within the system and are called morphostasis. There is another type of change called morphogenesis, in which the basic governing rules become altered. Some see these changes as irreversible (Smith 1984). Catastrophe theory (Zeeman 1976) suggests that morphogenetic changes are characterized by discontinuity of continuous processes. Any stable system can, on hitting an instability threshold, go through radical changes so that a new structure based on a new ordering principle emerges. From the perspective of the above theories, the idea is that not the fittest survive but those which are capable of symbiosis (creating a mutually sustaining network of relationships with other systems).

And, finally, studies and theories call for alternative ways of thinking about what is real. The phenomenological perspective on "organizing" (Weick 1979) and the theory of scientific revolution show how context shapes content and how what we see is determined by what we believe. From this perspective, self-transcendence is related to learning "how to jump over one's own shadow," as well as the capacity to change one's point of view and explore one's situation in a different light. Transformation entails learning to create or discover realities beyond the ones that are currently perceived and to choose one that fits one's needs.

We may describe second-order change from three perspectives:

1. Why: the driving forces of this type of change
2. How: the stages and process characteristics
3. What: the content of the change; what is changed.

WHY: THE DRIVING FORCES FOR CHANGE

This summary of the driving forces for change is based on a survey of research and case studies. The categorization used is guided by a classificatory scheme suggested by Lundberg (1984). The driving forces are seen as permitting, enabling, precipitating, and triggering events, processes, and conditions.

Permitting Conditions

Aspects of the internal organizational situation that allow transformation to occur are the following:

- The gathering of some surplus resources for managing the change. These additional resources may be managerial time and energy, or financial resources.
- Readiness and willingness of at least the dominant coalition to endure change. It refers to the managers' and members' willingness and ability to live with the anxiety that comes with anticipated uncertainty.
- Transformational leadership. This leadership is capable of providing new vision, aligning members with this vision, and mobilizing energy and commitment to the realization of this vision.

Enabling Conditions

External conditions that increase the likelihood of transformation occurring include the following:

- The degree of threat to the survival of the organization posed by its competitors, economic situation, and consumers.
- The degree of tolerance of metasystems for the transformation.
- The degree of radicalness of the change. It is hypothesized that too great an incongruence between the system and its domain will make the transformation seem overly threatening, overly risky.

Precipitating Conditions

Precipitating conditions include the following:

- The tendency of organizations to grow.
- The tendency of organizations to experience decline.
- Changes in the shared beliefs, meanings, understandings, or "interpretive schemes" that guide organizing.
- Feelings of pain and dissatisfaction by the organization members and the emergence of new, unmet needs.
- The pressure of stakeholders, consumers, clients, and of the claimants inside and outside the organization who have a vested interest in it.
- A real and perceived crisis (crisis appears in almost all cases as a driving force).
- An unexpected greater or lesser level of organizational performance.

Triggering Events

Among triggering events are the following:

- Events in the environment that abruptly create a calamity. Examples are sharp recessions, unexpected innovations by competitors, and natural disasters.
- Events in the environment that create opportunity. Examples are the discovery of unexpected market niches, the sudden availability of financial resources, and technological breakthroughs.
- Major unresolved conflicts or a crisis caused by a major management shake-up or blunder.
- A new manager or management team occupied with new vision and ideas. (In 80 percent of the case studies, the change was managed by a new manager.)
- A "coup d'état," "insurgency," or "mass movement" in the organization or in its metasystem.
- Political interference. New legislation or change in legislation.
- Corporate merger, acquisition, or takeover.

In summary, three types of conditions under which transformation occurs were specified: internal permitting conditions, external enabling conditions, and precipitating conditions. The first two types set an organization up for transformation, whereas the third type provides the pressures for transformation. Given these conditions, when trigger events occur, they initiate the unfolding of the transformation.

HOW: THE STAGES AND PROCESS OF SECOND-ORDER CHANGE

We have examined the process of second-order change in this book from two perspectives: (1) from the theoretical or empirical perspective, and (2) from the applied or practical perspective (planned and managed change). From the first perspective, the process of second-order change is characterized by decline and crisis, repeated failing efforts to correct the situation by first-order changes, chaos, efforts to go "back to basics," demise, discontinuity, reframing, a sudden shift in perception, insight, illumination, a discovery or creation of a new vision, and a jump to a higher order.

The second perspective had a "planned" and "managed" or "applied" viewpoint. Three important notions were added. The first was that in real-life situations, a new order is not suddenly or rapidly established. Although second-order change may involve momentary insights, a sudden illumination, or a sudden shift in perception, it nevertheless takes time, energy, and resources to translate ideas and visions into actual programs, procedures, and structures. The second notion was that the process of transformation can be facilitated and managed; we probably cannot stop or avoid social evolution, but we have the capabilities to shape its direction. The third notion was that understanding the principles of evolution of organizations enables us to develop strategies and technologies for deliberately participating in this process.

In Chapter 6 we suggested a two-stage model of second-order change. The first stage we termed "transformation"; the second stage we called "transition." Thinking in terms of change stages, we can develop it even further. Summarizing the literature on both second-order change and second-order planned change, the following four developmental stages emerge:

1. Crisis
2. Transformation
3. Transition
4. Stabilization and development.

Figure 13.1 describes the cycle of second-order change and its stages.

1. Crisis. External and internal pressures and needs are not appropriately met. Warning signals about the need for a radical

Figure   13.1.   The Cycle of Second-Order Planned Change

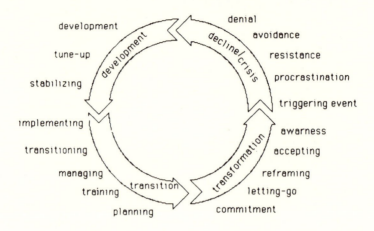

Source: Prepared by the authors.

reorganization are denied or avoided. Efforts to cope with problems by first-order change result in crisis, chaos, procrastination, efforts to go "back to basics," resistance to change, and anger. Through ever increasing fluctuation, the system reaches a critical point beyond which the alternative is demise or revitalization. We will need more study to clarify which transformations include the stage of decline, and which do not. The passage of an organization from good adaptive performance to a state of high performance and excellence need not include a stage of decline.

2. Transformation. This stage includes the acceptance of the need for change, discontinuity from the past, commitment to change, reframing processes, creating or discovering new realities, a sudden shift in perception, a moment of illumination, insight, and the emergence of a new possibility, a new direction, different quantitatively and qualitatively from the old one. This stage also involves departure from the old beliefs and habits, the process of "letting go," and unblocking energy needed for transformation.

3. Transition. This stage includes planned and managed efforts to translate ideas and visions into action steps, programs, structures, and procedures. The focus is on assessing solutions and their impact, and managing the transition from an unstable state to a new, stable state.

4. Stabilization and development. This is the time when the change of program is institutionalized, tuned up, maintained, and developed by first-order changes.

In this book the focus has been on the "transformation stage" from both the theoretical and the practical perspective.

The description of the process of second-order change, or of how this type of change occurs and evolves, is based on both micro and macro theoretical perspectives and studies from various fields. Wallace (1956), for example, in a cross-cultural study examines cultural changes that have occurred at various times and places. He then derives a series of idealized stages through which successful cultural transformations have passed. The stages are (1) steady state, (2) distortion, (3) revitalization and reformulation, (4) transformation, and (5) routinization. Wallace points to stress distortion, crisis, and leadership as factors needed for transformation. He argues that transformation usually occurs as a moment of insight, a brief period of realization of opportunities.

The stages described by Kuhn in which science develops, the stages described by Prigogine in which living systems develop, and the stages described by Marx in which social regimes are changed are all very similar and share some common characteristics with the process described by Wallace.

It should not be surprising that the creative process follows the same general stages, because basically creativity must somehow be at the core of transformational processes. Here the basic stages are (1) preparation, (2) incubation, (3) illumination, and (4) verification (J. L. Adams 1974). The creative process includes setting aside the assumptions that are conventionally made about reality and engaging in techniques or activities that open up one's self to more primal and direct perceptions of reality. Such perceptions often result from deliberate or accidental use of altered states of consciousness (Watzlawick et al. 1974).

Table 13.1 shows the sequential stages suggested by the above approaches. It summarizes the idealized stages of each of the varied processes through which human systems become transformed in response to environmental changes, internal changes, and deterministic, evolutionary processes. As shown in the table, the stages are, to a considerable degree, homologous. The elements of steady state — growth of perturbation, resulting in crisis and revolutionary change, in which a new order is established — are common to most of the above processes.

Table 13.1
The Transformation Process in Various Fields

Cultural Revitalization (Wallace)	Scientific Revolutions (Kuhn)	Dissipative Structures (Prigogine)	Historical Determinism (Marx)	Creative Process (Adams)
Steady state	Normal science	Fluctuations within defined boundaries	Steady state	Preparation
Cultural distortion	Growth of anomalies		Growing dissatisfaction	Incubation
		Fluctuations past a threshold		Illumination
Revitalization	Crisis		Conflicts	
				Verification
Reformulation	Revolution	Crisis	Crisis	
Transformation	Normal science within new	Jump to a higher, new order	Revolution	
Routinization	paradigm		New order	

Source: Prepared by the authors.

WHAT: WHAT IS CHANGED IN SECOND-ORDER CHANGE

Analyzing and summarizing cases, research, and theories for understanding what is changed in second-order change shows that there are basically four perspectives. Table 13.2 summarizes the four perspectives and classifies them according to the theoretical perspective, the organization's elements and dimensions that are changed, and the visibility to the organization's members of the existence and function of these elements.

1. Organizational paradigm. This is defined as the "metarules," presuppositions or underlying assumptions that unnoticeably shape perceptions, procedures, and behaviors. It includes the implicit ideals and ideas the organization lives by, the philosophy that provides a logical framework for organizing.
2. Organizational mission and purpose. This includes more explicitly stated programs for direction of action. It involves statements about "what business we are in," what the strategies are for achieving the organizational mission, goals, and policies.
3. Organizational culture. This includes the organization's beliefs, values, and norms. It also deals with symbolic action and elements

Table 13.2
The Content of Second-Order Change

Perspective	Changed Elements	Changed Dimension	Visibility
Evolution theory	Context, template, metarules, world view	Paradigm	Unnoticed
Management theory	Goals, reason for existence, policies, strategies	Core mission and purpose	Low
Planned change	Norms, values, beliefs	Culture	Medium
Systems theory	Input, output, throughput, processes	Functioning processes	High

Source: Provided by the authors.

such as myths, rituals, and ceremonies, the look and arrangement of the physical setting, and the style of management and relationships.

4. Functional processes. These include the organizational structure, management, technology, decision-making processes, recognition and rewards, and communication patterns. These are all processes generally dealt with in first-order change.

There are, of course, some overlaps between the above dimensions; however, it is suggested that each level is embedded in and shaped by higher levels. Figure 13.2 shows the four elements as organized in a "nested framework."

This model suggests that changing the organizational paradigm will necessarily entail changes in the organizational mission and purpose, culture, and functional processes. Changes in the organizational mission and purpose will entail changes in culture and functional processes, but not necessarily in the organizational paradigm. Hence, change in the organization's culture will entail changes in the organization's functional processes, but not necessarily in its mission and paradigm. And, last, changes in functional processes do not necessarily entail changes in culture, mission, and paradigm.

The model suggests that the efforts to change the organizational culture, as suggested by organizational development practitioners (Burke 1981), do not go deeply enough to facilitate second-order change.

Figure 13.2. The Content of Second-Order Change

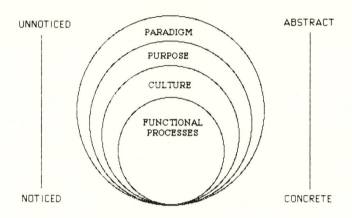

Source: Provided by the author.

Furthermore, it is possible that organizations will experience a rapid growth and expansion without changing their mission, purpose, and paradigm. This type of development is a typical first-order change. People Express experienced a dramatic growth in a very short time without changing its culture, mission, or paradigm; the change was relatively smooth and first-order in nature (Hackman 1984). The conclusion is that second-order change is basically a change in the organizational paradigm, ideology, underlying assumptions, or world view.

In this study, second-order change (or transformation) is described as change in all four dimensions: in functional processes, in mission and purpose, in culture, and in the organization's world view or paradigm. It is proposed that the organizational paradigm provides the context and logic for the organization's culture, purpose, and operations. Therefore, every change in the paradigm will inevitably entail changes in the other three dimensions. On the other hand, it is proposed that change in one of the other dimensions may, but will not necessarily, entail changes in the other dimensions. Functioning processes may change because of a new technology, new products, or new procedures, but they will not necessarily trigger changes in the other dimensions. Hence it is proposed that the less visible to top management the dimension is, the deeper the change and perhaps the greater the possibility that the change will be

Figure 13.3. Integrated Model for Understanding Second-Order Change

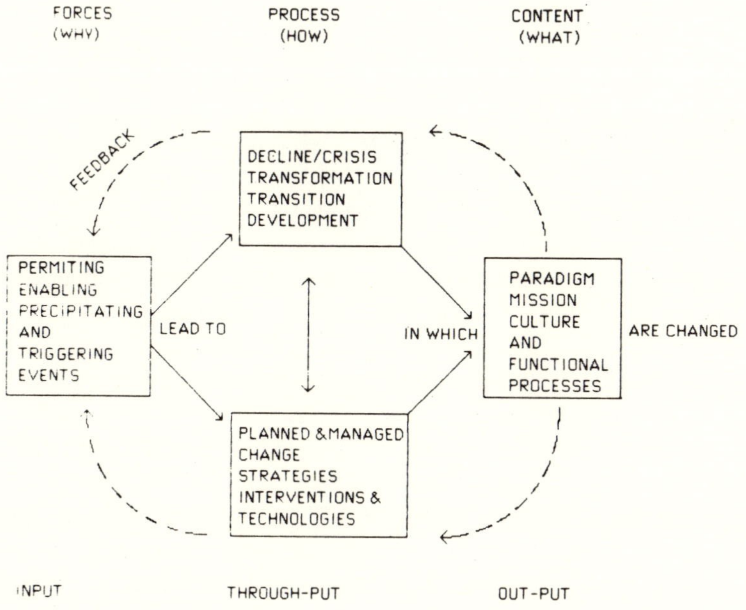

```
FORCES              PROCESS              CONTENT
(WHY)               (HOW)                (WHAT)
```

```
                         DECLINE/CRISIS
          FEEDBACK       TRANSFORMATION
                         TRANSITION
                         DEVELOPMENT

PERMITING                                          PARADIGM
ENABLING                                           MISSION
PRECIPITATING                                      CULTURE
AND          LEAD TO              IN WHICH         AND         ARE CHANGED
TRIGGERING                                         FUNCTIONAL
EVENTS                                             PROCESSES

                         PLANNED & MANAGED
                         CHANGE
                         STRATEGIES
                         INTERVENTIONS &
                         TECHNOLOGIES

INPUT               THROUGH-PUT          OUT-PUT
```

Source: Prepared by the authors.

irreversible. The three questions used for understanding the process of second-order change can be placed in a time sequence. Figure 13.3 shows the suggested relationships.

The driving forces for change can also be seen as input, where the process of change is the throughput and the change in the organizational paradigm is output. Taking the open-system perspective makes the model more dynamic and open, with feedback loops that affect conditions, processes, and change strategies.

The model suggests, for example, that at any moment in the process of second-order change, multitudes of strategies, approaches, and technologies are available for practitioners and managers who wish to facilitate and manage the process in the most effective way. Choosing a specific strategy and approach is dependent on or affected by the specific driving forces for change that exist, by the stage of the organization in the process of change, and by what dimension needs to be changed. On the other hand, using a specific approach affects the process of change and the content of change in a specific way. These ideas will be further developed in Chapter 14.

GENERAL ORIENTATIONS TO SECOND-ORDER PLANNED CHANGE

The strategies for facilitating transformation can be classified according to their implicit premises about determinism. Based on Ackoff's (1981) model and Sztompka's (1981) ideas on spontaneity and planning, we suggest a model that classifies strategies and approaches for facilitating second-order change by their implicit premises about whether the means (change approaches and processes) or the ends (the desired future) are given or can be chosen. The model is shown in Table 13.3.

The deterministic orientation holds that people have almost no influence on the desired future; all they can do is generate a variety of activities that will be selected by natural processes of evolution. Examples of this orientation are the natural selection perspective on the evolution of organizations (McKelvey 1982) and catastrophe theory (Thom 1975; Zeeman 1976).

The adaptive orientation holds that one cannot create a desired future but can only forecast or predict the future, and choose the means for forecasting and for preparing for the future. The implicit premise is that the future provides mainly negative trends (shocks, catastrophes, accelerating changes, ever growing and unmanageable complexities). The focus is on developing forecasting approaches, and on creating and designing structures and mechanisms that will minimize the shock of the

Table 13.3
Orientations to Second-Order Planned Change

Orientation	Means	Ends
Deterministic	Given	Given
Adaptive	Chosen	Given (negative)
Facilitative	Chosen	Given (positive)
Active	Given	Chosen
Proactive	Chosen	Chosen
Interactive	Chosen/given	Chosen/given

Source: Prepared by the authors.

coming future. An example is the "adaptation strategy" suggested by DeGreen (1982).

The facilitative orientation also holds that the future is given, but is basically positive. This perspective is taken by many New Age thinkers (Ferguson 1980; Markley & Harman 1982) and some organizational transformation scholars. Hence, what people can do is what Owen (1983b) calls "midwife the new," or help to bring it about.

The active orientation holds that the desired future is the creation of people. People can create a desired state by having a shared image of the future. Such an image shapes thoughts and actions, and thus "pulls" toward its fulfillment. The main effort is put on visualizing, creative thinking, and reframing (Boyce 1984).

The proactive orientation holds that both the desired future and the strategies for pursuing it are in the hands of people. People are the creators of their worlds. People can create in their minds a desired future, and then choose or design strategies for achieving this desired future. Examples of this orientation are the model developed by Burns and Nelson (1983), which combines strategies with desired paradigms, and the model of strategic change as suggested by Davis (1982).

The interactive orientation holds that the relationships between means and ends are mutually causal, and that there are some deterministic aspects in the evolution of social systems. Understanding these deterministic aspects will enable people to participate in and shape more freely both the means and the ends. The focus is on learning systems and self-organizing, self-transcending systems. Examples are the approaches of Argyris and Schon (1978), Jantsch (1980), and consciousness raising and changing (McWhinney 1980).

MODEL FOR CLASSIFYING SECOND-ORDER CHANGE APPROACHES

The last section dealt with orientations that guide and shape change strategies. This section goes one step further by analyzing strategies. The strategies in this study are categorized into two groups. The first, termed "transformation," consists of those approaches aimed at facilitating the first stages of the process of change. These approaches are aimed at raising awareness of the need for a radical change, at helping accept the need for change, at "letting go" processes, energizing, and reframing. The second group of approaches is termed "transition." These approaches are aimed at planning and managing the transition to a new state. Our point is that approaches can be classified according to the stage they aim to facilitate.

Therefore, second-order change approaches can be classified by the developmental stages at which they aim. In this chapter, four developmental stages are suggested: (1) crisis, (2) transformation, (3) transition, and (4) stabilization and development. The approaches can also be classified by their time span: by whether the approach is short or long. And approaches can be classified by their scope: how many aspects, dimensions, or people the approach is aimed at. Combining the three dimensions of stage, time, and scope, a second-order change approach cube can be constructed as shown in Figure 13.4.

In this book we have concentrated on transformation strategy and approaches. These approaches aim at facilitating and managing the transformation stage. Some of them are wide in their scope; others are narrow. Some are short in their time span; others are long. The dark lines in the cube mark the area most of the described approaches belong to. For example, reframing approaches can be classified as narrow, short, and transformational. They last only a short time, they focus on a specific symptom or problem, and they aim at creating new choices.

Obviously the alternative approaches presented in Figure 13.4 are extremes and no approach needs to adhere to them, for the middle course not only is possible but also may be desirable. The cube may be helpful

Figure 13.4. Second-Order Change Interventions

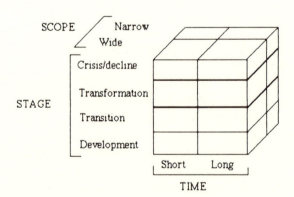

Source: Prepared by the authors.

for managers and consultants considering ways to facilitate second-order change. They may use these dimensions and the 16 alternatives as guides. We can now define the subject of this book, which was how to renew organizations and which focused on interventions aimed at facilitating the transformation stage. A summary of these approaches is made in Chapter 14.

14

Integrating Practice and Theory

In this book we have described research, theories, and approaches that deal with organization transformation. In this chapter we integrate practice and theory, transformation approaches and transformation theory. We begin the process with a summary of the transformation approaches.

TRANSFORMATION APPROACHES: SUMMARY

In this book six approaches for facilitating and managing the transformation stage have been described. The purpose of this section is to summarize, classify, and compare them. Table 14.1 classifies the six approaches by their specific change method and by the dimension on which they focus.

Table 14.1 helps us to postulate the following propositions:

1. Despite the differences in strategy and in approaching second-order planned change, the approaches shown in Table 14.1 share some important characteristics. First, the ultimate purpose of all of them is to change
the organization's "metarules"; underlying assumptions, world view, or what is defined in this work as paradigm. Second, they all ultimately attempt to create visions, choices, ideas, and directions that are beyond the confines of the current paradigm. Third, they all focus on the organization's members' perception of reality and what shapes this perception.

2. The basic difference between these approaches is that some of them focus on the organizational paradigm directly, while others deal with it indirectly. For example, facilitating the process of paradigmatic change Nicoll (1984a), introducing new paradigms (Burns & Nelson 1983), and introducing a new ideal type way of organizing, such as excellence (Peters & Waterman 1982) or metanoic (Kiefer & Stroh 1984), all focus directly on the organizational paradigm, its functions and dysfunctions, and on developing better alternatives.

3. The approaches that attempt to facilitate paradigmatic change indirectly focus on dimensions that are strongly related to the organizational paradigm and, in a broad sense, may be considered part of it. These dimensions are the belief system, the mission and purpose, symbolic aspects of the organizational culture (such as myths, metaphors, rituals), and second-order problems and symptoms. Figure 14.1 shows the proposed relationships among these elements.

4. Many scientists argue that organizational paradigms operate at the unconscious level. They shape perceptions, beliefs, values, and actions. However, paradigms are expressed in daily life by what members perceive as right or wrong, good or bad; by what they say about their organization; by what they perceive as basic problems; and by the mission and purpose of the organization. However, paradigms not only shape beliefs, purposes, problems, and stories; they are also shaped by

Figure 14.1. The Targeted Dimensions of Transformation Interventions

ORGANIZATIONAL PARADIGM

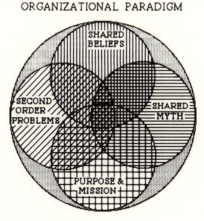

Source: Prepared by the authors.

Table 14.1
Transformation Approaches: Summary

Methods, Models, and Techniques	Target
1. CHANGING THE ORGANIZATIONAL PARADIGM	
Facilitating the process of paradigmatic change	
"delete design model" (Albert 1984)	Paradigm
"high performance programming" (Burns & Nelson 1983)	
"paradigm reframing" (Nicoll 1980)	
Strategic change	
"changing context" (Davis 1982)	Mission and Purpose
"purposing" (Vaill 1982)	
"strategic change" (Tichy 1983)	
Future envisioning	
"envisioning" (Boyce 1984; Rutte 1984)	Mission and Purpose
"fantasy theme analysis" (Mulligan & Kelly 1983)	
2. INTRODUCING EXCELLENCE	
Introducing new developed ideal types	
"excellence" (Peters & Waterman 1982)	Paradigm
"high performance" (Vaill 1978)	
"metanoic" (Kiefer & Senge 1984)	
"adaptive" (DeGreen 1982)	
"humanistic capitalism" (Harris 1983)	

3. CHANGING MYTHS AND RITUALS
   Changing the organizational myths
   "changing symbolic behavior" (Jones et al. 1983)
   "changing myths" (Boje et al. 1982; Owne 1983c; Stephens et al. 1983)
   "changing metaphors" (Sibbet & Cowood 1983; Smith 1982)

   Myths and Symbols

4. REFRAMING
   Reframing
   "paradoxical interventions" (Palazzoli 1978; Papp 1981)
   "problems reframing" (Watzlawick et al. 1974)
   "N.L.P." (Bandler & Grinder 1982)
   "short-term interventions" (Fisch et al. 1983; Minuchin & Fishman 1981)

   Second-order Problems

5. CONSCIOUSNESS RAISING AND CHANGING
   Transpersonal models and Eastern methods
   (Johnston 1983; Shapiro 1978)
   "psychosynthesis" (Brown 1983)
   "raising consciousness" (Culbert 1976; Freire 1970)
   "the alchemic" and "the paedogenic" models (McWhinney 1980, 1982)
   "creative thinking" (DeBono 1971; Adams 1974; Agor 1984; Tilden 1983)

   Beliefs, Logical Framework

6. ENERGIZING
   Energizing and rechanneling energy
   "the flow state" (Ackerman 1984)
   "spirited work & organization" (Ritscher 1983; Connelly 1984)
   "the alchemic model" (McWhinney 1983)
   "structural approaches" (Adams 1983)
   "Gestalt methods" (Nevis 1980; Merry & Brown 1986)

   Spirit, Motivation, Energy

Source: Prepared by the authors.

287

them. There are mutual relationships among these five elements, as Figure 14.1 suggests. With drastic changes in the environment and in the needs, they will begin telling new stories, the organization's purpose may prove to be irrelevant, and problems may reach a critical point. Changing one of these elements will entail changes in the other elements and will result in paradigmatic shift.

5. Second-order planned change, as mentioned before, is a long and exhausting process. A thorough examination of all the suggested approaches shows that there is no evidence that they can facilitate the whole process from its beginning (the unconscious stage) to its accomplishment (institutionalization). There is, however, some empirical and nonempirical (personal observations of scientists) evidence that each approach, intervention, and technology may facilitate one stage or phase of the process. Thus, for example, consciousness-expansion interventions may help members become aware of the current situation and of the need for a paradigmatic change, while presenting new ideal types may help them to choose and adopt a new paradigm.

6. The discussion about what is changed in second-order change brings us to the conclusion that if we want to facilitate this change, we probably should focus our efforts on changing the underlying assumptions and the abstract rules that shape and limit members' perceptions, beliefs, and behaviors. For that purpose, our interventions should be guided by, based on, and embedded in theories, models, and concepts that represent a new paradigm. We first need a paradigmatic change in the field of planned change.

7. Intervention models, approaches, technologies, and concepts that represent a new paradigm might at first appear illogical, blurred, and unfamiliar. They may even be rejected. That is because they are based on a different logical framework; they cannot be understood and judged within the old framework. Einstein's concepts may be perceived as illogical if they are understood and judged within the Newtonian logical framework. It takes time for a new scientific paradigm to establish itself. It is time-consuming to develop tools and methods of inquiry to provide empirical support for the new models and theories. It is assumed that once the paradigm of second-order planned change establishes itself, concepts such as organizational energy, paradigm, spirituality, and self-organization, which appear to be blurred, nonexistent, and unmeasurable, will be accepted and understood.

INTEGRATING THEORY AND PRACTICE

In this section an effort will be made to integrate the essence of the four subjects dealt with in this work in an integrating framework:

1. Approaches, technologies, and models
2. Strategies for facilitating second-order change
3. Studies of second-order change in organizations
4. Theoretical perspectives on the evolution of living systems.

The organizing framework is based on the main ideas of Kuhn's (1970) and Prigogine's (1984) theories, and on studies of evolutionary processes in organizations conducted by Elgin (1977), Miller (1982), Miller and Friesen (1980a, 1980b), and Nicoll (1980). The two theories were chosen because they include most of the ideas about the evolution of living systems. They are inclusive and well-integrated. The studies mentioned are based on longitudinal scientific research and provide empirical support for some of the basic ideas of the theories.

The organizing framework classifies the approaches according to their target for change or the organizational dimension on which they focus. From this perspective, we have four dimensions or targets for a transformation effort:

1. The efforts for change are focused on changing the organizational paradigm directly. This strategy includes the intervention model of Burns and Nelson (1983), the intervention approach of Nicoll (1980), and the approach of introducing new paradigms (such as "excellence") to the organization members.
2. The efforts for change are focused on changing the organization's mission and purpose. This strategy includes approaches such as "strategic change" (Davis 1982; Tichy 1983), "future envisioning" (Boyce 1984; Rutte 1984), "purposing" (Vaill 1982), and "strategic planning" (Lindman & Lippitt 1979).
3. The efforts for change are focused on changing myths, symbols, and metaphors. This strategy includes the change approaches of Owen (1983c), Boje (1982), Jones et al. (1983), and Stephens et al. (1983).
4. The change efforts are focused on second-order problems, symptoms, and attempted solutions. This strategy includes reframing approaches (Minuchin & Fishman 1981), short-term, here-and-now

interventions (Watzlawick et al. 1974), and paradoxical interventions (Palazzioli 1978).

From this perspective, consciousness expansion, awareness raising, and energizing are methods that may be used as part of each of the above approaches. The assumption is that in each approach, different activities facilitate a different stage of the process. Hence, they may be organized in a sequence according to their possible use in each stage of the change process. Thus, for example, it is assumed that presenting new paradigms (such as "excellence" or "spirited") to the organization's members is effective only after they are aware of the evolutionary process taking place in their organization, and after they have accepted the need for a major change. Therefore, in this case, consciousness expansion interventions must precede the paradigm-presenting intervention. The integrated framework is shown in Table 14.2. The table describes five developmental stages that constitute the process of second-order change in organizations.

Stage 1. Development and Change

Organizations are constantly fluctuating, making internal adjustments, incremental changes, and improvements. They constantly seek better ways to adapt to changes in their environment. At this stage, problems are solved within the current paradigm. Improvements do not change the purpose of the organization. Interventions are aimed at facilitating first-order changes, first-order solutions to problems. Depending on the degree and pace of environmental change and on members' needs, the organization could be in this stage for a long time.

Stage 2. Creating Awareness

Under circumstances of rapid and drastic environmental changes and changes in members' needs, first-order changes cannot provide satisfactory solutions to problems and adaptation to the new environment. Members tend to ignore the need for drastic changes or to postpone them. The results are sometimes "muddling through," vicious circles, and crises. To help members accept the need for a second-order change, interventions to raise awareness are needed. Each of the four strategies provides different types of interventions and technologies for raising awareness, and each suggests different targets on which members focus their attention.

One way is to increase people's awareness of symptoms, attempted solutions, second-order problems, and behaviors "here and now." A second way is to increase their awareness of the existence and impact of the current paradigm. A third way is to increase their awareness of the existence of purpose and mission, and the impact of these on procedures and behaviors. The fourth way is to bring their attention to symbolic aspects such as myths and rituals. Practitioners suggest a vast array of consciousness-raising techniques. Eastern techniques (such as meditation), psychosynthesis, and Gestalt are used by those who employ the "changing consciousness" approach. "Changing myths" raises awareness of the functions of the existing myths. "Paradigmatic change" has technologies that sharpen one's senses to the existence and functions of beliefs and underlying assumptions, while "reframing" suggests examining attempted solutions, dysfunctional behavior, and secondary gains as a way of increasing consciousness.

Stage 3. Midwifing the New

Fluctuations reach a critical point, and the organization may be trapped in a vicious circle and deep crisis. The organization may reach a critical point beyond which it could face demise or new possibilities, a new state of being. At this stage new ideas, representing a new paradigm, emerge at the periphery. There is still strong resistance to change, and acceptance of the belief that what worked in the past will also work in the future. Becoming more aware may lead to the acceptance of the need to change. In the third stage the main task is to encourage the search for, and discovery or creation of, new possibilities, new ideas, and new choices based on a higher-level paradigm.

Each of the four approaches provides a variety of technologies for the search and the discovery of new directions. "Reframing" offers technologies such as paradoxical methods, neurolinguistic programming, and creative thinking; "paradigmatic change" offers "ready-made" new paradigms that can be introduced by the consultant at this stage; the "changing mission" strategy offers technologies such as visioning, strategic planning, and purposing; and "changing myths" suggests searching for new myths and symbols.

Table 14.2
Integrating Theory and Practice

| | Intervention Strategy | | | | |
Reframing Problems Symptoms, Concepts	Changing Paradigm	Changing Myths, Symbols	Changing Mission, Purpose	The Process in Organization	Theory
STAGE 1: ORGANIZATIONAL PLANNED CHANGE AND DEVELOPMENT					
Efforts to adjust to the external and internal changes without changing the organization's purpose, myth, and world view				Changes in the environment and in the organization; adaptation efforts by development; step-by-step changes within the current belief system, purpose, and mission	*Kuhn*: normal science discoveries and inventions within current paradigm; scientific developments are guided and shaped by current paradigm. *Prigogine*: energy flow and fluctuations within certain limits
STAGE 2: CREATING AWARENESS					
Awareness of second-order problems and symptoms; awareness of attempted solutions and secondary gains	Awareness of present paradigm; awareness of process of paradigmatic change, identifying where organization is located in cycle of paradigmatic change	Awareness of existing myths and their functions; awareness of marginal and conflicting myths; awareness of the function of metaphors and symbolic language	Boundary clarification between the individual and the organization; consciousness expansion (Gestalt, transpersonal, psychosynthesis and Eastern technologies)	Incremental, minor changes cannot provide satisfactory solutions; call for "back to basics," and stick to the old, "muddling through"; crisis	*Kuhn*: growth of anomalies and crisis. *Prigogine*: through positive feedback, fluctuations are enhanced and reach a critical point

STAGE 3: CREATING READINESS FOR CHANGE: MIDWIFING THE NEW

Encouraging creative thinking; reframing; paradoxical interventions; N.L.P.	Encouraging marginality, vanguard roles, and new ideas; introducing new, developing paradigms, such as "excellence," "metanoic," "spirituality," "flow state"	Creating or strengthening new myths; developing new symbols, new metaphors, new symbolic language	Visioning; future envisioning; strategic change; purposing; strategic planning	New ideas emerge at the periphery and are diffused, or new leadership suggests new vision and direction; struggle for informal legitimization	*Kuhn:* able individuals working at the margin suggest ideas and explanations based on a new paradigm *Prigogine:* the system is perturbed and stands before new possibilities of order or death

STAGE 4: CREATING ENERGY FOR CHANGE: CREATING AN OPEN SPACE

Encouraging cross-fertilization Democratization Legitimization in system and metasystem Letting go of the old			
"Networking" "Fusion team"	Alignment; attunement	The new ideas are subject to political campaign and conflicts; struggle for formal legitimization results in a sudden shift and the acceptance of the new order	*Kuhn:* scientific revolution; a sudden shift to a new paradigm *Prigogine:* the system jumps into a higher order, more complex and qualitatively different

STAGE 5: FACILITATING TRANSITION

From changes in perceptions and beliefs to changes in behavior	Establish two management structures Task teams and steering committees Design the desired state Organize and plan for the change Impact analysis Training Implement the change program Evaluation and tune-up	The new ideas are translated to rules, regulations, procedures, and structures; developing socialization mechanism	*Kuhn:* scientific theories provide guidelines for applied research; development of schools, research institutions, tools, technologies, and language; institutionalization

Source: Prepared by the authors.

Stage 4. Creating an Open Space

When new ideas are diffused, they become subject to political campaign and conflicts. Conflicts can be a paralyzing force, and may deepen the crisis unless communication channels are open and democratic processes take place. The main task at this stage is to encourage the formal system and leadership to attend to these new ideas, to examine their utility for the organization, and to set the stage for democratic processes. Moreover, legitimization is also needed at the metasystem level. The main suggestion here is that facilitating second-order change involves issues such as power struggles, conflicts, interest groups, and political campaigns — processes most practitioners tend to ignore. Democratization implies setting the stage or creating an open space for new ideas to be heard, examined, and accepted or rejected. And, last but not least, it is important to assure support and legitimization at the metasystem level; otherwise, the change probably will not persist for long. This stage also involves "letting go" and "holding on" processes.

Stage 5. Facilitating Transition to the New State

The process of searching for, creating, discovering, and accepting new ideas has been termed "transformation." Translating these ideas into actual programs and implementing the change has been termed "transition" (see Chapter 8). For transition to be facilitated, many complex actions are involved, such as establishing task forces, translating ideas into programs, analyzing the impact of the future state on the present state, developing training programs, training, budgeting, restructuring, and reorganizing. Much has been written on facilitating the transition phase (Ackerman 1982; Beckhard & Harris 1977; Kimberly & Quinn 1984; Nadler 1982), and the main focus of this book has been on transformation approaches rather than transition approaches. Like the transformation phase, the transition phase may be divided into developmental stages such as planning, implementing, institutionalizing, and tuning up, as suggested in the model presented previously.

To summarize, Table 14.2 suggests that the type of approach one chooses to use to facilitate second-order change is determined by the developmental stage of the organization. At each stage, multiple approaches and technologies are available for moving the organization to the next stage. The use of these approaches depends on the consultant's skills, the type and the readiness of the organization, the attitudes of metasystems, and the expected outcomes of the intervention. We will discuss later how the type of approach used should take into account the type of transformation that is taking place.

SUMMARY OF CASE STUDIES ANALYSIS

In this book more than 30 case studies, representing second-order change efforts, have been reviewed. Ten of these cases are described and analyzed, and the others briefly mentioned for the purpose of understanding specific issues. The cases represent a vast array of organizations, such as prisons (Gluckstern & Packard 1977); mental hospitals (Sheldon 1979); hospitals (Tichy 1977); schools (Dwyer et al. 1983); colleges (Warren 1984); communes (Levy 1980); public services, such as the Post Office (Biggart 1977) and the telephone company (Nadler 1982); religious organizations (Bartunek 1984); and business organizations (Ackerman 1982).

Many of these case studies take an empirical theoretical perspective or a management perspective. They study the process of change and aspects of management. Few case studies describe the whole process of second-order planned change. It is, therefore, too early to evaluate second-order planned change efforts. It is, however, possible and useful to summarize common themes or to state generalizations based on a survey of the case studies. The following are generalizations based on a review of the case studies.

Resistance to and Persistence of the Change

Unlike first-order changes, second-order changes involve two fronts of strong resistance. The first is within the organization; the second is without. When the change is too radical and the system is vastly different from its domain, it threatens its environment and generates strong resistance. Thus, the case studies point out that it is probably easier to transform organizations by creating a new system or a new unit for which new personnel are recruited and trained, than to renew existing systems. However, in both strategies the system must confront the resistance of its domain. Thus, it is easier to create a new, innovative, open, alternative school than it is to renew one. It is very difficult to keep the innovative school from reverting to being a regular public school, as the studies of Gold and Miles (1981) and Dwyer et al. (1983) pointed out. Our conclusion is, therefore, that second-order change efforts must be measured by the persistence of the change, not by institutionalization.

The Persistence of the Change

Elements that distinguish between reversible and irreversible second-order change are (1) the support of the system's stakeholders, clients, consumers, or customers (parents' support, in the cases of the alternative elementary school and clients in the cases of the alternative health system), and (2) the support of metasystems (district, state, and federal levels in the cases of changes in a local school). However, while these two conditions are necessary, they are not sufficient. Customers, metasystems, and stakeholders tend to change. To assure long-term environmental support and metasystems' support, they must have a positive attitude or at least be indifferent to the change.

Where second-order change in a specific system is not supported by the metasystem, and is confronted with resistance and hostility, the transformed system must find, or even create, what Aldrich (1979) calls a new niche. The system has to establish a new network of support; to find systems with similar world views and to collaborate with them; to find a new environment more supportive of and favorable to the change; to develop its own resources; and/or to develop a new domain. The system must close its boundaries to its previous incoming information, people, and matter, and open it to new resources. The system must develop selection mechanisms and socialization systems to assure its survival. Alternative, open, and creative educational systems already represent such behavior (the Montessori network, for example; see also Broad 1977).

Time and Cost

The case studies show that the process of second-order planned change is a long and expensive one. It may take between two and ten years or more to accomplish such a process. The process may include moments of insight and a relatively sudden shift in views, perceptions, and attitudes; however, there is a long way to go until ideas are translated into rules, procedures, technologies, and structures, and until a new order is established. A study evaluating the cost of planned change shows that it demands the establishment of steering committees, task forces, and, in many cases, two parallel management systems. Those who are the target of a change are obliged to devote part of their time to participating in the process as observers, planners, implementers. They must spend time in "reeducation" programs and workshops. The estimated average cost of the process may be 5–10 percent of the annual budget or production volume of each change unit per year.

SOME FINAL THOUGHTS AND SUGGESTIONS FOR FURTHER STUDY

Transformation is a new domain of practice and study. Most of the material described in the book is only in the beginning stages of development, study, and research. There are many open questions, and it is difficult to single out areas particularly in need of study — the whole field needs much study. Nevertheless, we have a number of concerns and a number of open questions that we are curious about and that seem worthy of particular attention.

System and Subsystem Transformation

One of the main questions about transformation is the relationship between a transformation in a system and in one of its subsystems. Much work remains to be done on the relationship between an organization and a transformation in one of its parts. In system terms, what is the effect of a transformation of a subsystem on its system?

A second-order change in a subsystem does not mean that there is a second-order change in the system to which it belongs. A transformation of the sales department does not mean there is transformation in the company. The change in sales necessitates changes in its relationships with other departments and the company as a whole. But this does not mean a transformation of the entire company. The change probably necessitates a degree of support from the company, and support, or at least indifference, from other parts of the organization, but this is not transformation.

The level by which we define a change as "first order" or "second order" depends on our viewpoint from within a system hierarchy. From the department level and below (teams and individuals), the change in the department is second-level. From all levels above the department (the company, the consortium), the change in the department is first-level or not noted at all. The change in the department may not have been of concern to the consortium to which the company belongs. A second-order change in a work team in the department may affect the department but no more than that. An individual in that team may pass through a transformation, but that does not transform the team, and may leave no mark on the department.

Does a second-order change in a subsystem necessarily lead to a first-order change in the system? Possibly yes, possibly no. The effect of the change in the subsystem on the system probably depends on the centrality of the subsystem and how tightly it is coupled with other parts of the system. The more peripheral a department and the less tightly it is coupled with the rest of the organization, the less effect will any change within it have on the rest of the organization.

A transformation in a subsystem may also lead to a transformation in the system. Cutting out an appendix seems to have little effect on the body as a whole; removing a limb or a major organ can lead to a major change in the body. A heart attack can lead to a personal transformation. Similarly, at the organizational level, could a second-order change in one subsystem lead to a second-order change in the organization as a whole? Could transformation in the management or in the production of a subsystem lead to a transformation in the organization? What is clear is that we do not know enough about this subject, which needs study and research.

Also unclear is the relationship between transformation in a number of subsystems and change in the system as a whole. Which subsystems? How many subsystems need to go through a second-order change for the system as a whole to be transformed? Can one draw an analogy between the heart attack and the organizational level? Relative to individuals, organizations are not tightly coupled systems. It is possible that in organizations, transformation cannot come about through subsystem transformation. Perhaps in organizations, transformation can occur only by a change in a dimension that affects all subsystems. This points in the direction of the approaches detailed in this book: changing the paradigm, core processes, the mission.

This leads to recognizing the complexity of the subject and how little we know about it. At one level, with individuals, transforming a subsystem sometimes does, and sometimes does not, transform the person. We do not know if this holds at the organizational level. In short, we know little of this subject, and it deserves study.

Is Transformation Always to a Higher Level of Complexity?

According to Prigogine and the consciousness evolution approach, at a certain point — when the perturbations of a system reach the elastic limit — the system faces a choice of either transforming to a higher level of complexity or of disintegrating. Do organizations and other human and social systems face only these two possibilities, or do they have other choices?

A common possibility is that of an organization which is continually dysfunctioning — with outputs lower than inputs — and yet is being maintained by its suprasystem. A large concern may maintain a losing company for reasons of prestige or tax advantages. A philanthropic organization may maintain one of its branches although by all acceptable standards it should be disbanded.

Another example of a different choice is when the outputs of an organization are difficult to measure. A university, a therapy institute, a research organization, and a school are examples of organizations whose outputs are difficult to evaluate. In these cases the organization seems able to continue dysfunctioning almost endlessly, without either transforming or disintegrating. A monopolistic organization can also get by with continued dysfunctioning, increasing costs, and lower outputs, without facing the moment of truth and choice between change and demise.

It can be argued that in all the above cases, the organization has not passed its elastic limits or that they cannot be defined. In the case of the losing company, it or its continued existence must have value of some kind to its parent concern — otherwise resources would stop pouring in. In the case of the university, it may be argued that the elastic limits have not been passed because they are undefinable. In the case of the monopoly, the elastic limits may be described as ever expanding. With these arguments, Prigogine's theory holds for the social system.

Is this the case with the movement to greater complexity? Do human systems always transfer to higher levels of complexity, to greater differentiation and more interdependence? Granted, this has been empirically proved with chemical compounds that are dissipative structures. Does this also hold for the higher levels of human systems? Does not the emergent property of choice allow the human system the possibility of transforming to a lower level of complexity?

A large company reaches its elastic limits and decides to break up into a number of subsidiaries, each of which is a separate profit center; all of them are tied together very loosely by a common board. Is this a transformation to a higher or a lower level of complexity? The movement from large laundries that did customers' washing and ironing to individually owned washing machines and laundromats appears to be a transformation to lower levels of complexity — that is, less interdependence among the elements in the system. The change to automatic bank machines is also one to a less interdependent, less differentiated way of banking. The case of the transformation from communal sleeping arrangements to children sleeping with their parents also appears not to be a movement to a higher level of complexity. All these cases of transformation are not toward increasing differentiation and interdependence, but toward decreasing interdependence. The parts of the organization interact less with each other and are less dependent on each other.

This leads to the possibility that in human systems, transformation can be both to higher and to lower levels of complexity. When we deal with human systems, we are dealing with self-organizing, autopoietic systems that determine their own form, structure, and functioning. Such systems have choice. They are not determined by forces beyond their control. An organization can envision and plan its future form; it can grow or contract, centralize functions or distribute them, increase interdependence of units or couple them loosely. It appears that organizations can transform themselves both to higher and to lower levels of complexity.

In the social system, the two forms of transformation may occur at the same time. Some organizations may be transforming to higher levels of complexity while concurrently other organizations may be changing into simpler and less interdependent forms. To a certain degree this is similar to the concurrent polarized processes of integration and differentiation that affect all organizations.

This aspect of organizational transformation is in need of study and clarification.

Transformation Reversibility and Environmental Support

Some scholars have characterized second-order change, in contrast with first-order change, as being irreversible. Time flows in one direction; systems transform from lower levels of complexity to higher levels. We cannot reverse this trend in a particular system. The system cannot return to its former state.

While this may be so with nonhuman systems, does it hold for human systems? The case study in Chapter 9 describes a school that was transformed and later returned to its initial state. Should we say that since the school returned to its initial state, it was therefore not transformed — a second-order change did not take place because it was reversible?

Can it be that transformation in human systems is reversible? Does the emergent property of choice grant humans and their organizations the ability to reverse transformations? Is it not feasible that organizations and societies can undo what they have done, no matter how radical the initial change? We can point out cases where societies were transformed to higher levels of complexity and later the trend was reversed. The new economic policy of Communist China appears to be such a reverse. As ponted out in the case study, we find this happening in organizations.

Irreversibility does not appear to be a defining characteristic of transformation. It may be most difficult to reverse a transformation, but this does not mean it does not happen. Under what circumstances is a transformation reversible? Could this depend on the organization's environment? If other organizations on which the transformed organization depends strongly oppose the transformation, might they not be able to reverse the change?

This leads to another area that deserves study: the measure of dependence of a transformation on the support of the environment. It would seem that an organization will have difficulty transforming if there is strong resistance from relevant organizations in its environment. If the suprasystem to which the organization belongs, its mother company, is against the change, the organization will have major difficulty going through with it. The same probably holds for the resistance of other organizations on which the organization is dependent. If they strongly resist the transformation, this may be a major block. Alternatively, the organization may succeed in transforming itself, then later have to reverse the change because of environmental resistance. Yet organizations do transform themselves in the face of resistance. Political life provides many cases to prove this. A political party transforms itself and "forces" its environment to accept the transformation.

When can transformation be achieved if there is environmental opposition? What factors affect this? These questions need research.

Different Types of Transformation

Are there different types of transformation? Throughout this book transformation is treated as if it is a single phenomenon with specific characteristics. It is possible that we are dealing with a number of different phenomena having commonalities but also with differences that deserve attention. Let us try to sharpen this issue. Are the following transformations similar?

1. The transformation of a declining organization facing demise into a well-functioning, adaptive organization
2. The transformation of a well-functioning organization of one kind into a well-functioning organization of another kind, because of an environmental change of major impact
3. The transformation of a well-functioning organization of one kind into a well-functioning organization of another kind, because of a change in management
4. The transformation of a well-functioning organization into a high-performing, excellent organization
5. The transformation of an organization by rank and file in the face of management's opposition.

Each of these cases has a character different from the others. Sometimes the initial condition is different, sometimes the level of change is different, sometimes the triggering event, and sometimes the field of forces in the organization.

In the first case, the organization is disintegrating and facing the choice of extinction or renewal. It probably lacks energy and other resources necessary for transformation to a more adaptive state of functioning. This will not be the situation in some of the other cases, where the organization is functioning well. In the first case, outside forces are pushing for a transformation, while in the fourth — the well-functioning organization — internal, autopoietic forces have energized the organization to transform itself. If we take the third and fifth cases, the differences are also not negligible. It seems feasible that the transformation of an organization in which top management supports the move will be very different from a transformation engineered by rank and file in the face of managerial opposition.

This leads to another question: Will the form of the transformation, its stages, and characteristics be the same in all the cases described above? A cursory examination tends to lead to a negative answer. In different types of transformations, the process of the transformation and its characteristics will be dissimilar. In what way different types of transformation are similar to or different from each other is in need of research, study, and analysis.

Applying Different Approaches to Different Types of Transformation

Are all the approaches to transformation described in Part I of this book equally relevant to different types of transformation? Or is it possible that a different type of transformation necessitates different approaches and interventions?

An example will clarify this issue. A declining organization facing disintegration and demise is generally in a state of total energy depletion. The organization has used up most of its reserve resources of human energy and motivation: It is in a period of internal conflict, firefighting management, abortive change efforts, and the loss of capable entrepreneurial people. An organization in this state is in dire need, in the first stage of transformation, of finding ways to mobilize and rechannel energy. If it cannot mobilize the energy needed for action and support, it cannot initiate the change process. In contrast with this, a well-functioning organization embarking on a transformation to a high-performing/excellent state lacks no energy and motivation resources for the initial stage of the change. In the first case, a transformation project would have to focus on approaches and interventions that create motivation, mobilize support, and rechannel energy. In the second case, there would be no need to deal with this issue, and approaches and interventions for mobilizing energy would not be needed.

Some organizations going through a crisis are aware of the need for a transformation but do not know into what to transform themselves. They do not know which direction to take, what to become. All possibilities may appear equally formidable and threatening. An approach used to facilitate transformation in a case like this would be very different from that of a declining organization wishing to move to a well-functioning, adaptive state or a well-functioning organization transforming to an excellent state. In these two cases, the organization knows where it wants to go, what the direction is, what it wants to become.

Different approaches to transformation would probably be more effective in different sets of circumstances. In one case, an approach through myths might be most effective. In another organization, working directly on a paradigm shift may be the best strategy. Reframing may be most relevant to one type of transformation and entirely irrelevant to another.

Transformation theory and practice are still in their infancy. Much experimentation, practice, thought, and research are still needed to clarify this fuzzy area.

The Need to Integrate Different Views on Organizational Change

One of the major disagreements is about the inevitability of radical change and its function. A recurrent theme in the literature is that organizations can, and should, avoid second-order change because it is disruptive, expensive, and risky, and may generate unpredictable results. Much praise is therefore to be found for organizations that can be responsive to dynamic environments. These organizations are believed to have structures, procedures, and mechanisms that enable them to adapt to environmental changes through incremental, first-order changes, and thus avoid second-order change. "Organic," "loosely coupled," "matrix," "adaptive," "innovative," "resilient," and "excellent" all refer to organizations capable of quick response and adaptation to a dynamic environment without the need to pass through second-order change.

Most literature on organizations is focused on understanding stablity and integration. The recurrent theme is that despite the changes in the organizational world, most organizations do not change much. The Catholic church, for example, survived for centuries without changing dramatically. The same is true of universities, schools, and many public bureaucracies. Open systems theory, which is the dominant theory in the field of organizations, provides the theoretical framework for understanding organizations as homeostatic systems, capable of readjustments through feedback mechanisms. The notion here is that open systems can survive long and remain the same by going through constant readjustments.

These perceptions are challenged by others. They argue that the future holds a totally new world for organizations. Living in this new world entails transformation. Hence, second-order change is inevitable for all organizations, be they "organic" or "matrix." The survival of the organization in the future world will be dependent on its capacity to pass through dramatic changes in its purpose, culture, functioning, and world view. The field studies of Miller (1982) and Miller and Friesen (1983) showed that in turbulent, uncertain environments, first-order changes are dysfunctional, disruptive, and expensive, and should be delayed until clear trends and choices are available, and a certain level of readiness for change is attained. In this case, second-order change is preferable because it is less risky and less expensive. It avoids the need for constant readjustments.

Disagreements also exist among those who have attempted to explain why and how change occurs over time. Some emphasize that organizations emerge and dissolve, grow and decline, and go through periods of stabilization, transition, and transformation. However, they disagree on why and how these processes occur. In Chapters 11 and 12 many different perspectives are presented. These perspectives differ in their level of analysis (micro or macro), in their view on the source of the change (internal, interface, external), on the question of determinism and voluntarism (choice or determined) and on how change occurs (evolution or revolution).

From a practical standpoint, observation of organizational behavior suggests that there is a "ring of truth" to each of these perspectives. Over time, employees and managers are confronted with problems requiring them to operate within and to switch among the different perspectives. In addition, a given problem can be viewed from a number of perspectives, and the way these problems are defined will significantly influence how they will be addressed. Thus, the managerial problem is not only diagnosing what view is appropriate for dealing with a given problem but also being sufficiently flexible to switch views from one issue to another over time.

Which perspective represents the most appropriate model for understanding organizations? The problem with this question is that it ignores the fact that each view by itself is incomplete; the weaknesses of one appear as strengths in another. The question overlooks the reality of dialectical problems, tensions, paradoxes, and directions that are a normal and inherent part of behavior in complex organizations. Should the different perspectives be integrated? The answer depends upon one's purposes. Many organizational problems can be pursued in a more robust way by deepening each perspective's distinctiveness, and by recognizing the existence of the separate views. However, a partial integration of the different perspectives might have benefits for developing a theory of change in organizations.

It might be useful to have a more comprehensive and dynamic perspective on organizations than is available from any one of the perspectives alone. Such theory should meet the following desiderata:

1. It should explain both the statics and the dynamics of organizational functioning by including factors that account for both stability or equilibrium and instability or disequilibrium.
2. It should identify and explain the sources of change both from within the organization and from outside it.
3. It should include macro and micro factors, and show reciprocal relations among them (part-whole relations).
4. It should include time or a historical accounting system that explains the lead and lag effects of changes in micro and macro organizational characteristics.
5. It should include gradual, incremental, evolutionary changes as well as rapid, abrupt, revolutionary changes.

The Need to Develop Ideal Ways of Organizing Based on the Interactive Orientation

The organization's end state, the hoped-for outcomes of transformation, and the ideal type transformed organization (excellent, metanoic, high performance) represent models, concepts, and procedures that might be insufficient for organizational adaptation and growth. Excellent organizations, for example, under some circumstances might find it difficult to adapt to radical changes in their environment.* Studies and theoretical perspectives on change and evolution in living systems provide an overview of the necessity for establishing and maintaining a dynamic "fit" among the organization's subsystems (technical, political, cultural, psychological) and the organization as a whole, and a "fit"

---

*Who's excellent now? *Businessweek,* November 1984, pp. 76-88.

between the organization and its environment (natural, technological, human resources, economical, political).

These studies and theories suggest that the evolution of living systems involves decline, crises, discontinuities, and sudden breakoffs. It involves the emergence of new qualities, internal fluctuations and environmental turbulence, and ever growing complexities at an ever increasing pace. Changes seem to occur in cycles, and at an ever increasing pace and volume. What is the optimal way of organizing (in terms of organization survival and human development and growth) under these circumstances? The models and concepts that were found to be relevant for addressing this issue are learning systems, and self-organizing, self-transcending, and anticipatory systems. These concepts are interrelated, even overlapping.

The modern organization must be able to sense the dynamic processes within itself and in its environment, to assess future trends, and to sense signs of decline and crisis. The organization must be capable of continuous learning, and this learning must continually be reflected in updated plans and policies. Information must flow openly, vertically and horizontally, and must be digested and analyzed from different perspectives (different conceptions, beliefs), and integrated. Learning must come from the future as well as from the past and present. The organization must be potentially quick and flexible in its ability to change structures, procedures, and policies.

However, the process of adaptation and growth should be guided not only by an adaptive orientation, but also by an interactive orientation to change. Preparing for the future (good or bad) is not sufficient. The future can, and must, be shaped by human thought and action. Self-transcendent systems and learning systems are those capable of creating environments that satisfy ever increasing and higher needs. Human needs, values, and ethical considerations should be an inseparable part of the desired future.

The above concepts are highly abstract and theoretical. There is a need to reduce them to more concrete, practical, measurable concepts and processes. There is a need to study ideal ways of organizing from an interactive perspective. We are now on the verge of understanding and being aware of the evolutionary process affecting our organizations and our lives. The next step is to consciously participate in this process and shape it.

Bibliography

Ackerman L. S. 1982. Transition management: An indepth look at managing complex change. *Organizational Dynamics,* Summer, pp. 46–47.

____. 1983. The drama unfolds: Development, transition, or transformation? In E. Kosower (ed.), *Beyond our boundaries: Presenters' papers.* Los Angeles: O.D. Network.

____. 1984. The flow state: A new view of organizations and managing. In J. D. Adams (ed.), *Transforming work.* Alexandria, Virginia: Miles River Press.

Ackerman, L. S., and Whitney, D. K. 1984. The fusion team: A model of organic and shared leadership. In J. D. Adams (ed.), *Transforming work.* Alexandria, Virginia: Miles River Press.

Ackoff, R. L. 1981. *Creating the corporate future.* New York: John Wiley & Sons.

Adams, J. D. 1983. Networking and the emerging culture: A transformational process. Arlington, Virginia: TWG Publications. (Mimeo.)

____. 1984a. Achieving and maintaining personal peak performance. In J. D. Adams (ed.), *Transforming work.* Alexandria, Virginia: Miles River Press.

____ (ed.). 1984b. *Transforming work: A collection of organizational transformation readings.* Alexandria, Virginia: Miles River Press.

Adams, J. L. 1974. *Conceptual blockbusting.* New York: W. W. Norton.

Adizes, I. 1979a. *How to solve the mismanagement crisis.* Homewood, Illinois: Dow Jones-Irwin.

____. 1979b. Organizational passages. *Organizational Dynamics,* Summer, pp. 3–25.

Agor, W. H. 1984. *Intuitive management: Integrating left and right brain management skills.* San Francisco: Prentice-Hall.

Albert, S. 1984. A delete design model for successful transitions. In J. R. Kimberly and R. E. Quinn (eds.), *New futures: The challenge of managing corporate transitions.* Homewood, Illinois: Dow Jones-Irwin.

Aldrich, H. E. 1979. *Organizations and environments.* Englewood Cliffs, New Jersey: Prentice-Hall.

Aldrich, H. E., and Fish, D. 1981. Origins of organizational forms: Births, deaths, and transformation. Working paper, Department of Sociology, Cornell University. (Mimeo.)

Aldrich, H. E., and Pfeffer, J. 1976. Environments of organizations. *Annual Review of Sociology* 2:79–105.

Alinsky, S. D. 1972. *Rules for radicals.* New York: Random House.

Allen, R. F., and Kraft, C. 1982. *The organizational unconscious.* Englewood Cliffs, New Jersey: Prentice-Hall.

Argyris, C. 1977. Double loop learning in organizations. *Harvard Business Review* 55:115–125.

Argyris, C., and Schon, D. 1978. *Organizational learning: A theory of action perspective.* Reading, Massachusetts: Addison-Wesley.

Assagioli, R. 1971. *Psychosynthesis.* New York: Viking Press.

Ayres, R. U. 1984. *The next industrial revolution.* Cambridge, Massachusetts: Ballinger.

Baldock, P. 1980. Community action and the achievement of popular power. In D. A. Chekki (ed.), *Community development.* New Delhi: Vikas.

Bandler, R., and Grinder, J. 1982. *Reframing: Neuro linguistic programming and the transformation of meaning.* Moab, Utah: Real People Press.

Barbee, M. 1983. Energy and mythology. In J. D. Adams (ed.), *Working transformation.* Durham: University of New Hampshire Press.

Barrett, L., and Cammann, C. 1984. Transitioning to change: Lessons from NSC. In J. Kimberly and R. Quinn (eds.), *New futures: The challenge of managing corporate transitions.* Homewood, Illinois: Dow Jones-Irwin.

Bartunek, J. M. 1984. Changing interpretive schemes and organizational restructuring: The example of a religious order. *Administrative Science Quarterly 29*:355–372.

Bass, B. M. 1985. Leadership: Good, better, best. *Organizational Dynamics,* Winter, pp. 26–40.

Bass, G. V. 1978. *A study of alternatives in American education.* Santa Monica, California: Rand Corp.

Bateson, G. 1972. *Steps to an ecology of mind.* New York: Random House.

Beckhard, R. 1975. Strategies for large system change. *Sloan Management Review* *16*:43–55.

Beckhard, R., and Harris, H. T. 1977. *Organizational transitions: Managing complex change.* Reading, Massachusetts: Addison-Wesley.

Beer, M. A. 1980. *Organizational change and development: A system's view.* Glenview, Illinois: Scott, Foresman.

____. 1981. A social systems model for O.D. In T. G. Cummings (ed.), *System theory for organization development.* Chichester, England: John Wiley.

Bennis, W. G. 1970. A funny thing happened on the way to the future. *American Psychologist 45*:595–608.

____. 1973. The decline of bureaucracy and organizations of the future. In *Beyond bureaucracy: Essays on the development and evolution of human organizations.* New York: McGraw-Hill.

____. 1982. Leadership transforms vision into action. *Industry Week,* May 31.

Bennis, W., Benne, K., Chin, R., and Corey, K. (eds.). 1976. *The planning of change.* 3rd ed. New York: Holt, Rinehart, and Winston.

Berger, D. 1984. The emergence of organization consciousness. In *2nd O.T. symposium.* Columbia, Maryland: O.T. Network.

Berger, P. L., and Luckman, T. 1967. *The social construction of reality.* New York: Anchor Books.

Bettelheim, B. 1969. *The children of the dream.* New York: Macmillan.

Bibeault, D. B. 1982. *Corporate turnaround: How managers turn losers into winners.* New York: McGraw-Hill.

Bigelow, T. 1982. A catastrophe model of organizational change. *Behavioral Science 27*:26–42.

Biggart, N. W. 1977. The creative-destructive process of organizational change: The case of the Post Office. *Administrative Science Quarterly 22*:410–426.

Blake, R., and Mouton, J. 1976. *Consultation.* Reading, Massachusetts: Addison-Wesley.

____. 1978. *The new managerial grid.* Houston: Gulf.

Blodgett, T. B. 1984. Changing the system. *Harvard Business Review,* January–February, pp. 12–14.

Boje, M. D., Fedor, D. B., and Rowland, K. M. 1982. Myth making: A qualitative step in O.D. intervention. *Journal of Applied Behavioral Science 1*:17–28.

Boskin, C., and Phillips, C. 1983. Transformation: A core technology. In E. Kosower (ed.), *Beyond our boundaries: Presenters' papers.* Los Angeles: O.D. Network.

Boulding, E. 1976. Learning to image the future. In W. G. Bennis, K. D. Benne, R. Chin, and K. E. Corey (eds.), *The planning of change.* 3rd ed. New York: Holt, Rinehart, and Winston.

Boulding, K. 1978. *Ecodynamics: A new theory of social evolution.* Beverly Hills, California: Sage.

Boyce, M. E. 1984. *Envisioning the future: An approach to institutional change.* Glendora, California: Raymond Rood and Associates.

Bradford, D. L., and Cohen, A. R. 1984. *Managing for excellence: The guide to developing high performance in contemporary organizations.* New York: John Wiley & Sons.

Bradford, D. L., and Harvey, J. B. 1970. Dealing with dysfunctional organizational myths. *Training and Development Journal 24*:2–6.

Brimm, M. 1972. When is a change not a change? *Journal of Applied Behavioral Science 8*:102–106.

Brittain, J. W., and Freeman, J. H. 1980. Organizational proliferation and density. In J. R. Kimberly and R. H. Miles (eds.), *The organizational life cycle.* San Francisco: Jossey-Bass.

Broad, L. 1977. *Alternative schools: Why, what, where, and how much.* Arlington, Virginia: National School Boards.

Brown, A., and Weiner, E. 1984. *Supermanaging.* New York: McGraw-Hill.

Brown, M. H. Psychosynthesis: An approach to organization transformation. Springfield, Virginia. (Mimeo.)

Brown, R. H. 1978. Bureaucracy as praxis: Toward a political phenomenology. *Administrative Science Quarterly 23*:365–382.

Buckley, K. W., and Perkins, D. 1984. Managing the complexity of organizational transformation. In J. D. Adams (ed.), *Transforming work.* Alexandria, Virginia: Miles River Press.

Burke, W. 1981. *Organizational development: Principles and practices.* Boston: Little, Brown.

Burns, F., and Nelson, L. 1983. High performance programming. Alexandria, Virginia: High Performance Systems Consulting. (Mimeo.)

Burns, J. 1978. *Leadership*. New York: Harper & Row.

Burns, T., and Stalker, G. 1961. *The management of innovation*. London: Tavistock.

Campbell, D. T. 1969. Variation and selective retention in socio cultural evolution. *Central Systems 16*:69–85.

Capra, F. 1982. *The turning point*. New York: Simon and Schuster.

Carneiro, R. 1968. Ascertaining, testing, and interpreting sequences of cultural development. *Southern Journal of Anthropology 24*:354–374.

_____. 1981. Successive reequilibration as a mechanism of cultural evolution. In W. Schieve and P. Allen (eds.), *Self-organization in dissipative structures*. Austin: University of Texas Press.

Caroll, G. R. 1981. Dynamics of organizational expansion in national system of education. *American Sociology Review 46*:585–599.

Carr, J. C., Grambs, J. D., and Campbell, E. G. 1977. *Pygmalion or Frankenstein? Alternative schooling in American education*. Reading, Massachusetts: Addison-Wesley.

Carrillo, R. P., Lumbley, J. L., and Westbrook, J. D. 1984. Effective networking: The roles of the consultant. *Consultation 3*:37–42.

Casti, J. 1979. *Connectivity, complexity, and catastrophe in large scale systems*. New York: John Wiley & Sons.

Chandler, A. D. 1977. *The visible hand*. Cambridge, Massachusetts: Harvard University Press.

Chase, T. 1983. Some thoughts on O.T. *T.W.G. Newsletter 2*:1–2.

Child, J. 1972. Organizational structure, environment, and performance. The role of strategic choice. *Sociology 6*:1–22.

Chin, R. 1976. The utility of system models and developmental models for practitioners. In W. Bennis, K. Benne, R. Chin, and K. Corey (eds.), *The planning of change*. New York: Holt, Rinehart, and Winston.

Clapp, W. N. 1983. Shared delusions on the path to shared values. *O.D. Practitioner 15*:1–5.

Clark, B. R. 1972. The organization saga in higher education. *Administrative Science Quarterly 17*:178–184.

Clark, L. P., and Burke, W. W. 1984. Successful O.D.: A matter of execution. *O.D. Practitioner 16*:1–5.

Cobb, L., Ramohan, K., and Ash, B. 1978. Applications of catastrophe theory in the behavioral and life sciences. *Behavioral Sciences 5*. (Entire special issue.)

Coke, M. A., and Mierau, D. M. 1984. A formula for corporate fitness. In J. D. Adams (ed.), *Transforming work*. Alexandria, Virginia: Miles River Press.

Connelly, S. L. 1982. The fusion team: An experimental group management technology. In L. L. Franklin (ed.), *An army of excellence: Visions of our future force*. Carlisle Barracks, Pennsylvania: Delta Force.

———. 1984. Work spirit. Ph.D. dissertation, George Washington University.

Cross. F. B. 1982. Scientific theories suggest a light at the end of the tunnel. *The Tarrytown Letter,* March, pp. 2–19.

Culbert, S. 1976. Consciousness-raising: A five stage model for social and organizational change. In C. Cooper (ed.), *Theories of group processes*. London: John Wiley & Sons.

Cumming, E., Clancy, L. W., and Cummings, T. G. 1977. Improving patient care through organizational changes in the mental hospital. In T. G. Cummings and E. S. Molloy (eds.), *Improving productivity and quality of work life*. New York: Praeger.

Cummings, T. G. (ed.). 1980. *Systems theory for O.D*. New York: John Wiley & Sons.

Curvin, R., and Porter, B. 1977. *New York blackout, July 13, 1977*. New York: Gardner Press.

Daft, R. L. 1978. A dual core model of organizational innovation. *Academy of Management Journal 21*:193–210.

Daft, R. L., and Weick, K. E. 1984. Toward a model of organizations as interpretation systems. *Academy of Management Review 9*:284–295.

Dahrendorf, R. 1959. *Class and class conflict in industrial society*. Stanford, California: Stanford University Press.

Davis, S. 1982. Transforming organizations: The key to strategy is context. *Organizational Dynamics,* Winter, pp. 64–80.

Deal, T., and Kennedy, A. 1982. *Corporate cultures*. Reading, Massachusetts: Addison-Wesley.

deBono, E. 1971. *Lateral thinking for management*. New York: American Management Association.

De Green, K. 1982. *The adaptive organization*. New York: John Wiley & Sons.

Dell, P., and Goolishian, H. 1981. An evolutionary epistemology for cohesive phenomena. *Family Dynamics 6*:104–122.

Deluca, J. 1984. Managing the sociopolitical context in planned change efforts. In A. Kakabadse and C. Parker (eds.), *Power, politics, and organizations*. New York: John Wiley.

Denhardt, R. B. 1971. The organization as a political system. *Western Political Science Quarterly 24*:675–686.

de Vries, K., and Miller, D. M. 1982. Neurotic style and organizational pathology. Montreal: Faculty of Management, McGill University. (Mimeo.)

DuBick, M. A. 1978. The organizational structure of newspapers in relation to their metropolitan environment. *Administrative Science Quarterly 23*:418–432.

Dunn, W., and Swierczek, F. 1977. Planned organizational change: Toward grounded theory. *Journal of Applied Behavioral Science 13*:135–157.

Durkheim, E. 1947. *The division of labor in society*. Glencoe, Illinois: Free Press.

Dwyer, D. C., Smith, L. M., and Prunty, J. J. 1983. *Innovation and change in American education, Kensington revisited: A fifteen-year follow-up of an innovative elementary school*. St. Louis: Washington University Press.

Elgin, D. 1977. Limits to the management of large, complex systems. *Assessment of future national and international problem areas*. Part IV, volume 2. Menlo Park, California: Center for the Study of Social Policy, Stanford Research International.

Etzioni, A. 1964. *Modern organizations*. Englewood Cliffs, New Jersey: Prentice-Hall.

Evered, R. 1980. Consequences of and prospects for systems thinking in organizational change. In T. G. Cummings (ed.), *Systems theory for O.D.* New York: John Wiley & Sons.

Ferguson, M. 1980. *The Aquarian conspiracy*. Los Angeles: Tarcher.

Fink, S. L., Beak, J., and Taddeo, K. 1971. Organization crisis and change. *Journal of Applied Behavioral Science 7*:15–37.

Fisch, R., Weakland, J. H., and Segal, L. 1983. *The tactics of change.* San Francisco: Jossey-Bass.

Flaxman, A., and Homestead, K. C. 1978. *1977–78 national directory of public alternative schools.* Amherst: University of Massachusetts Press.

Fraser, T. 1984. Gestalt for managers. In C. Cox and J. Beck (eds.), *Management development: Advances in practice and theory.* Chichester, England: John Wiley.

Freeman, J., and Hannan, M. 1975. Growth and decline processes in organizations. *American Sociology Review 40*:215–220.

Freire, P. 1970. *Pedagogy of the oppressed.* New York: Seabury Press.

Frew, D. R. 1974. Transcendental meditation and productivity. *Academy of Management Journal 17*:362–368.

Gergan, K. J. 1982. *Toward transformation in social knowledge.* New York: Springer Verlg.

Gerlach, L., and Hines, V. 1973. *The dynamics of change in America.* Minneapolis: University of Minnesota Press.

Glaser, E. M., Abelson, H. H., and Garrison, N. K. 1983. *Putting knowledge to use.* San Francisco: Jossey-Bass.

Gluckstern, N. B., and Packard, R. W. 1977. Bringing change to a "closed institution"; a case study on a county jail. *Journal of Applied Behavioral Science 13*:41–53.

Goffman, E. 1961. On the characteristics of total institutions. In D. R. Cressey (ed.), *The prison.* New York: Holt, Rinehart, and Winston.

Gold, B., and Miles, M. 1981. *Whose school is it, anyway?* New York: Praeger.

Golembievsky, R., Billingsley, K., and Yaeger, S. 1976. Measuring change and persistence in human affairs: Types of change generated by O.D. designs. *Journal of Applied Behavioral Science 12*:133–154.

Goodman, P. S., and Associates (eds.). 1982. *Change in organizations.* San Francisco: Jossey-Bass.

Goodman, P. S., and James, W. D. 1982. Creating long term organizational change. In P. S. Goodman and Associates (eds.), *Change in organizations.* San Francisco: Jossey-Bass.

Gould, J. S. 1983. *Hen's teeth and horses' toes.* New York: W. W. Norton.

Grabow, S., and Heskin, A. 1973. Foundations for a radical concept of planning. *Journal of the American Institute of Planners* no. 392 (March):472–483.

Greiner, L. 1972. Evolution and revolution as organizations grow. *Harvard Business Review 50*:39–46.

Guastello, S. J. 1984. Catastrophe theory, evaluation of a policy to control job absence. *Behavioral Science 29*:263–269.

Hackman, R. J. 1984. The transition that hasn't happened. In J. Kimberly and R. Quinn (eds.), *New futures: The challenge of managing corporate transitions.* Homewood, Illinois: Dow Jones-Irwin.

Hage, J. 1980. *Theories of organizations.* New York: John Wiley & Sons.

Hage, J., and Dewer, R. 1973. Elite values versus organizational structures in predicting innovation. *Administrative Science Quarterly 18*:279–290.

Haire, M. 1959. Biological models and empirical histories of the growth of organizations. In M. Haire (ed.), *Modern organization theory.* New York: John Wiley & Sons.

Haller, T. 1984. Authority: Changing patterns, changing times. In J. Adams (eds.), *Transforming work.* Alexandria, Virginia: Miles River Press.

Halley, J., and Hoffman, L. 1967. *Techniques of family therapy.* New York: Basic Books.

Hannan, M. T., and Freeman, J. 1977. The population ecology of organizations. *American Journal of Sociology 82*:929–965.

Harris, P. R. 1983. *New world, new ways, new management.* New York: AMACOM.

Harrison, R. 1972. Understanding your organization's character, *Harvard Business Review,* May–June, pp. 97-112.

____. 1984. Leadership and strategy for New-Age. In J. Adams (ed.), *Transforming work.* Alexandria, Virginia: Miles River Press.

Harrison, R. G., and Pitt, D. C. 1984. Organizational development: A missing political dimension? In A. Kakabadse and C. Parker (eds.), *Power, politics, and organizations.* New York: John Wiley & Sons.

Harvey, J. B., and Albertson, R. D. 1971. Neurotic organizations: Causes and symptoms. *Personnel Journal 9*:694–699.

Hawley, J. 1982. Transforming organizations through vertical linking. *Organizational Dynamics,* Winter, pp. 68–80.

_____. 1983. O.T.: Organization transformation as life welling forth. *O.D. Practitioner* *15* (December):9–10.

Hedberg, B. L. 1981. How organizations learn and unlearn. In P. C. Nystrom and W. H. Starbuck (eds.), *The handbook of organization design: Adapting organizations to their environments.* Vol. 1. New York: Oxford University Press.

Hedberg, B. L., and Johnston, S. A. 1977. Strategy formulation as a discontinuous process. *International studies of management and organizations* 7:89–109.

Hedberg, B. L., Nystrom, P. C., and Starbuck, W. H. 1976. Camping on seesaws: Prescriptions for a self-designed organization. *Administrative Science Quarterly* *21*:41–65.

Heller, K., and Monahan, J. 1977. *Psychology and community change.* Homewood, Illinois: Irwin-Dorkey.

Heller, T. 1984. Authority: Changing pattern, changing times. In J. Adams (ed.), *Transforming work.* Alexandria, Virginia: Miles River Press.

Herman, M. S., and Kornich, M. 1977. *Authentic management.* Reading, Massachusetts: Addison-Wesley.

Hernes, G. 1976. Structural change in social processes. *American Journal of Sociology 82*:513–547.

Holling, S. 1976. Resilience and stability of ecosystems. In E. Jantsch and C. Waddington (eds.), *Evolution and consciousness: Human systems in transition.* Reading, Massachusetts: Addison-Wesley.

Hubbard, B. M. 1982. *The evolutionary journey.* San Francisco: Evolutionary Press.

Huff, A. S. 1980. Organizations as political systems: Implications for diagnosis, change and stability. In T. G. Cummings (ed.), *Systems theory for organizational development.* New York: John Wiley & Sons.

Hultman, K. E. 1979. *The path to least resistance.* Austin, Texas: Learning Concepts.

Huse, E. 1982. *Organizational development and change.* 2nd ed. Englewood Cliffs, New Jersey: Prentice-Hall.

Iannaccone, L. 1977. *The politics of education.* Chicago: University of Chicago Press.

Jackson, J. H., and Morgan, C. P. 1982. *Organization theory.* 2nd ed. Englewood Cliffs, New Jersey: Prentice-Hall.

Jantsch, E. 1975. *Design for evolution: Self-organization and planning in the life of human systems.* New York: Braziller.

____. 1976. Self-transcendence: New light on the evolutionary paradigm. In E. Jantsch and C. H. Waddington (eds.), *Evolution and consciousness: Human systems in transition*. Reading, Massachusetts: Addison-Wesley.

____. 1980. *The self-organizing universe: Scientific and human implications of the emerging paradigm of evolution*. New York: Pergamon Press.

Jayaram, K. 1976. Open system planning. In W. Bennis, K. Benne, R. Chin, and K. Corey (eds.), *The planning of change*. 3rd ed. New York: Holt, Rinehart, and Winston.

Johnston, R. W. 1983. Tools for organization transformation. Los Angeles. (Mimeo.)

____. 1984. Integrating O.D. with spirituality. *Vision and Action 41*:6–9.

Jones, M. O., Boje, D., Wolfe, T., Moore, M., Krell, R., Gordon, S., and Christiansen, D. 1983. Dealing with symbolic expression in organizations. In E. Kosower (ed.), *Beyond our boundaries: Presenters' papers*. Los Angeles: O.D. Network.

Kahn, R. 1974. Organizational development: Some problems and proposals. *Journal of Applied Behavioral Science 10*:485–502.

Kakabadse, A. 1982. Politics in organizations: Reexamination of O.D. *Leadership and Organization Development Journal 3(2)*:(Monograph).

____. 1984. Politics of a process consultant. In A. Kakabadse and C. Parker (eds.), *Power, politics and organizations*. New York: John Wiley.

Kakabadse, A., and Parker, C. 1984. Towards a theory of political behavior in organizations. In A. Kakabadse and C. Parker (eds.), *Power, politics, and organizations*. New York: John Wiley.

Kaluzny, A., Veney, J., and Gentry, J. 1974. Innovation in health services. *Milbank Memorial Fund Quarterly 52*:51–82.

Kamens, D. H. 1977. Legitimizing myths and educational organizations. *American Sociology Review 42*:208–219.

Kanter, R. M. 1983. *The change masters*. New York: Simon and Schuster.

Karp, H. B. 1976. A Gestalt approach to collaboration in organizations. In W. J. Pfeiffer and J. E. Jones (eds.), *The 1976 annual handbook for group facilitators*. San Diego: University Associates.

Katz, O., and Kahn, R. 1978. *The social psychology of organizations*. New York: John Wiley & Sons.

Khandwalla, P. M. 1976. The techno-economic ecology of corporate strategy. *Journal of Management Studies 13*:62–75.

Kiefer, C. F., and Senge, P. M. 1984. Metanoic organizations. In J. D. Adams (ed.), *Transforming work.* Alexandria, Virginia: Miles River Press.

Kiefer, C. F., and Stroh, P. 1984. A new paradigm for developing organizations. In J. D. Adams (eds.), *Transforming work.* Alexandria, Virginia: Miles River Press.

Kimberly, J. F., and Evanesco, M. J. 1981. The influence of individual, organizational, and contextual factors on hospital adoption of technological and administrative innovations. *Academy of Management Journal 24*:689–713.

Kimberly, J. F., and Miles, R. H. (eds.). 1980. *The organizational life cycle.* San Francisco: Jossey-Bass.

Kimberly, J. R., and Quinn, R. E. (eds.). *New futures: The challenge of managing corporate transitions.* Homewood, Illinois: Dow Jones-Irwin.

Kindler, H. S. 1979a. The effects of meditation relaxation techniques on group problem solving effectiveness. *Journal of Applied Behavioral Science 15*:527–534.

_____. 1979b. Two planning strategies: Incremental change and transformational change. *Group and Organization Studies 4*:476–484.

King, A. S. 1979. Expectations effects in organizational change. *Administrative Science Quarterly 19*:221–230.

Kirton, M. 1980. Adaptors and innovators in organizations. *Human Relations 33*:213–223.

Knight, K. 1967. A descriptive model of the intra-firm innovation process. *Journal of Business 40*:478–496.

Kohlberg, L. 1969. *Stages in the development of moral thought and action.* New York: Holt, Rinehart, and Winston.

Kolb, D. A. 1981. Experiential learning theory and the learning style inventory. *Academy of Management Review 4(2)*:289–296.

Krippner, S. 1972. Altered states of consciousness. In J. White (ed.), *The highest state of consciousness.* New York: Doubleday.

Kropovsky, J. E. 1983. Cultural myths: Clues to effective management. *Organizational Dynamics,* Autumn, pp. 39–51.

Kuhn, T. 1970. *The structure of scientific revolution.* 2nd ed. Chicago: University of Chicago Press.

Kurke, L. B. 1981. Adaptability in organizations: The role of environmental change. Ph.D. dissertation, Graduate School of Public Administration, Cornell University.

Land, G. T. L. 1973. *Grow or die: The unifying principles of transformation.* New York: Random House.

Lavoie, D., and Culbert, S. 1978. Stages in organization and development. *Human Relations 31*:417–438.

Lawrence, P., and Lorsch, J. 1976. *Organization and environment.* Cambridge, Massachusetts: Harvard University Press.

Lawrence, W. G. 1979. *Exploring individual and organizational boundaries.* Chichester, England: John Wiley & Sons.

Leavitt, H. J. 1978. *Managerial psychology.* 4th ed. Chicago: University of Chicago Press.

Lees, R., and Mayo, M. 1984. *Community action for change.* London: Routledge.

Levinson, H. 1972. *Organizational diagnosis.* Cambridge, Massachusetts: Harvard University Press.

Levy, A. 1979. *Parents and sons: A structured intervention.* Tel Aviv: Kibbutz O.D. Institute. (Hebrew.)

———. 1980. *Developmental stages in the transition from communal to familial sleeping accommodation system in the kibbutz.* Tel Aviv: Kibbutz Committee for Social Affairs. (Hebrew.)

Lewis, J., and Lewis, M. 1977. *Community counseling: A human services approach.* New York: John Wiley.

Lindblom, C. 1959. The science of muddling through. *Public Administration Review 21*:78–88.

Lindman, E., and Lippitt, R. 1979. *Choosing the future you prefer.* Washington, D.C.: Development Publishers.

Lindsay, W. M., and Rue, L. W. 1980. Impact of the organizational environment on the long-range planning process: A contingency view. *Academy of Management Journal 23*:385–404.

Lippitt, G. 1969. *Organizational renewal.* New York: Appleton-Century-Crofts.

Lippitt, R. 1982. Futuring as part of long-range planning. (Mimeo.)

Lippitt, R., Watson, J., and Westley, B. 1958. *Planned change: A comparative study of principles and techniques.* New York: Harcourt, Brace, and World.

Loevinger, J. 1976. *Ego development.* San Francisco: Jossey-Bass.

Lundberg, C. C. 1984. Strategies for organizational transitioning. In J. R. Kimberly and R. E. Quinn (eds.), *New futures: The challenge of managing corporate transitions.* Homewood, Illinois: Dow Jones-Irwin.

McCleery, R. H. 1957. *Policy change in prison management.* East Lansing: Michigan State University Press.

McGregor, D. M. 1960. *The human side of enterprise.* New York: McGraw-Hill.

McKelvey, B. 1982. *Organizational systematics.* Los Angeles: University of California Press.

McKnight, R. 1984. Spirituality in the work place: Developing business with heart. In J. D. Adams (ed.), *Transforming organizations.* Alexandria, Virginia: Miles River Press.

McClean, J., Sims, D., Mangham, I., and Tuffield, D. 1982. *Organization development in transition.* New York: John Wiley.

McWaters, B. 1982. *Conscious evolution: Personal and planetary transformation.* San Francisco: Evolutionary Press.

McWhinney, W. 1980. Paedogenesis and other modes of design. In T. Cummings (ed.), *Systems theory for organization development.* New York: John Wiley & Sons.

____. 1982. "The alchemic." Venice, California: Enthusion. (Mimeo.)

____. 1984. Mythology and O.D. *Vision and Action* 3:1–7.

Maccoby, M. 1976. *The gamesman.* New York: Bantam Books.

Mangham, I. L. 1979. *The politics of organizational change.* Westport, Connecticut: Greenwood Press.

____. 1984. The management of creativity. In C. Cox and J. Beck (eds.), *Management development: Advances in practice and theory.* Chichester: John Wiley.

March, J. G. 1981. Footnotes to organizational change. *Administrative Science Quarterly* 26:563–577.

Margulis, W. 1977. Make the most of your corporate identity. *Harvard Business Review 55*:184–201.

Margulies, N., and Raia, A. 1978. *Conceptual foundations of organization development.* New York: McGraw-Hill.

Markley, O. W. 1976. Human consciousness in transformation. In E. Jantsch and C. H. Waddington (eds.), *Evolution and consciousness: Human systems in transition.* Reading, Massachusetts: Addison-Wesley.

Markley, O. W., and Harman. W. W. 1982. *Changing image of man.* New York: Pergamon Press.

Marks, U. 1977. Organizational adjustment to uncertainty. *Journal of Management Studies 14*:1–15.

Maruyama, M. 1963. The second cybernetics: Deviation amplifying mutual causal processes. *American Scientist 51*:164–179.

Maslow, A. H. 1971. *The farther reaches of human nature.* New York: Viking Press.

May, R. 1969. *Love and will.* New York: W. W. Norton.

_____. 1972. *Power and innocence.* New York: Dell.

_____. 1981. *Freedom and destiny.* New York: W. W. Norton.

Mayor, J., and Rowan, B. 1977. Institutional organizations: Formal structure as myth and ceremony. *American Journal of Sociology 83*:340–363.

Meadows, D. H., Richardson, J., and Bruckman, G. 1982. *Groping in the dark: The first decade of global modelling.* New York: John Wiley & Sons.

Merry, U. 1983. The neurosis of organizations. Ph.D. dissertation, University of California at Santa Barbara.

Merry, U., and Brown, G. I. 1986. *The neurotic behavior of organizations.* New York: Gardner Press.

Meyer, M. W. 1979. *Change in public bureaucracies.* Cambridge, Massachusetts: Harvard University Press.

Miles, R. E., and Snow, C. C. 1978. *Organizational strategy, structure, and process.* New York: McGraw-Hill.

Miller, D. 1982. Evolution and revolution: A quantum view of structural change in organizations. *Journal of Management Studies 19*:131–151.

Miller, D., and Friesen, P. H. 1980a. Archetypes of organizational transition. *Administrative Science Quarterly 25*:263–299.

_____. 1980b. Momentum and revolution in organizational adaptation. *Academy of Management Journal 23*:591–614.

_____. 1983. A longitudinal study of the corporate life cycle. Unpublished research. Montreal: McGill University.

Miller, J. 1978. *Living systems.* New York: McGraw-Hill.

Mintzberg, H. 1975. The manager's job: Folklore and facts. *Harvard Business Review 53*:187–198.

_____. 1979. *The structuring of organizations.* Englewood Cliffs, New Jersey: Prentice-Hall.

Minuchin, S., and Fishman, C. F. 1981. *Family therapy techniques.* Cambridge, Massachusetts: Harvard University Press.

Moch, M. K. 1976. Structure and organizational resource allocation. *Administrative Science Quarterly 21*:661–674.

Morgan, G., and Ramirez, R. 1984. Action learning: A holographic metaphor for guiding social change. *Human relations 37*:1–28.

Mulligan, M., and Kelly, J. W. 1983. Fantasy theme analysis: A method to assess organizational culture. In E. Kosower (ed.), *Beyond our boundaries: Presenters' papers.* Los Angeles: O.D. Network.

Nadler, A. D. 1982. Managing transitions to uncertain future states. *Organizational Dynamics,* Summer, pp. 37–46.

Naisbitt, J. 1982. *Megatrends.* New York: Warner Books.

Nevis, E. C. 1980. *Gestalt awareness process in organizational assessment.* Boston: MIT Press. (Reprint.)

Nicoll, D. 1980. Paradigm reframing. In P. Mico (ed.), *Presenters' papers, fall 1980.* San Francisco: O.D. Network.

_____. 1984a. Consulting to organizational transformation. In J. D. Adams (ed.), *Transforming work.* Alexandria, Virginia: Miles River Press.

_____. 1984b. Grace beyond the rules. In J. D. Adams (ed.), *Transforming work.* Alexandria, Virginia: Miles River Press.

Nielsen, F., and Hannan, M. T. 1977. The expansion of national education systems: Tests of a population ecology model. *American Sociological Review 42*:479–490.

Niv, A. 1980. Organization disintegration: Roots, processes and types. In J. Kimberly and R. Miles (eds.), *The organizational life cycle*. San Francisco: Jossey-Bass.

Nold, M. 1983. Myth in progress: The chronicle of the transformation of an organization. In J. D. Adams (ed.), *Working transformation*. Durham: University of New Hampshire Press.

Nord, W. 1976. The failure of current applied behavioral science: A Marxian perspective. *Journal of Applied Behavioral Science 10*:557–578.

Olivia, T. A., Peters, M. H., and Murthy, H. S. 1981. A preliminary empirical test of a cusp catastrophe model in the social sciences. *Behavioral Science 26*:153–162.

Ouchi, W. G. 1981. *Theory Z*. New York: Aron Books.

Owen, H. 1983a. *Facilitating organization transformation: The uses of myths and rituals*. Arlington, Virginia: T.W.G.

_____. 1983b. The intellectual roots of O.T. *Vision and Action 3(2)*:7–8.

_____. 1983c. *Open space: Introduction to O.T. and the use of myths and ritual*. Arlington, Virginia: H. Owen and Co.

_____. 1984. Excellence, myth and organization. *Vision and Action 9(3)*:7–10.

Padgett, J. F. 1981. Hierarchy and ecological control in federal budgetary decision making. *American Journal of Sociology 87*:75–129.

Palazzoli, M. S. 1978. *Paradox and counter paradox*. New York: Jason Aronson.

Papp, P. 1981. Paradoxes. In S. Minuchin and C. F. Fishman (eds.), *Family therapy techniques*. Cambridge, Massachusetts: Harvard University Press.

Peck, J. 1980. Changing a manager's construction of reality. In J. E. Beck and C. J. Cox (eds.), *Advances in management education*. Chichester: John Wiley.

Peck, R. D. 1983. *Future focusing: An alternative to long-range planning*. Washington, D.C.: Council of Independent Colleges.

Pelletier, K., and Garfield, C. 1976. *Consciousness: East and West*. New York: Harper & Row.

Perls, F. 1981. *The Gestalt approach*. 5th ed. New York: Bantam Books.

Peters, D. R. 1982. *Organization change and development and related fields: A reader guide to selected documents.* Malibu, California: School of Business and Management, Pepperdine University.

Peters, T. J. 1978. Symbols, patterns and settings: An optimistic case for getting things done. *Organizational Dynamics,* Autumn pp. 3–23.

Peters, T., and Waterman, R. 1982. *In search of excellence.* New York: Harper & Row.

Pfeffer, J. 1981. Management as symbolic action: The creation and maintenance of organizational paradigm. In L. Cummings and B. Staw (eds.), *Research in organizational behavior.* Vol. 3. Greenwich, Connecticut: JAI Press.

Pfeffer, J., and Salancik, G. 1978. *The external control of organizations.* New York: Harper & Row.

Polack, F. 1973. *The image of the future.* San Francisco: Jossey-Bass.

Pondy, L. R. 1967. Organization conflicts: Concepts and models. *Administrative Science Quarterly 12:*296–320.

Pondy, L., and Mitroff, I. 1979. Beyond open systems models of organization. In L. Cummings and B. Staw (eds.), *Research in organizational behavior.* Greenwich, Connecticut: JAI Press.

Postle, D. 1980. *Catastrophe theory.* Glasgow: William Collins.

Prigogine, I. 1984. *Order out of chaos.* New York: Bantam Books.

Prigogine, I., and Allen, P. 1981. The challenge of complexity. In W. Schieve and P. Allen (eds.), *Self-organization in dissipative structures.* Austin: University of Texas Press.

Prigogine, I., and Gregoire, N. 1977. *Self organization in nonequilibrium systems: From dissipative structures to order through fluctuation.* New York: John Wiley & Sons.

Putney, S. 1972. *The conquest of society.* Belmont, California: Wadsworth.

Quinn, R., and Anderson, D. 1984. Formalization as crisis: Transition planning for a young organization. In J. Kimberly and R. Quinn (eds.), *New futures: The challenge of managing corporate transitions.* Homewood, Illinois: Dow Jones-Irwin.

Quinn, R., and Cameron, K. 1983. Organizational life cycles and shifting criteria of effectiveness: Some preliminary evidence. *Management Science,* January, pp. 33-51.

Ramaprasad, A. 1982. Revolutionary change and strategic management. *Behavioral Science* 27:387–392.

Ramos, A. G. 1981. *The new science of organizations.* Toronto: University of Toronto Press.

Ranson, S., Hinings, B., and Greenwood, R. 1980. The structuring of organizational futures. *Administrative Science Quarterly* 25:1–17.

Reason, P. 1984. Is organization development possible in power culture? In A. Kakabadse and C. Parker (eds.), *Power, politics, and organizations.* New York: John Wiley & Sons.

Ritscher, J. A. 1983. Applying spiritual principles to organizations. Brookline, Massachusetts: James A. Ritscher Associates. (Mimeo.)

Rothman, J. 1974. *Strategies of community organization.* Itasca, Illinois: Peacock.

_____. 1979. *Planning and organizing for social change.* New York: Columbia University Press.

Rundall, T., and McClain, J. 1982. Environmental selection and physician supply. *American Journal of Sociology* 87:1090–1112.

Rutte, M. 1984. Turning vision into reality. In *The second symposium on O.T.* Columbia, Maryland: T.W.G.

Sahlins, M. D. 1960. *Evolution and culture.* Ann Arbor: University of Michigan Press.

Sales, A., and Mirvis, P. 1984. When cultures collide: Issues in acquisition. In J. Kimberly and R. Quinn (eds.), *New futures: The challenge of managing corporate transitions.* Homewood, Illinois: Dow Jones-Irwin.

Sarason, S. G. 1972. *The creation of settings.* San Francisco: Jossey-Bass.

Satir, V. 1967. *Conjoint family therapy: A guide to theory and techniques.* Palo Alto, California: Science and Behavior Books.

Schattschneider, E. E. 1975. *The semisovereign people.* Hinsdale, Illinois: The Dryden Press.

Schein, V. E. 1977. Individual power and political behaviors in organizations. *Academy of Management Review* 2:64-72.

Segal, M. 1974. Organization and environment: A typology of adaptability and structure. *Public Administration Review* 34:212–220.

Selznick, P. 1976. *TVA and the grass roots: A study in the sociology of formal organizations.* New York: Harper & Row.

Shapiro, D. H., Jr. 1978. Behavioral and attitudinal changes resulting from a Zen experience workshop and Zen meditation. *Journal of Humanistic Psychology 18(3)*:21–29.

Sheldon, A. 1979. *Managing change and collaboration in the health system.* Cambridge, Massachusetts: O, G, and H.

_____. 1980. Organizational paradigms: A theory of organizational change. *Organizational Dynamics,* Winter, pp. 61-80.

Sheldrake, R. 1982. *A new science of life: The hypothesis of formative causation.* Los Angeles: J. P. Tarcher.

Sheridan, J. E. 1985. A catastrophe model of employee withdrawal leading to low job performance, high absenteeism, and job turnover. *Academy of Management Journal 1*:88–109.

Shortell, S., Wickizer, T., and Wheeler, J. 1984. *Hospital physician joint ventures: Results and lessons from a national demonstration.* Ann Arbor, Michigan: Health Administration Press.

Skibbins, G. 1974. *Organization evolution.* New York: Amacon.

Slater, P. 1974. *Earthwalk.* Garden City, New York: Anchor Books.

Smith, K. K. 1982. Philosophical problems in thinking about organizational change. In P. S. Goodman and Associates (eds.), *Change in organizations.* San Francisco: Jossey-Bass.

_____. 1984. Rabbits, lynxes, and organizational transitions. In J. Kimberly and R. Quinn (eds.), *New futures: The challenge of managing corporate transitions.* Homewood, Illinois: Dow Jones-Irwin.

Sproul, L. S. 1981. Beliefs in organizations. In P. C. Nystrom and W. H. Starbuck (eds.), *Handbook of organization design.* Vol. 2. Oxford: Oxford University Press.

Sproul, L., and Weiner, S. 1976. *Easier "seen" than "done": The function of cognitive images in establishing a new bureaucracy.* Unpublished manuscript, Stanford University.

Starbuck, W. H. 1982. Congealing oil: Inventing ideologies to justify acting ideologies out. *Journal of Management Studies 19*:3–27.

Steele, F., and Jenks, S. 1977. *The feel of the work place.* Reading, Massachusetts: Addison-Wesley.

Stephens, D., Eisen, S., and Ensign, S. 1983. Organizational mythology: Working with the collective superconscious. In E. Kosower (ed.), *Beyond our boundaries: Presenters' papers.* Los Angeles: O.D. Network.

Stinchcomb, A. L. 1965. Social structure and organizations. In J. G. March (ed.), *Handbook on organizations.* Chicago: Rand-McNally.

Strassman, P. 1976. Stages of growth. *Datamation* 22:46–50.

Sztompka, P. 1981. The dialectics of spontaneity and planning. In U. Himmelstrand (ed.), *Spontaneity and planning in social development.* Beverly Hills, California: Sage.

Talbot, R. J., and Rickards, T. 1984. Developing creativity. In C. Cox and J. Beck (eds.), *Management development: Advances in practice and theory.* Chichester, England: John Wiley.

Talmon, Y. G. 1972. *Family and community in the kibbutz.* Cambridge, Massachusetts: Harvard University Press.

Tannenbaum, R. 1974. Organizational change has to come through individual change. *Innovations,* August, pp. 36–43.

____. 1980. A new perspective on change: Holding on, letting go and moving on. In P. Mico (ed.), *Presenters' papers, fall 1980.* San Francisco: O.D. Network.

Tart, D. T. 1972. *Altered states of consciousness.* Garden City, New York: Anchor Books.

Teilhard de Chardin, P. 1959. *The phenomenon of man.* New York: Harper and Brothers.

Thom, R. 1975. *Structural stability and morphogenesis.* Reading, Massachusetts: Benjamin.

Thompson, V. A. 1969. *Bureaucracy and innovation.* Tuscaloosa: University of Alabama Press.

Tichy, N. M. 1977. *Organization design for primary health care: The case of the Dr. Martin Luther King, Jr. health center.* New York: Praeger.

____. 1980. A social network perspective for O.D. In T. Cummings (ed.), *Systems theory for organization development.* New York: John Wiley & Sons.

____. 1983. *Managing strategic change.* New York: John Wiley & Sons.

Tichy, N. M., and Ulrich, D. 1984. Revitalizing organizations: The leadership role. In J. Kimberly and R. Quinn (eds.), *New futures: The challenge of managing corporate transitions.* Homewood, Illinois: Dow Jones-Irwin.

Tilden, R. 1983. Legitimizing intuition in a scientific setting: Transforming organizations from insight . . . out. In E. Kosower (ed.), *Beyond our boundaries: Presenters' papers*. Los Angeles: O.D. Network.

Toffler, A. 1981. *The third wave*. New York: Bantam Books.

Tonnies, F. 1964. Gemeinschaft and gesellschaft: Community and society. In A. Etzioni and E. Etzioni (eds.), *Social change*. New York: Basic Books.

Tuchman, M. L. 1977. A political approach to organizations: A review and rationale. *Academy of Management Review* 2:206–216.

Tuchman, M. L., and Romandelli, E. 1985. Organization evolution: A metamorphosis model of convergence and reorientation. In L. L. Cummings and B. M. Staw (eds.), *Research in organizational behavior*. Volume 2. Greenwich, Connecticut: JAI Press.

Vaill, P. 1978. Toward a behavioral description of high performing systems. In M. McCall and M. Lombardo (eds.), *Leadership: Where else can we go?* Durham, North Carolina: Duke University Press.

_____. 1982. The purposing of high performing systems. *Organization Dynamics,* Autumn, pp. 23-40.

Van de Ven, H., and Joice, W. 1981. *Perspectives on organization design and behavior*. New York: John Wiley & Sons.

Vaughan, F. 1979. *Awakening intuition*. New York: Doubleday.

Vickers, G. 1965. *The art of judgment*. New York: Basic Books.

Wallace, A. F. C. 1956. Revitalization movements. *American Anthropologist,* pp. 264–281.

Walsh, R., and Vaughn, J. 1980. *Beyond the ego*. Los Angeles: J. P. Tarcher.

Walsh, R., and Shapiro, D., Jr. 1983. *Beyond health and normality*. New York: Van Nostrand Reinhold.

Walton, R. E. 1975. The diffusion of new work structures: Explaining why success didn't take. *Organizational Dynamics,* Winter, pp. 3–22.

Warren, D. L. 1984. Managing in crisis: Nine principles for successful transition. In J. Kimberly and R. Quinn (eds.), *New futures: The challenge of managing corporate transitions*. Homewood, Illinois: Dow Jones-Irwin.

Watzlawick, P., Weakland, J., and Fisch, R. 1974. *Change*. New York: W. W. Norton.

Weick, K. E. 1979. *The social psychology of organizing*. Reading, Massachusetts: Addison-Wesley.

Westerlund, G., and Sjostrand, S. 1979. *Organizational myths*. New York: Harper & Row.

Whetton, D. A. 1980. Sources, responses and effects of organizational decline. In J. R. Kimberly and R. H. Miles (eds.), *The organizational life cycle*. San Francisco: Jossey-Bass.

Whitaker, C. 1976. The hindrance of theory in clinical work. In P. J. Genuerin (ed.), *Family therapy: Theory and practice*. New York: Gardner Press.

Wilber, K. 1981. *Up from Eden: A transpersonal view of human evolution*. New York: Doubleday.

_____. 1983. The evolution of consciousness. In R. Walsh and D. Shapiro (eds.), *Beyond health and normality*. New York: Van Nostrand Reinhold.

Wilner, E. 1975. *Gathering the winds: Visionary imagination and radical transformation*. Baltimore: Johns Hopkins University Press.

Williams, T. 1982. *Learning to manage our future*. New York: John Wiley & Sons.

Woodward, T. 1965. *Industrial organizations: Theory and practice*. Oxford: Oxford University Press.

Zald, M., and Berger, M. 1978. Social movements in organizations: Coup d'état, insurgency, and mass-movements. *American Journal of Sociology 83*:823–861.

Zaltman, G., Duncan, R., and Holbeck, J. 1973. *Innovations in organizations*. New York: John Wiley & Sons.

Zeeman, C. 1976. Catastrophe theory. *Scientific American 234*:65–83.

Zeleny, M., and Pierre, N. 1976. Simulation of self-renewing systems. In E. Jantsch and C. Waddington (eds.), *Evolution and consciousness: Human systems in transition*. Reading, Massachusetts: Addison-Wesley.

Zucker, L. G. 1977. The role of institutionalization in cultural persistence. *American Sociological Review 42*:726–743.

Index

About the Authors

Amir Levy holds a B.A. in sociology, an MBA magna cum laude from the University of Tel-Aviv, and Ph.D. from the University of California, Santa Barbara. He consults with communities and complex organizations on organizational restructuring and reorganizing. He has also taught and done research at the University of California, Santa Barbara. Dr. Levy has published over 20 articles in the fields of organizational behavior, training and development, management and organizational development. He pursues research in managing and facilitating radical changes in complex organizations.

Uri Merry has a B.A. magna cum laude in sociology and anthropology. His Ph.D. dissertation at the University of California, Santa Barbara was on organizational pathology. He has consulted with and led change and development projects in many industries, communities, and educational institutions. He has developed and facilitated numerous workshops for executives, management teams, and other organizational units. Dr. Merry teaches, trains, and supervises organizational consultants and socio-technical consulting teams. He has taught at the graduate level at the University of California. Dr. Merry has published over 100 research training and theoretical articles in the fields of management and behavioral science. Two of his previous books include: *Developing Teams and Organization* and *The Neurotic Behavior of Organizations*.